i-Ready Classroom
Mathematics

Grade 6 • Volume 1

NOT FOR RESALE

978-1-7280-1298-8
©2021–Curriculum Associates, LLC
North Billerica, MA 01862
No part of this book may be reproduced
by any means without written permission
from the publisher.
All Rights Reserved. Printed in USA.
4 5 6 7 8 9 10 11 12 13 14 15   22 21

BTS21

Curriculum Associates

800471

Contents

Rises 2 meters every second

120 m

Item	Coins Needed
Dance move	175
Costume	850

UNIT 2

Decimals and Fractions

Base-Ten Operations, Division with Fractions, and Volume

Contents (continued)

UNIT 3

Ratio Reasoning

Ratio Concepts and Equivalent Ratios

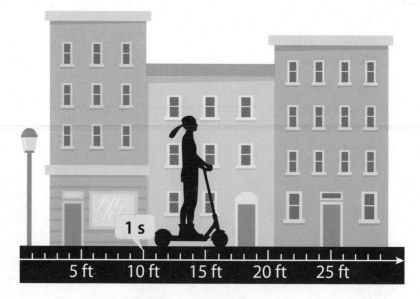

UNIT 4

Ratio Reasoning

Unit Rates and Percent

Contents (continued)

UNIT 5

Algebraic Thinking

Equivalent Expressions and Equations with Variables

Positive and Negative Numbers

Absolute Value, Inequalities, and the Coordinate Plane

Contents (continued)

©Curriculum Associates, LLC   Copying is not permitted.

Unit 1

Expressions and Equations

Area, Algebraic Expressions, and Exponents

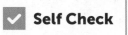 **Self Check** | Before starting this unit, check off the skills you know below.
As you complete each lesson, see how many more skills you can check off!

I can . . .	Before	After
Find the area of parallelograms.	☐	☐
Find the area of triangles and other polygons.	☐	☐
Identify and draw a net for a three-dimensional figure.	☐	☐
Find the surface area of a three-dimensional figure.	☐	☐
Write and evaluate algebraic expressions.	☐	☐
Write and evaluate numerical and algebraic expressions, including those with whole-number exponents.	☐	☐
Find the greatest common factor (GCF) and least common multiple (LCM) of two whole numbers to solve real-world problems.	☐	☐
Actively participate in discussions by asking questions and rephrasing or building on classmates' ideas.	☐	☐

Prepare for Area, Algebraic Expressions, and Exponents

➤ **Use the table to list what you know about perimeter, area, and volume.**

	Perimeter	Area	Volume
Shape			
What the measurement is			
How to find the measurement for the shape shown			
Formula(s) for the shape shown			
Example units			
Situation the measurement could be used for			
Related words	border length, around, width		

Dear Family,

In earlier grades, your student learned that a rectangle is a type of parallelogram. One way to find the area of a rectangle is to multiply the length (**base**) and width (**height**) of the rectangle.

To find the area of a parallelogram, you can decompose, or break apart, the parallelogram and compose the parts into a rectangle.

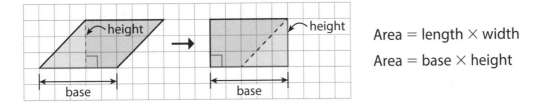

Area = length × width

Area = base × height

The base and height of a parallelogram are always perpendicular, forming right angles. The height can be measured inside or outside the parallelogram.

Your student will be learning how to solve problems like the one below.

What is the area of the parallelogram?

2 ft

2.25 ft

➤ **ONE WAY** to find the area is to rearrange the parallelogram into a rectangle.

$A = \ell \cdot w$

$= 2.25 \cdot 2$

$= 4.5$

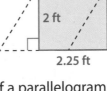

2 ft

2.25 ft

➤ **ANOTHER WAY** is to use the formula for the area of a parallelogram.

$A = b \cdot h$

$= 2.25 \cdot 2$

$= 4.5$

2 ft

2.25 ft

Using either method, the area is 4.5 ft².

▶ Use the next page to start a conversation about parallelograms.

Activity Decomposing Parallelograms

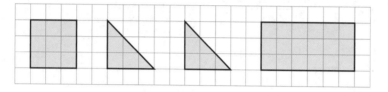

➤ **Do this activity together to investigate different ways of decomposing a parallelogram.**

Have you ever noticed you can decompose a parallelogram into smaller shapes? Decomposing a parallelogram allows you to rearrange the pieces into other familiar shapes. Use any combination of the following shapes to draw as many parallelograms as you can.

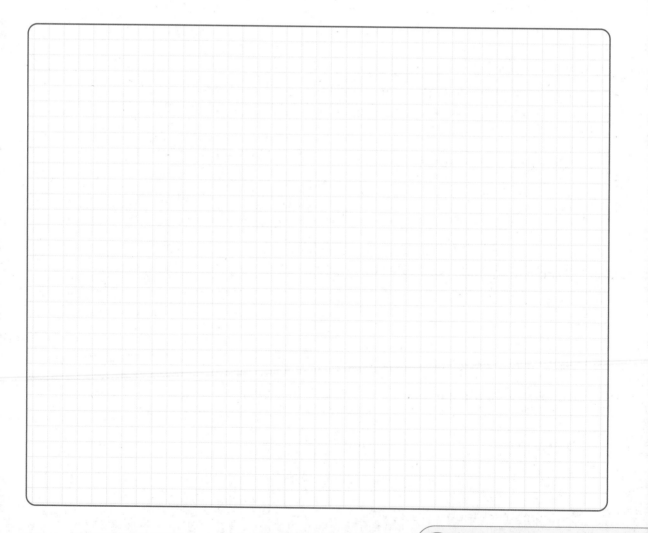

? What do you notice that is the same about all your shapes?

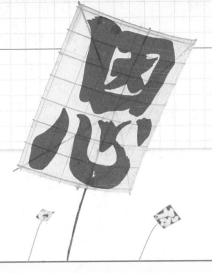

Explore The Area of a Parallelogram

Previously, you learned how to find the area of a rectangle. In this lesson, you will learn how to find the area of a parallelogram.

➤ **Use what you know to try to solve the problem below.**

Kenji and Alec are making paper kites for a kite fight. Kenji's kite is a rectangle and Alec's kite is a parallelogram that is not a rectangle. Each boy draws a model of his kite on grid paper. Does Alec's kite use more paper than Kenji's kite?

TRY IT   **Math Toolkit** geoboards, grid paper, tracing paper, unit tiles

DISCUSS IT

Ask: How would you explain what the problem is asking in your own words?

Share: The problem is asking . . .

◎ **Learning Target**   SMP 1, SMP 2, SMP 3, SMP 4, SMP 5, SMP 6
Find the area of right triangles, other triangles, special quadrilaterals, and polygons by composing into rectangles or decomposing into triangles and other shapes; apply these techniques in the context of solving real-world and mathematical problems.

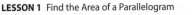

CONNECT IT

1 **Look Back** Does Alec's kite use more paper than Kenji's kite? Explain.

2 **Look Ahead** The words *length* and *width* are often used to describe the dimensions of a rectangle. When describing the dimensions of a parallelogram, you use **base** and **height**.

Any side of a parallelogram can be called the base. You can draw a corresponding height inside or outside the parallelogram. The base and height are perpendicular.

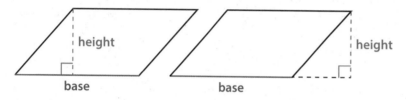

For each parallelogram, draw and label a height that corresponds to the side labeled as the base. Then write the length of the base and the height.

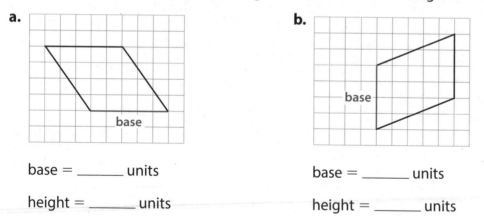

a.

base = _____ units

height = _____ units

b.

base = _____ units

height = _____ units

3 **Reflect** In problem 2a, would the length of the height change if you measured it from a different point on the same base? Explain.

Prepare for Finding the Area of a Parallelogram

1 Think about what you know about area. Fill in each box. Use words, numbers, and pictures. Show as many ideas as you can.

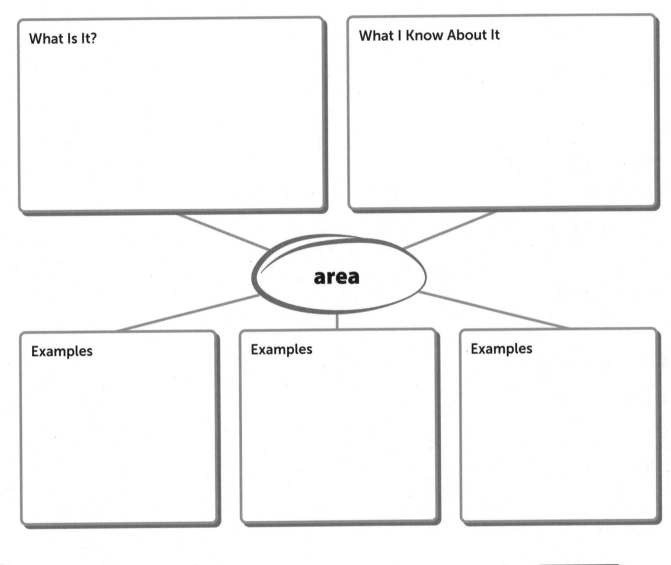

What Is It?

What I Know About It

area

Examples

Examples

Examples

2 Doug says the area of the figure is 20 square units. What is the correct area of the figure? What mistake might Doug have made?

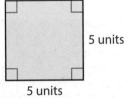

5 units

5 units

3 A parking lot has two types of parking spaces. Some parking spaces are rectangles and other spaces are parallelograms. Plans for the parking spaces are drawn on grid paper.

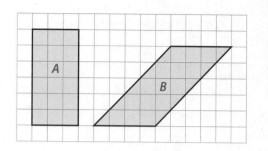

a. Which parking space covers the greater area, *space A* or *space B*? Show your work.

SOLUTION _____

b. Check your answer to problem 3a. Show your work.

Develop Finding the Area of a Parallelogram

➤ **Read and try to solve the problem below.**

On a star map, Neena sees that four stars in the constellation Lyra appear to form a parallelogram. Neena draws a model of the constellation on 1-centimeter grid paper. What is the area of Neena's parallelogram?

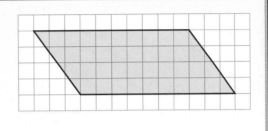

TRY IT

Math Toolkit geoboards, grid paper, tangrams, tracing paper

DISCUSS IT

Ask: How is your strategy for finding the area of the parallelogram similar to mine? How is it different?

Share: My strategy is similar to yours . . . It is different . . .

➤ **Explore different ways to find the area of a parallelogram.**

On a star map, Neena sees that four stars in the constellation Lyra appear to form a parallelogram. Neena draws a model of the constellation on 1-centimeter grid paper. What is the area of Neena's parallelogram?

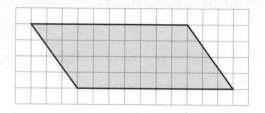

Picture It

You can find the area of a parallelogram by breaking it into parts and rearranging the parts into rectangles.

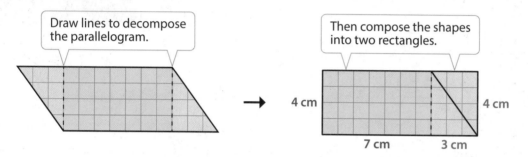

Draw lines to decompose the parallelogram.

Then compose the shapes into two rectangles.

4 cm

4 cm

7 cm   3 cm

Area of parallelogram = **Area of left rectangle + Area of right rectangle**

= **(length × width) + (length × width)**

= **28 cm² + 12 cm²**

Model It

You can use a formula to find the area of a parallelogram.

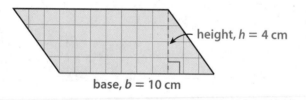

height, *h* = 4 cm

base, *b* = 10 cm

Area of parallelogram = **base × height**

$A = b \times h$

$= 10 \times 4$

You can also write the formula $A = b \times h$ as $A = b \cdot h$ or $A = bh$.

> **Use the problem from the previous page to help you understand how to find the area of a parallelogram.**

1 Look at **Picture It**. What is the combined area of the two rectangles? Why is this the same as the area of Neena's parallelogram?

2 In **Model It**, one side of the parallelogram is labeled as the base. How is the length of the base related to the lengths of the two rectangles in **Picture It**?

3 Neena's parallelogram can be rearranged into a rectangle. Use this to explain the formula for the area of a parallelogram.

4 Explain why you can also use the formula $A = b \cdot h$ to find the area of a rectangle.

5 **Reflect** Think about all the models and strategies you have discussed today. Describe how one of them helped you better understand how to find the area of a parallelogram.

Apply It

➤ **Use what you learned to solve these problems.**

6 Cyrus makes Greek spinach pie, called spanakopita, with his grandfather. They cut the pie into pieces shaped like parallelograms. The dimensions of one piece are shown. What is the area of the top of this piece of spinach pie? Show your work.

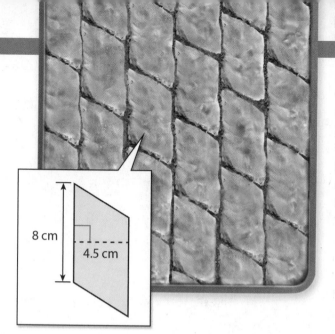

8 cm

4.5 cm

SOLUTION _____

7 A parallelogram has an area of 48 square units. Which dimensions could it have? Select all that apply.

A base = 8 units, height = 6 units

B height = 24 units, base = 24 units

C base = 4 units, height = 12 units

D base = 12 units, height = 36 units

E height = 4 units, base = 12 units

8 What is the area of the parallelogram? Show your work.

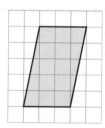

SOLUTION _____

12   **LESSON 1** Find the Area of a Parallelogram

Practice Finding the Area of a Parallelogram

➤ **Study the Example showing how to find the area of a parallelogram. Then solve problems 1–5.**

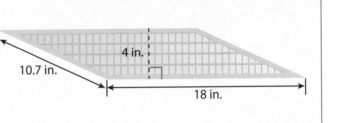

Example

Grace is making a model of a building that is shaped like a parallelogram. The dimensions of the parallelogram in her model are shown. What is the area of the parallelogram in Grace's model?

The segment labeled 4 in. is perpendicular to the side labeled 18 in. So, the **base** of the parallelogram is **18 in.** and the **height** is **4 in.**

You can use the formula for the area of a parallelogram.

$A = b \cdot h$

$A = 18 \cdot 4$

$ = 72$

The area of the parallelogram in Grace's model is 72 in.^{2}.

1. Look at the parallelogram in the Example. Describe a way to decompose the parallelogram and rearrange the parts to form a rectangle.

 2. What is the area of the parallelogram? Show your work.

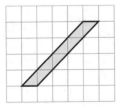

Vocabulary

decompose
to break into parts. You can break apart numbers and shapes.

parallelogram
a quadrilateral with opposite sides parallel and equal in length.

perpendicular
meeting to form right angles.

SOLUTION _____

3 The parallelogram shown on the grid represents a mirror. The mirror hangs on a wall that is covered with square tiles. Each grid square represents one tile. The side length of each square tile is 4 in. What is the area of the mirror? Show your work.

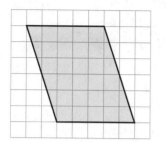

SOLUTION _____

4 Explain how you know which line segments are a base and height of the parallelogram.

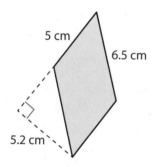

5 cm
6.5 cm
5.2 cm

5 The Eagle Express Shipping Service logo is in the shape of a parallelogram. The side lengths of the logo painted on a delivery truck are shown. The perpendicular distance from the bottom of the logo to the top of the logo is 3 ft. What is the area of the logo on the truck? Show your work.

3.2 ft
3 ft
3.1 ft

SOLUTION _____

Refine Finding the Area of a Parallelogram

➤ **Complete the Example below. Then solve problems 1–9.**

Example

The area of a parallelogram is 288 in.² . The base of the parallelogram is 24 in. What is the height of the parallelogram?

Look at how you can use a diagram and equations to show your work.

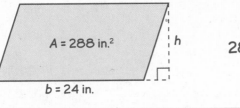

$$A = b \cdot h$$
$$288 = 24 \cdot h$$
$$h = 288 \div 24$$

SOLUTION _____

Apply It

1 What is the area of the figure? Show your work.

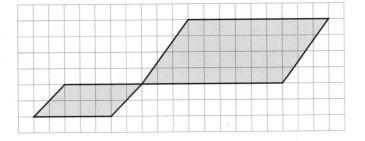

SOLUTION _____

2 Find the area of the parallelogram. Show your work.

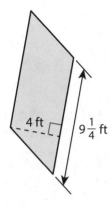

4 ft $9\frac{1}{4}$ ft

SOLUTION _____

3 A small window in a barn is shaped like a parallelogram. The height of the window is half the length of the base of the window. The base of the window is 12 in. The length of the other side of the window is 10 in. What is the area of the window?

A 22 in.^{2}

B 60 in.^{2}

C 72 in.^{2}

D 120 in.^{2}

Juanita chose D as the correct answer. How might she have gotten that answer?

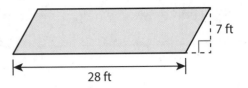

4 Kimani plans to paint the background of a mural on a wall in her school's cafeteria. The mural will be in the shape of a parallelogram. One quart of paint covers 100 square feet. How many quarts of paint does Kimani need? Show your work.

7 ft

28 ft

SOLUTION _____

5 The area of a parallelogram is 18 square units. One side of the parallelogram is 24 units long. The other side is 6 units long. Which could be the parallelogram's height? Select all that apply.

A $\frac{3}{4}$ unit

B $\frac{4}{3}$ units

C 3 units

D 4 units

E 12 units

6 A road sign is a rectangle with the dimensions shown. The sign has two identical black parallelograms joined together. Each parallelogram has a base of 14 in. and a height of 17 in. Find the area of the sign that is not black. Show your work.

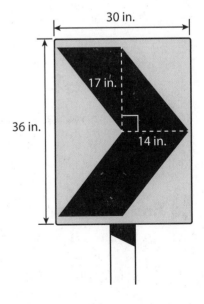

30 in.

17 in.

36 in.

14 in.

SOLUTION _____

7 Leon draws the height shown in the parallelogram. He estimates that the height is about 5 units long. Is Leon's estimate reasonable? Explain.

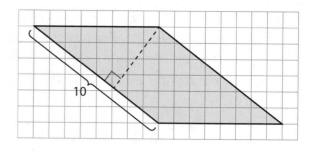

8 What is the area of the parallelogram in square centimeters?

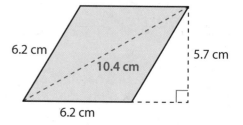

6.2 cm   5.7 cm

10.4 cm

6.2 cm

9 **Math Journal** Draw two different parallelograms that each have an area of 12 square centimeters. Label the base and height of each parallelogram.

✓ End of Lesson Checklist

☐ **INTERACTIVE GLOSSARY** Find the entries for *base* and *height* of a parallelogram. Write definitions for a younger student. Show an example and label the *base* and *height*.

☐ **SELF CHECK** Go back to the Unit 1 Opener and see what you can check off.

Dear Family,

This week your student is learning to find the area of triangles and other polygons. You can use formulas to find the area of some polygons.

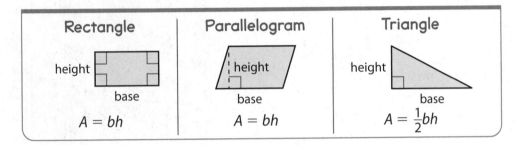

Rectangle	Parallelogram	Triangle
height / base / $A = bh$	height / base / $A = bh$	height / base / $A = \frac{1}{2}bh$

The area of other polygons can be found by breaking apart, or decomposing, the shape into triangles, rectangles, and parallelograms. Your student will be learning to solve problems like the one below.

What is the area of the polygon?

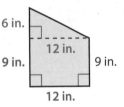

15 in.

9 in.

12 in.

➤ **ONE WAY** to find the area of a polygon is to decompose the shape and add areas.

Area of polygon = Area of rectangle + Area of triangle

$$= 12 \cdot 9 + \frac{1}{2}(12 \cdot 6)$$

$$= 108 + 36$$

$$= 144$$

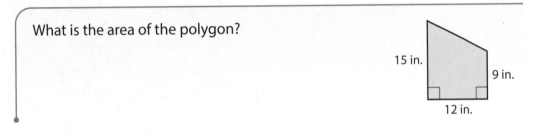

6 in.

12 in.

9 in.   9 in.

12 in.

➤ **ANOTHER WAY** is to subtract areas.

Area of polygon = Area of rectangle − Area of triangle

$$= 12 \cdot 15 - \frac{1}{2}(12 \cdot 6)$$

$$= 180 - 36$$

$$= 144$$

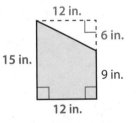

12 in.

6 in.

15 in.

9 in.

12 in.

Using either method, the area of the polygon is 144 in.²

▶ Use the next page to start a conversation about triangles.

Activity Exploring Triangles and Parallelograms

➤ **Do this activity together to investigate the relationship between triangles and parallelograms.**

Have you noticed that a parallelogram can be decomposed into two identical triangles? You can also arrange two identical triangles into a parallelogram. Look at each shape below. What similarities and differences do you notice?

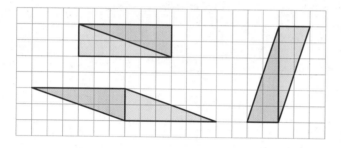

? What are other ways you can arrange two triangles?

Explore The Area of a Triangle

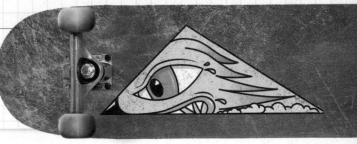

Previously, you learned about finding the area of a parallelogram.
In this lesson, you will learn about finding the area of a triangle.

➤ **Use what you know to try to solve the problem below.**

Caitlyn has two decals shaped like the triangles shown. She arranges them on the back of her skateboard to form a parallelogram. Each grid square represents 1 square inch. What area do the two decals cover?

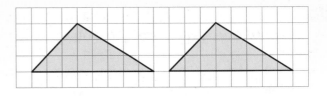

TRY IT

Math Toolkit grid paper, tracing paper, unit tiles

DISCUSS IT

Ask: What did you do first to find the area that the decals cover? Why?

Share: I started by . . . because . . .

◎ **Learning Target**   SMP 1, SMP 2, SMP 3, SMP 4, SMP 5, SMP 6, SMP 7
Find the area of right triangles, other triangles, special quadrilaterals, and polygons by composing into rectangles or decomposing into triangles and other shapes; apply these techniques in the context of solving real-world and mathematical problems.

CONNECT IT

1 **Look Back** What area do Caitlyn's two decals cover? Explain how you know.

2 **Look Ahead** As in a parallelogram, the **base** and **height of a triangle** are perpendicular. Any side of a triangle can be called the base. The corresponding height is drawn from the vertex that is opposite the base.

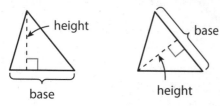

a. Use the triangle at the right. Draw the height that corresponds to the side labeled as the base. Then write the lengths of the base and height.

base = _____ units   height = _____ units

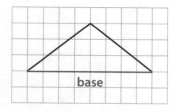

b. Use the triangle at the right. Draw the height that corresponds to the side labeled as the base.

c. Choose one side of the triangle at the right to be the base of the triangle. Then draw the height that corresponds to that base. Label the base *b* and the height *h*.

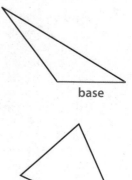

3 **Reflect** Look at the right triangle. Which pair of sides can be called a base and height for the triangle? Explain.

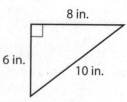

Prepare for Finding the Area of Triangles and Other Polygons

1 Think about what you know about parallelograms. Fill in each box. Use words, numbers, and pictures. Show as many ideas as you can.

In My Own Words	My Illustrations

parallelogram

Examples	Non-Examples

2 Is this polygon a parallelogram? Explain.

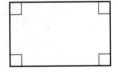

3 An artist makes a sculpture by joining together two triangular pieces of metal to form a parallelogram. The shape of the triangles is shown below. Each grid square represents 1 square foot.

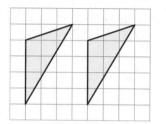

a. What is the area of the parallelogram that the artist makes? Show your work.

SOLUTION _____

b. Check your answer to problem 3a. Show your work.

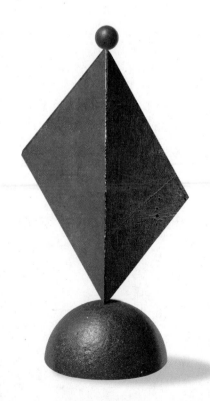

Develop Finding the Area of a Triangle

➤ **Read and try to solve the problem below.**

Maria's class is painting a mural on a school wall. Staff at an Acoma cultural center help Maria copy an Acoma Pueblo pottery design to use in the mural.

Maria draws her design on 1-centimeter grid paper. She begins with one of the triangles. What is the area of Maria's triangle?

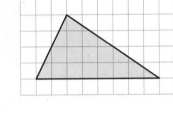

TRY IT

🖉 **Math Toolkit** grid paper, tracing paper, unit tiles

DISCUSS IT

Ask: How is your strategy for finding the area similar to mine?

Share: My strategy is similar to yours because . . .

➤ **Explore different ways to find the area of a triangle.**

Maria's class is painting a mural on a school wall. Staff at an Acoma cultural center help Maria copy an Acoma Pueblo pottery design to use in the mural.

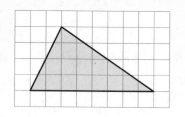

Maria draws her design on 1-centimeter grid paper. She begins with one of the triangles. What is the area of Maria's triangle?

Model It

You can find the area of a triangle by decomposing it into two right triangles.

Think of each right triangle as one half of a rectangle.

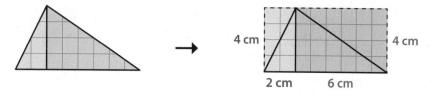

Write an expression for the area of Maria's triangle.

$$\frac{1}{2}(2 \cdot 4) + \frac{1}{2}(6 \cdot 4)$$

Model It

You can find the area of a triangle by composing the triangle with a copy of itself to form a parallelogram.

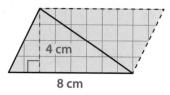

The area of the triangle is half the area of the parallelogram.

$$A = \frac{1}{2}(8 \cdot 4)$$

➤ **Use the problem from the previous page to help you understand how to find the area of a triangle.**

1 How can thinking of a right triangle as half of a rectangle help you find the area of the right triangle?

2 Look at the expression in the first **Model It**.

   a. What does the product $\frac{1}{2}(2 \cdot 4)$ represent? How do you know?

   b. Use the expression to find the area of Maria's triangle.

3 Look at the second **Model It**. How are the base and height of Maria's triangle related to the base and height of the parallelogram? Explain.

4 The formula for the area of a parallelogram is $A = bh$. Explain why the formula for the area of a triangle is $A = \frac{1}{2}bh$.

5 **Reflect** Think about all the models and strategies you have discussed today. Describe how one of them helped you better understand how to find the area of a triangle.

Apply It

➤ **Use what you learned to solve these problems.**

6 Forest managers plant trees in a triangular section of a state park. The managers model the area on grid paper. Each grid square represents 1 km². What is the area of the section that the forest managers plant with trees? Show your work.

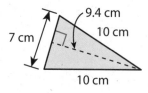

SOLUTION _____

7 What is the area of the triangle? Show your work.

9.4 cm
10 cm
7 cm
10 cm

SOLUTION _____

8 Elena claims that the expression $\frac{1}{2}(4)(5)$ represents the area of the triangle, in square inches. Explain why Elena is not correct. Then explain how to correct her error and find the area of the triangle.

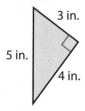

3 in.
5 in.
4 in.

Name: _____

Practice Finding the Area of a Triangle

➤ **Study the Example showing how to find the area of a triangle. Then solve problems 1–5.**

Example

Students in an art club are painting a design on a wall of their school. Rodrigo paints the triangle shown. What is the area of the triangle?

You can use a formula to find the area. Use the side labeled **4 ft** as the base. Then the height is **3 ft**.

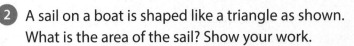

$$A = \frac{1}{2}bh$$

$$= \frac{1}{2}(4)(3)$$

$$= \frac{1}{2}(12)$$

$$= 6$$

The area of the triangle is 6 ft².

1. Suppose the height of Rodrigo's triangle in the Example is doubled. Will the area of the triangle also double? Explain how you know.

2. A sail on a boat is shaped like a triangle as shown. What is the area of the sail? Show your work.

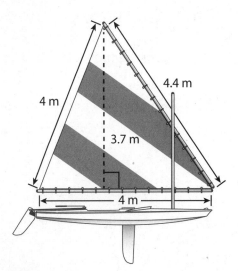

SOLUTION _____

3 **a.** Three sidewalks in a schoolyard form a triangle. Explain how the expression

$\frac{1}{2}(40)(30) + \frac{1}{2}(40)(20)$ represents the area inside the three sidewalks.

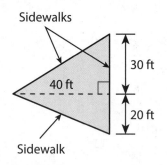

Sidewalks

30 ft

40 ft

20 ft

Sidewalk

b. What is the area inside the sidewalks? Show your work.

SOLUTION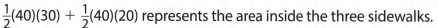

4 Which expressions represent the area of the triangle in square feet? Select all that apply.

A $\frac{1}{2} \cdot 48 \cdot 9$

B $\frac{1}{2}(6 + 8)(9)$

C $(14 \cdot 9) \div 2$

D $\frac{1}{2}(6)(9) + \frac{1}{2}(8)(9)$

E $(6)(9) + (8)(9) \div 2$

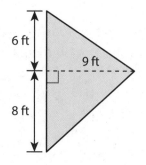

6 ft

9 ft

8 ft

5 Explain how you know that the two triangles have the same area.

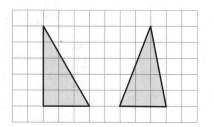

Develop Finding the Area of a Polygon

➤ **Read and try to solve the problem below.**

A costume designer is making a superhero costume for a movie. The costume will have a logo on the front. The designer draws a plan for the logo on 1-inch grid paper. What is the area of the logo in the drawing?

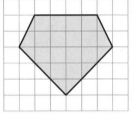

TRY IT

Math Toolkit grid paper, tracing paper, unit tiles

DISCUSS IT

Ask: Why did you choose that strategy to find the area of the logo?

Share: I chose that strategy because . . .

➤ **Explore different ways to find the area of a polygon.**

A costume designer is making a superhero costume for a movie. The costume will have a logo on the front. The designer draws a plan for the logo on 1-inch grid paper. What is the area of the logo in the drawing?

Model It

You can find the area of a polygon by using addition.

Decompose the logo into two triangles and a parallelogram.

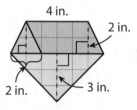

Shape	Formula	Area
Large triangle	$A = \frac{1}{2}bh$	$\frac{1}{2}(6)(3) = 9$
Small triangle	$A = \frac{1}{2}bh$	$\frac{1}{2}(2)(2) = 2$
Parallelogram	$A = bh$	$(4)(2) = 8$

Write an addition expression for the area of the logo.

Area of the logo $= 9 + 2 + 8$

Model It

You can find the area of a polygon by using subtraction.

Draw a rectangle around the logo.

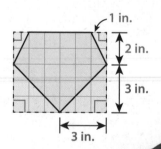

The rectangle is composed of the shape of the logo and four right triangles.

Write a subtraction expression for the area of the logo.

$(6 \cdot 5) - 2 \cdot \left(\frac{1}{2} \cdot 3 \cdot 3 \right) - 2 \cdot \left(\frac{1}{2} \cdot 1 \cdot 2 \right)$

Area of the logo $= 30 - 9 - 2$

➤ **Use the problem from the previous page to help you understand how to find the area of a polygon.**

1 Look at the first **Model It**. Why might you choose to divide the logo into triangles and a parallelogram?

2 Look at the expression in the second **Model It**. The product $6 \cdot 5$ represents the area of the rectangle. What does the product $2 \cdot \left(\frac{1}{2} \cdot 3 \cdot 3 \right)$ represent? Why is this product subtracted from the area of the rectangle?

3 What is the area of the logo? How is the strategy of adding to find the area similar to the strategy of subtracting to find the area? How are these strategies different?

4 How can you find the area of a polygon when you do not know a formula for the area of that polygon?

5 **Reflect** Think about all the models and strategies you have discussed today. Describe how one of them helped you better understand how to find the area of a polygon.

Apply It

➤ **Use what you learned to solve these problems.**

6 What is the area of the polygon in square units? Show your work.

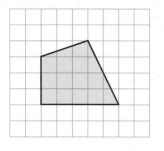

SOLUTION _____

7 To find the area of a trapezoid, Badru decomposes it into two triangles as shown. He says the area of the trapezoid is two times the area of the top triangle. Is Badru correct? Why or why not?

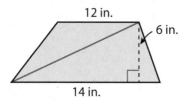

12 in.

6 in.

14 in.

8 The polygon represents the top of a desk. What is the area of the top of the desk? Show your work.

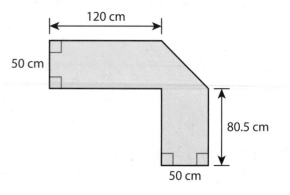

120 cm

50 cm

80.5 cm

50 cm

SOLUTION _____

Practice Finding the Area of a Polygon

➤ **Study the Example showing how to find the area of a polygon. Then solve problems 1–5.**

Example

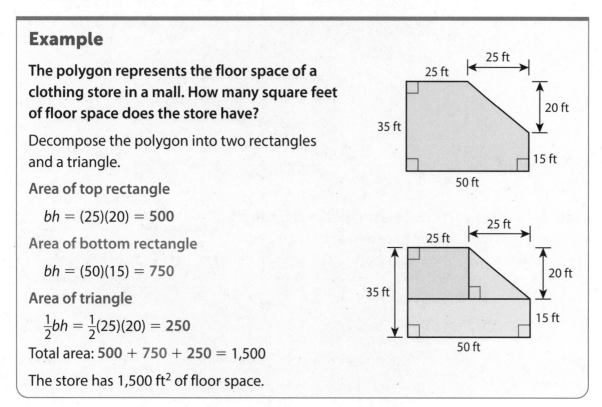

The polygon represents the floor space of a clothing store in a mall. How many square feet of floor space does the store have?

Decompose the polygon into two rectangles and a triangle.

Area of top rectangle

$bh = (25)(20) = 500$

Area of bottom rectangle

$bh = (50)(15) = 750$

Area of triangle

$\frac{1}{2}bh = \frac{1}{2}(25)(20) = 250$

Total area: $500 + 750 + 250 = 1,500$

The store has 1,500 ft² of floor space.

1 Show another way to find the number of square feet of floor space for the store in the Example.

2 Teresa wants to find the area of a wall in her attic. The wall is shaped like the polygons at the right. Show two different ways Teresa could decompose the wall into triangles, rectangles, or both.

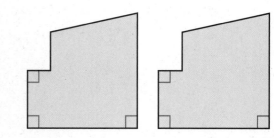

3 What is the area of the polygon? Show your work.

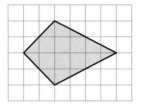

SOLUTION _____

4 A tarp covers the grass on part of a baseball field during batting practice. The tarp is shaped like the trapezoid at the right. What is the area of the tarp? Show your work.

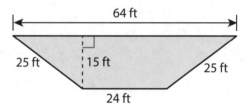

SOLUTION _____

5 A stage for a concert is shaped like the polygon shown. What is the area of the stage? Show your work.

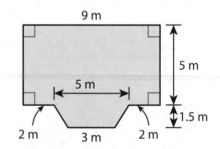

SOLUTION _____

Refine Finding the Area of Triangles and Other Polygons

➤ **Complete the Example below. Then solve problems 1–9.**

Example

Rachel has a poster board. She cuts away a triangle and a rectangle from two corners. What is the area of the poster board that remains?

Look at how you could use a table to organize your work.

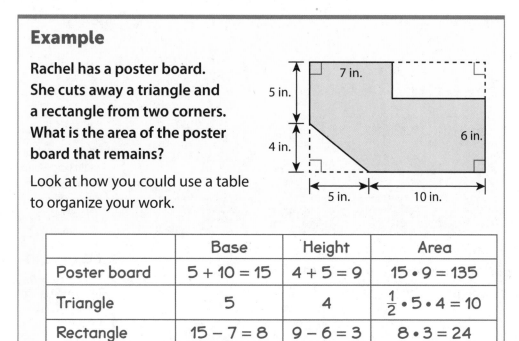

	Base	Height	Area
Poster board	5 + 10 = 15	4 + 5 = 9	15 • 9 = 135
Triangle	5	4	$\frac{1}{2}$ • 5 • 4 = 10
Rectangle	15 − 7 = 8	9 − 6 = 3	8 • 3 = 24
Remaining area			135 − 10 − 24

CONSIDER THIS . . .
You can use lengths you know to find lengths that are not labeled.

PAIR/SHARE
How could you solve the problem another way?

SOLUTION _____

Apply It

1 Find the area of the triangle. Show your work.

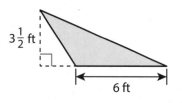

$3\frac{1}{2}$ ft

6 ft

CONSIDER THIS . . .
How can you multiply a mixed number by a whole number?

PAIR/SHARE
How would your answer change if the base of the triangle were 3 ft instead of 6 ft?

SOLUTION _____

2 Each grid square represents 1 cm². What is the area of the polygon? Show your work.

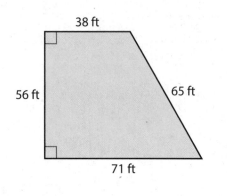

CONSIDER THIS...
How could you use subtraction to help you find the area?

SOLUTION _____

PAIR/SHARE
What other strategy could you use to find the area of the polygon?

3 The carpet in a school library needs to be replaced. The dimensions of the library floor are shown. Each square foot of new carpet costs $1.25. What is the total cost of the new carpet for the library?

CONSIDER THIS...
How can you use the cost for each square foot to find the total cost?

```
        38 ft
    ┌─────────────┐
    │              ╲
56 ft│               ╲ 65 ft
    │                 ╲
    └───────────────────┘
        71 ft
```

A $3,052

B $3,815

C $4,970

D $5,145

Daniel chose A as the correct answer. How might he have gotten that answer?

PAIR/SHARE
How can you check your answer?

4 A rancher has a field in the shape of the polygon shown. The rancher plans to keep one sheep in the field for every 2,000 m². Based on this plan, how many sheep can the rancher keep in the field? Show your work.

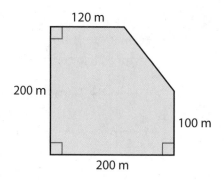

120 m

200 m

100 m

200 m

SOLUTION _____

5 What is the difference between the area of Figure *A* and the area of Figure *B*? Each grid square represents 1 square foot.

A 2 ft²

B 4 ft²

C 8 ft²

D 10 ft²

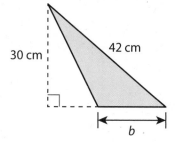

6 The height of the triangle is 12 cm greater than the base of the triangle, *b*. What is the area of the triangle? Show your work.

30 cm

42 cm

b

SOLUTION _____

7 Seth is making panes for a stained-glass window. He makes a triangular pane shaped like the triangle shown. Which of these rectangular panes has the same area as the triangular pane? Select all that apply.

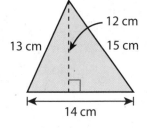

12 cm

13 cm   15 cm

14 cm

A a 12-cm by 7-cm rectangle

B a 15-cm by 7-cm rectangle

C a 21-cm by 4-cm rectangle

D a 21-cm by 8-cm rectangle

E a 28-cm by 6-cm rectangle

8 Jaime makes a rectangular flag in his school colors.

One section of the flag is a triangle. He says the area of the triangle is $\frac{16}{24}$ of the area of the flag. Do you agree? Explain.

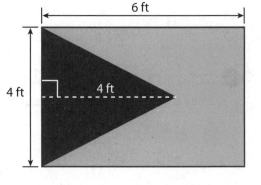

6 ft

4 ft   4 ft

9 **Math Journal** Draw a polygon with at least 5 sides on the grid. Show one way to find the area of your polygon.

End of Lesson Checklist

☐ **INTERACTIVE GLOSSARY** Write a new entry for *represent*. Tell what you do when you use an expression to *represent* the area of a triangle.

☐ **SELF CHECK** Go back to the Unit 1 Opener and see what you can check off.

Dear Family,

This week your student is learning about nets and finding the surface area of three-dimensional figures. **Surface area** is the combined area of all the faces, or sides, of a three-dimensional figure.

Imagine cutting a three-dimensional figure along some of its edges and unfolding it. The flat, unfolded figure is called a **net**. You can use the net to find the surface area of the three-dimensional figure.

Your student will be learning to solve problems like the one below.

What is the surface area of the right rectangular prism?

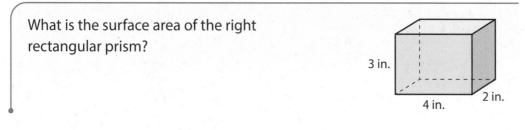

➤ **ONE WAY** to find the surface area is to make a net.

You can find the area of each rectangular face. Then find the sum of the areas.

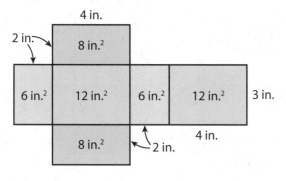

$$12 + 12 + 6 + 6 + 8 + 8 = 52$$

➤ **ANOTHER WAY** is to write and evaluate an expression.

Notice that the prism has three pairs of identical faces. The faces in each pair have the same area.

$$2(4 \cdot 3) + 2(2 \cdot 3) + 2(4 \cdot 2) = 24 + 12 + 16$$
$$= 52$$

Using either method, the surface area is 52 in.²

 Use the next page to start a conversation about surface area.

Activity Thinking About Surface Area Around You

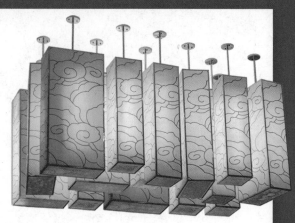

➤ **Do this activity together to investigate surface area in the real world.**

Have you ever seen lights or lanterns covered in patterned fabric or paper? Have you ever wondered how much fabric or paper is used to cover each lantern?

Surface area is a useful way to find the exact amount of fabric needed to make these types of lights. Without knowing the surface area, you might end up with too much or too little fabric.

? What other shapes around you could you find the surface area for?

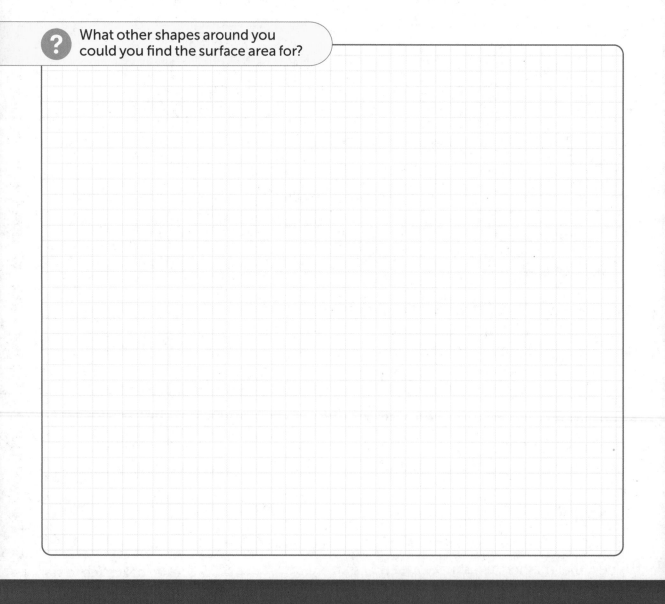

Explore Nets of Three-Dimensional Figures

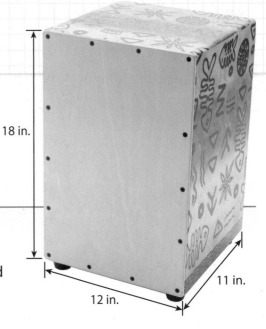

18 in.

12 in.

11 in.

Previously, you learned about the area of two-dimensional figures. In this lesson, you will learn about the surface area of three-dimensional figures.

➤ **Use what you know to try to solve the problem below.**

Brian learned to build a cajón from his grandfather. A cajón is a box-shaped drum that you play by slapping the front. Brian builds the cajón shown. How much wood will Brian need to build the four vertical sides but not the top or bottom?

TRY IT

🖊 **Math Toolkit** dot paper, geometric solids, grid paper

DISCUSS IT

Ask: How would you explain what the problem is asking in your own words?

Share: The problem is asking . . .

◎ **Learning Target** SMP 1, SMP 2, SMP 3, SMP 4, SMP 5, SMP 6
Represent three-dimensional figures using nets made up of rectangles and triangles, and use the nets to find the surface area of these figures. Apply these techniques in the context of solving real-world and mathematical problems.

CONNECT IT

1 **Look Back** How much wood will Brian need to build the four vertical sides of the cajón? How can you find the amount he needs?

2 **Look Ahead** Brian's cajón is a **right rectangular prism.** If you cut along some of the edges of a right rectangular prism, you can unfold the **prism** into a **net.**

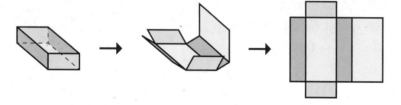

a. How do the sizes and shapes of the rectangles in the net compare to the faces, or sides, of the right rectangular prism? Explain how you know.

b. Where in the net do you see the edges of the right rectangular prism?

c. You can make nets for other three-dimensional figures. Look at the prism and the **pyramid.** How are they alike? How are they different?

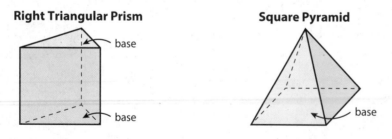

Right Triangular Prism

base

base

Square Pyramid

base

3 **Reflect** How many triangles and how many rectangles are in a net for a right triangular prism? How do you know?

Prepare for Using Nets to Find Surface Area

1 Think about what you know about three-dimensional figures. Fill in each box. Use words, numbers, and pictures. Show as many ideas as you can.

Word	In My Own Words	Example
face		
edge		
vertex		

2 Neva writes the following in her math notebook.

A right rectangular prism has 6 rectangular faces. Each rectangle has 4 sides. This means the prism has 6 • 4 = 24 edges. Each rectangle also has 4 vertices. That means the prism also has 6 • 4 = 24 vertices.

Do you agree or disagree? Explain.

Kiara is covering part of this rectangular box with duct tape. She is covering the four sides but not the top or bottom.

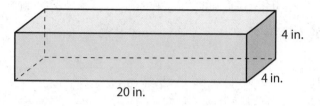

a. What is the total area that Kiara will cover with duct tape? Show your work.

SOLUTION _____

b. Check your answer to problem 3a. Show your work.

Develop Representing a Three-Dimensional Figure with a Net

➤ **Read and try to solve the problem below.**

Amelia wants to make a model of the Great Pyramid of Giza. Her model will be in the shape of a square pyramid. Which of the nets shown can she use to make her model? How do you know?

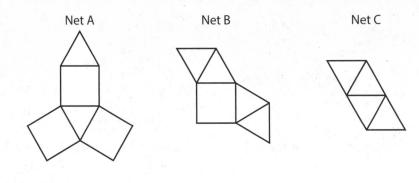

Net A   Net B   Net C

TRY IT

Math Toolkit geometric solids, grid paper, templates

➤ **Explore different ways to find a net for a three-dimensional figure.**

Amelia wants to make a model of the Great Pyramid of Giza. Her model will be in the shape of a square pyramid. Which of the nets shown can she use to make her model? How do you know?

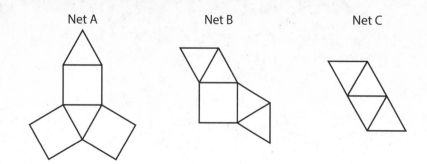

Net A Net B Net C

Analyze It

You can use reasoning to help you identify the net for a three-dimensional figure.

A square pyramid has one square face.

Net C does not include a square, so Net C cannot be used to make the model.

Net A has three squares, which is too many. Net A cannot be used to make the model.

Analyze It

You can make a table to organize information about the shapes.

Figure	Number of Triangles	Number of Squares
Pyramid	4	1
Net A	2	3
Net B	4	1
Net C	4	0

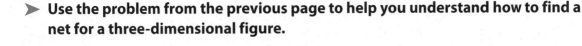
➤ **Use the problem from the previous page to help you understand how to find a net for a three-dimensional figure.**

1 Look at the first **Analyze It**. How does reasoning help you find the correct net?

2 Which of the nets can Amelia use to make her model? How does the table help you choose a net that can be used to make the pyramid?

3 The nets at the right each have one square and four identical triangles. A student says that both nets can be used to form a pyramid. Do you agree? Explain.

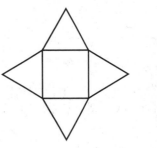

4 What must be true about the shapes in a net for a three-dimensional figure?

5 **Reflect** Think about all the models and strategies you have discussed today. Describe how one of them helped you better understand nets.

Apply It

➤ **Use what you learned to solve these problems.**

6 Each line segment in the net shown is labeled with a letter.
The net will be cut out and folded to form a triangular pyramid.
Which line segment will match up with segment *A* to form an
edge of the pyramid? Show your work.

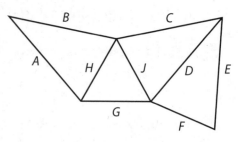

SOLUTION _____

7 Issay cuts out the net shown and folds it to make a three-dimensional
shape. Which three-dimensional shape does Issay make?

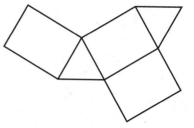

A Right triangular prism

B Right rectangular prism

C Pyramid with a triangular base

D Pyramid with a rectangular base

8 Sketch a net for the right triangular prism shown. Explain how you know your net
represents the prism.

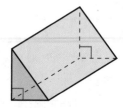

Practice Representing a Three-Dimensional Figure with a Net

➤ **Study the Example showing how to draw a net for a three-dimensional figure. Then solve problems 1–5.**

Example

An artist needs a sheet of copper that can be bent to form a cube. Draw a net the artist can use to make the cube.

Imagine cutting a cube apart along some of the edges and unfolding it.

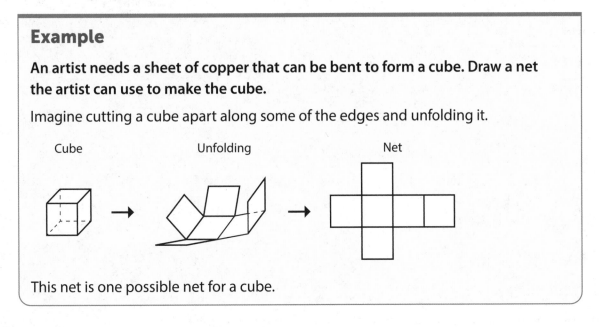

This net is one possible net for a cube.

1 a. What shapes are in any net for a cube? Explain.

b. You could cut the cube in the Example along other edges to make a net with a different arrangement of squares. Draw an example of another net for a cube.

2 Hai says that every net for a prism is made up of exactly six faces. Explain why Hai's statement is incorrect.

Vocabulary

cube
a rectangular prism in which each face of the prism is a square.

prism
a three-dimensional figure with two parallel bases that are the same size and shape. A prism is named by the shape of the base.

3 Shanika is designing a wooden trunk. She wants the trunk to be a right rectangular prism with two square sides. Shanika starts drawing a net on dot paper. Complete Shanika's net.

4 Draw a net for the triangular pyramid.

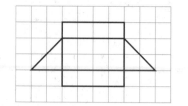

5 Salvador draws a figure on grid paper. He says it is a net for a three-dimensional figure. Explain if Salvador is correct. If he is, identify the figure in your explanation.

Develop Finding the Surface Area of a Three-Dimensional Figure

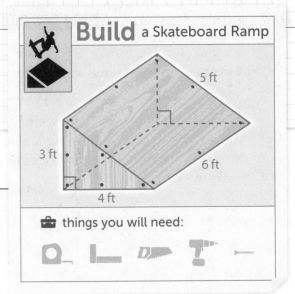

Build a Skateboard Ramp

5 ft
3 ft
6 ft
4 ft

🧰 things you will need:

➤ **Read and try to solve the problem below.**

Oliver is using plywood to build the skateboard ramp shown. Three sides of the ramp are rectangles. How many square feet of plywood does Oliver need to build the ramp?

TRY IT

Math Toolkit dot paper, geometric solids, grid paper

DISCUSS IT

Ask: Why did you choose that strategy to find the square feet of the plywood needed to build the ramp?

Share: My strategy helped me to . . .

➤ **Explore different ways to find the surface area of a three-dimensional figure.**

Oliver is using plywood to build the skateboard ramp shown. Three sides of the ramp are rectangles. How many square feet of plywood does Oliver need to build the ramp?

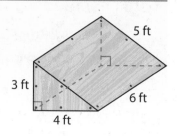

Picture It

You can draw a net to help you find the **surface area** a three-dimensional figure.

The ramp has two triangular faces and three rectangular faces. Label the net with the dimensions from the triangular prism.

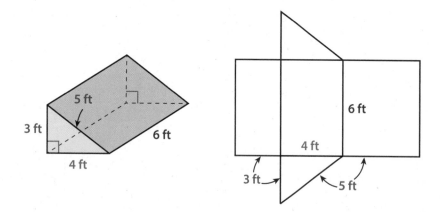

Model It

You can write an expression to find the surface area of a three-dimensional figure.

Use area formulas to write an expression for the sum of the areas of the faces.

$$\frac{1}{2} \cdot (4 \cdot 3) + \frac{1}{2} \cdot (4 \cdot 3) + (3 \cdot 6) + (4 \cdot 6) + (5 \cdot 6)$$

➤ **Use the problem from the previous page to help you understand how to find the surface area of a three-dimensional figure.**

1 Look at the **Picture It**. Two line segments in the net are labeled as being 5 ft long. Where do you see these line segments in the prism?

2 The length of one line segment in the net is labeled as 6 ft. Which other line segments in the net could be labeled as 6 ft? How do you know?

3 Aisha wrote the expression $2\left(\frac{1}{2}\right)(4 \cdot 3) + 6(3 + 4 + 5)$ for the area of the net.

Explain why the expression represents the area of the net.

4 What is the area of the plywood Oliver needs for the ramp? Explain how a net can help you find the ramp's surface area.

5 How can you use what you know about two-dimensional shapes to find the surface area of a three-dimensional figure?

6 **Reflect** Think about all the models and strategies you have discussed today. Describe how one of them helped you better understand how to solve the **Try It** problem.

Apply It

➤ **Use what you learned to solve these problems.**

7 What is the surface area of the cereal box? Show your work.

10 in.

7 in.   2 in.

SOLUTION _____

8 Which expressions can be used to find the surface area of the right rectangular prism? Select all that apply.

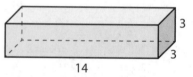

3
3
14

A $14(3 + 3 + 3 + 3) + (3 \cdot 3) + (3 \cdot 3)$

B $(4 \cdot 14 \cdot 3) + (2 \cdot 3 \cdot 3)$

C $(14 \cdot 3) + (14 \cdot 3) + (14 \cdot 3) + (14 \cdot 3)$

D $14 \cdot 3 \cdot 3$

E $2(14 \cdot 3) + 2(14 \cdot 3) + 2(3 \cdot 3)$

9 All of the faces of the triangular pyramid are identical. What is the surface area of the pyramid? Show your work.

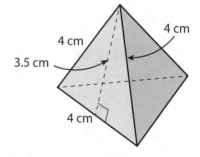

4 cm
4 cm
3.5 cm
4 cm

SOLUTION _____

Practice Finding the Surface Area of a Three-Dimensional Figure

➤ **Study the Example showing how to find the surface area of a three-dimensional figure. Then solve problems 1–5.**

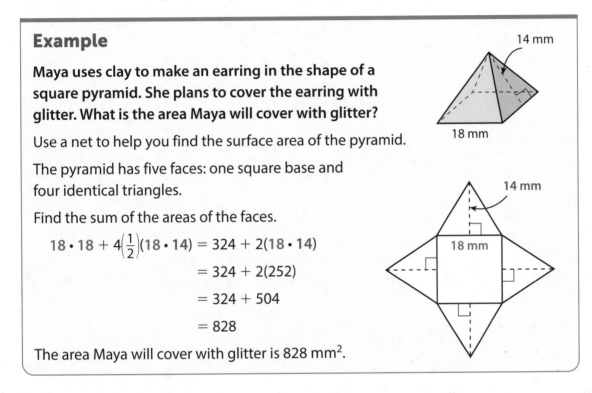

Example

Maya uses clay to make an earring in the shape of a square pyramid. She plans to cover the earring with glitter. What is the area Maya will cover with glitter?

Use a net to help you find the surface area of the pyramid.

The pyramid has five faces: one square base and four identical triangles.

Find the sum of the areas of the faces.

$18 \cdot 18 + 4\left(\frac{1}{2}\right)(18 \cdot 14) = 324 + 2(18 \cdot 14)$

$= 324 + 2(252)$

$= 324 + 504$

$= 828$

The area Maya will cover with glitter is 828 mm².

14 mm

14 mm

18 mm

18 mm

---

1 Ayana wrote the expression below. Does this expression represent the surface area of Maya's earring in the Example? Explain.

$2(18 \cdot 18) + 2\left(\frac{1}{2}\right)(18 \cdot 14) + 2\left(\frac{1}{2}\right)(18 \cdot 14)$

2 What is the surface area of the right rectangular prism? Show your work.

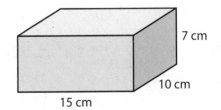

7 cm

10 cm

15 cm

SOLUTION _____

3 What is the surface area of the right triangular prism? Show your work.

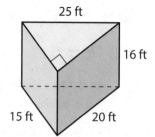

25 ft

16 ft

15 ft   20 ft

SOLUTION _____

4 An artist uses metal to make a sculpture in the shape of a cube. What is the total amount of metal, in square meters, used in the sculpture? Show your work.

$\frac{1}{2}$ m

SOLUTION _____

5 The figure shows a net for a three-dimensional figure. The net includes three squares.

a. What is the three-dimensional figure?

b. What is the surface area of the figure? Show your work.

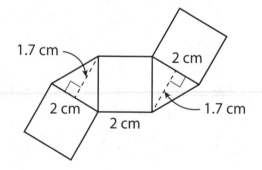

1.7 cm

2 cm

2 cm

1.7 cm

2 cm   2 cm

SOLUTION _____

Refine Using Nets to Find Surface Area

➤ **Complete the Example below. Then solve problems 1–7.**

Example

Alyssa paints the ceiling and the walls of a storage room. The ceiling is a rectangle that is 12 feet long and 9 feet wide. The walls are 10 feet tall, with no windows. What is the area Alyssa paints?

Look at how you could show your work using a net.

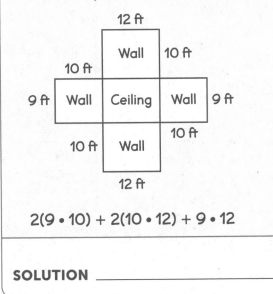

$2(9 \cdot 10) + 2(10 \cdot 12) + 9 \cdot 12$

SOLUTION _____

CONSIDER THIS . . .
Alyssa is inside a right rectangular prism, but she is only painting five of the faces.

PAIR/SHARE
What is a different expression you can write to find the surface area?

Apply It

1 Circle the net for a right triangular prism. Explain how you know.

 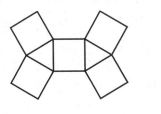 

CONSIDER THIS . . .
How many faces of a triangular prism are triangles?

PAIR/SHARE
Is one of the other two figures a net for a pyramid? How do you know?

2 A net for a three-dimensional figure is shown on grid paper. Each square of the grid paper represents one square foot. What is the surface area of the three-dimensional figure? Show your work.

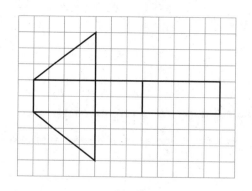

CONSIDER THIS . . .
What shapes make up the net?

PAIR/SHARE
Is the three-dimensional figure a *prism* or a *pyramid*? How do you know?

SOLUTION _____

3 Elisa has a rectangular block of wood with the dimensions shown. She plans to cover it with paper to make a piece of dollhouse furniture. What is the total surface area to be covered with paper?

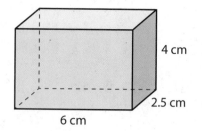

CONSIDER THIS . . .
The block of wood is in the shape of a right rectangular prism.

A 49 cm²

B 60 cm²

C 78 cm²

D 98 cm²

Kyle chose B as the correct answer. How might he have gotten that answer?

PAIR/SHARE
How can you estimate to see if your answer is reasonable?

4 Which figure is a net for a cube?

A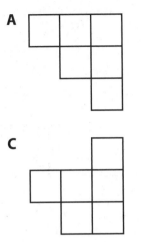

B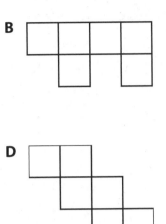

C

D

5 Pedro uses cardboard to make a model of a square pyramid. The edges of the base of the model are 5 in. long. The height of each triangular face is 4 in. What is the area of the cardboard in Pedro's model? Show your work.

Pyramid of the Sun, Teotihuacán, Mexico

SOLUTION _____

6 The figure shows the dimensions of a compost bin. Can the expression below be used to find the surface area of the compost bin? Explain. Include a net in your explanation.

$$6 \cdot 5 + 4 \cdot 5 + 3 \cdot 5 + 5 \cdot 5 + 2\left[3 \cdot 4 + \frac{1}{2}(3 \cdot 4)\right]$$

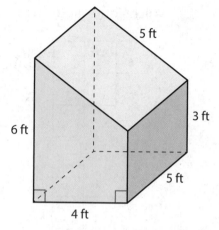

7 **Math Journal** Write a real-world problem that involves finding the surface area of a right rectangular prism. Show how to find the surface area of your prism.

✔ **End of Lesson Checklist**

☐ **INTERACTIVE GLOSSARY** Find the entry for *surface area*. Write the definition in your own words using the word *area*.

☐ **SELF CHECK** Go back to the Unit 1 Opener and see what you can check off.

Dear Family,

This week your student is learning to write and evaluate algebraic expressions.

An algebraic expression is like a numerical expression, except that it contains variables. A **variable** is a letter that represents an unknown quantity. Variables are useful for representing real-world situations such as the one below.

When you go bowling, each game costs $5 and it costs $3 to rent shoes. The total cost to play x games can be represented with the algebraic expression $5x + 3$.

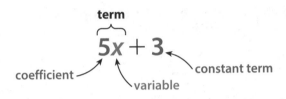

term

$5x + 3$

coefficient — variable — constant term

Your student will be learning how to solve problems like the one below.

At a certain theater, movie tickets cost $9 each. There is a $4 fee to buy tickets online. The expression $9x + 4$ represents the total cost, in dollars, to buy x tickets online. What is the total cost to buy 3 tickets online?

➤ **ONE WAY** to find the cost is to use a table.

1 ticket + fee	2 tickets + fee	3 tickets + fee
$9 + $4 = $13	$9 + $9 + $4 = $22	$9 + $9 + $9 + $4 = $31

➤ **ANOTHER WAY** is to evaluate the expression by substituting 3 for x.

$9x + 4 = 9(3) + 4$

$= 27 + 4$

$= 31$

Using either method, the total cost is $31.

 Use the next page to start a conversation about algebraic expressions.

Activity Exploring Algebraic Expressions

➤ **Do this activity together to explore how algebraic expressions can represent real-world situations.**

One use of algebraic expressions is to represent situations in which some quantities change and others do not. Then once you know the value of the quantity that is changing, you can quickly find the total amount. Look at the expressions below. What could each expression represent?

SITUATION	EXPRESSION	WHAT COULD IT REPRESENT?
How much it costs to buy a salad with additional toppings	$6 + 0.25x$	A salad costs $6 and each additional topping costs $0.25.
How much it costs to order pizzas with a coupon	$8p - 3$	Each pizza costs $8 and . . .
How much it costs for a school field trip to the museum with teachers and students	$10t + 5s$	
How much it costs to buy notebooks on sale	$(4 - 0.50) \cdot n$	

? Did it help to figure out what the variable represents first or the numbers?

Explore Algebraic Expressions

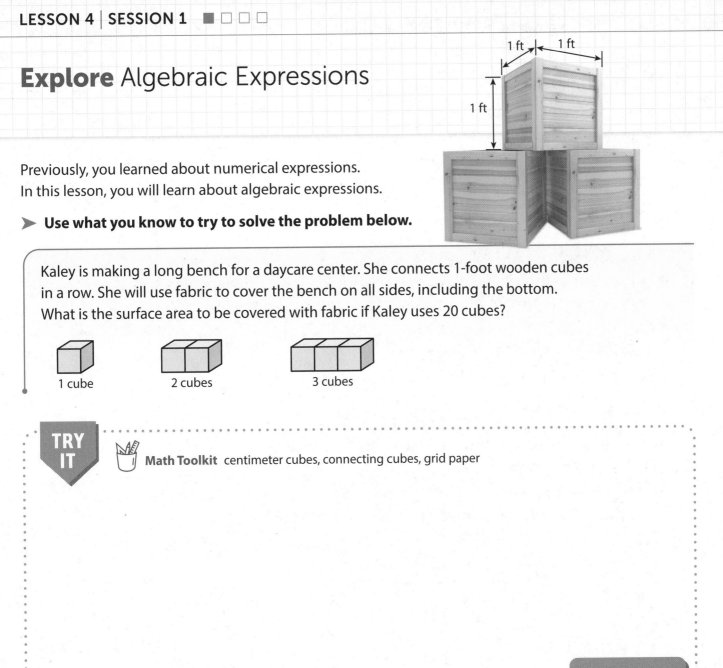

Previously, you learned about numerical expressions.
In this lesson, you will learn about algebraic expressions.

➤ **Use what you know to try to solve the problem below.**

Kaley is making a long bench for a daycare center. She connects 1-foot wooden cubes in a row. She will use fabric to cover the bench on all sides, including the bottom. What is the surface area to be covered with fabric if Kaley uses 20 cubes?

1 cube   2 cubes   3 cubes

TRY IT

Math Toolkit centimeter cubes, connecting cubes, grid paper

DISCUSS IT

Ask: How does your model or strategy show the number of cubes?

Share: My model or strategy shows . . .

◎ **Learning Targets** SMP 1, SMP 2, SMP 3, SMP 4, SMP 5, SMP 6
  • Write expressions that record operations with numbers and with letters standing for numbers.
  • Identify parts of an expression using mathematical terms; view a part of an expression as a single entity.
  • Evaluate expressions at specific values of their variables.
  • Understand that a variable can represent an unknown number, or any number in a specified set.

CONNECT IT

1 **Look Back** What is the surface area Kaley will cover with fabric? What strategy or model can you use to find the answer?

2 **Look Ahead** Each time Kaley adds another cube to the row, the amount of fabric she needs changes. The algebraic expression $4c + 2$ uses the **variable** c to represent any number of 1-foot cubes that Kaley can use in her bench.

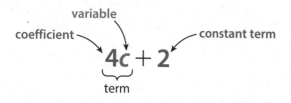

The expression $4c + 2$ is a sum of two **terms**. The numerical factor 4 of the variable term is the term's **coefficient.**

a. Which term of the expression $4c + 2$ is a product? What part of the surface area of Kaley's bench does this product represent? How do you know?

b. Look at the constant term, 2. What part of the surface area of Kaley's bench does it represent?

3 **Reflect** The formula for the area of a triangle includes the algebraic expression $\frac{1}{2}bh$. What is the coefficient in this expression? What are the variables? What do the variables represent?

Prepare for Working with Algebraic Expressions

1 Think about what you know about parts of numerical expressions. Fill in each box.
Use words, numbers, and pictures. Show as many ideas as you can.

Word	In My Own Words	Example
sum		
difference		
product		
factor		
quotient		

2 **a.** Write a numerical expression for this word phrase.

the product of 4 and the difference of 9 and 2

b. Find the value of your expression.

3 Jamal places 1-centimeter cubes in pairs. Then he uses the pairs of cubes to make rows of different lengths.

  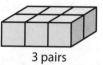

1 pair   2 pairs   3 pairs

a. What is the surface area of a row made of 30 pairs of cubes? Show your work.

SOLUTION _____

b. Check your answer to problem 3a. Show your work.

Develop Writing and Interpreting Algebraic Expressions

➤ **Read and try to solve the problem below.**

The Ramirez family is making tamales. They wrap the tamales in corn husks for baking. They already have 8 corn husks. Isabel is bringing 3 bags of corn husks. Each bag has the same number of corn husks.

How can you use an algebraic expression to show the total number of corn husks the Ramirez family will have after Isabel arrives?

TRY IT

Math Toolkit algebra tiles, number lines, sticky notes

DISCUSS IT

Ask: How does your model show that each bag has the same number of corn husks?

Share: My model shows . . .

➤ **Explore different ways to write and interpret an algebraic expression.**

The Ramirez family is making tamales. They wrap the tamales in corn husks for baking. They already have 8 corn husks. Isabel is bringing 3 bags of corn husks. Each bag has the same number of corn husks.

How can you use an algebraic expression to show the total number of corn husks the Ramirez family will have after Isabel arrives?

Model It

You can use algebra tiles to model the quantities in a problem.

Each small square algebra tile represents 1.

Each rectangular algebra tile represents the same unknown quantity.

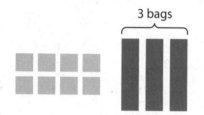

3 bags

Model It

You can use words to help you write an algebraic expression.

Describe how to find the total number of corn husks.

Add the number of corn husks the Ramirez family has to the number of husks in the 3 bags Isabel brings.

number they have	plus	3 times the number in 1 bag
8	+	3 • **number in 1 bag**

Use a variable for the unknown quantity.

➤ **Use the problem from the previous page to help you understand how to write and interpret an algebraic expression.**

1 Look at the algebra tiles in the first **Model It**. What do the small square tiles represent? What unknown quantity does each large rectangular tile represent?

2 Use the variable *x* to represent each large rectangular tile. What algebraic expression can you write to represent the situation?

3 Gavin looks at the second **Model It** and uses the variable *h* to write the expression $8 + 3h$. How many terms does the expression have? Which term is a product? Identify the variable and the coefficient and explain what each represents.

4 Jade writes the expression for the total number of corn husks as $3c + 8$. Elias writes it as $8 + c + c + c$. Are both expressions correct? Explain.

5 How can you write an algebraic expression to represent a situation in which there is an unknown quantity?

 6 **Reflect** Think about all the models and strategies you have discussed today. Describe how one of them helped you better understand how to solve the **Try It** problem.

Apply It

➤ **Use what you learned to solve these problems.**

7 Gaspar writes the algebraic expression $5b + 3.79$. It represents the total cost, in dollars, of buying 5 bagels and a container of cream cheese. Identify any variables, coefficients, and terms in the expression. Tell what each represents.

8 **a.** Write an algebraic expression for the word phrase below. Which factor of your expression is a sum of two terms?

the product of 5.8 and the sum of 9 and a number n

b. Write an algebraic expression for the word phrase below. Is your expression a *difference* or a *quotient?* Explain.

subtract a number x from 15 and then divide by 2

9 Laqueta has a $50 gift card for an online music store. Each song costs s dollars. Write an algebraic expression that represents the amount left on the card after Laqueta buys 7 songs. Show your work.

SOLUTION _____

Practice Writing and Interpreting Algebraic Expressions

➤ **Study the Example showing how to write an algebraic expression. Then solve problems 1–6.**

Example

Noah reads a book and an article. The article is 12 pages long. He completes all the reading in 8 days, and he reads the same number of pages each day. Write an algebraic expression for the number of pages Noah reads each day.

Use the variable b to represent the unknown number of pages in the book.

Add to write an expression for the total number of pages Noah reads.

b + the number of pages in the article $= b + 12$

Divide by 8 to write an expression for the number of pages Noah reads each day.

$(b + 12) \div 8$

1 Julio says that the expression $(b + 12) \div 8$ in the Example can be written as the fraction $\frac{b + 12}{8}$. Do you agree? Explain.

2 Write an algebraic expression for each word phrase.

   a. 5 less than 3.1 times a number n

   b. four more than the quotient of 12 and a number x

3 Ava has a part-time job at a store. She earns a weekly salary. She also earns a $0.60 bonus for each gift card she sells. The expression $165 + 0.60g$ shows Ava's total weekly earnings. Identify any variables, coefficients, and terms in the expression. Tell what each represents.

Vocabulary

coefficient
a number that is multiplied by a variable.

term
a number, a variable, or a product of numbers, variables, and/or expressions.

variable
a letter that represents an unknown number. In some cases, a variable may represent more than one number.

4 Dario looks at the parallelogram and writes the expression $(x + 3)(9)$.

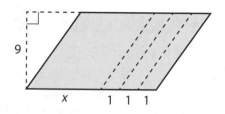

a. Is Dario's expression a *sum*, a *product*, a *difference*, or a *quotient*? Explain.

b. What are the factors of the expression $(x + 3)(9)$? What does each factor represent about the parallelogram?

c. What does the expression $(x + 3)(9)$ represent? Why?

5 Three friends go to a restaurant. They share a meal. They decide to split the cost of the meal equally. Each friend also contributes $2 for the tip. Write an algebraic expression for the amount each friend pays. Show your work.

SOLUTION _____

6 Leah runs m miles every day during the week except for Wednesday and Sunday.

a. Write an algebraic expression that represents the total number of miles Leah runs each week.

b. There are 52 weeks in a year. Write an algebraic expression that represents the total number of miles Leah runs in a year.

Develop Evaluating Algebraic Expressions

$38 Spent on Tickets

➤ **Read and try to solve the problem below.**

A county fair has different ticket prices for adults and children. The expression $6a + 5c$ represents the total cost in dollars of tickets for a adults and c children.

The Patel family spends $38 on tickets. How many adult tickets and child tickets do they buy?

TRY IT

Math Toolkit counters, number lines, sticky notes

DISCUSS IT

Ask: How did you use the expression $6a + 5c$ in your solution?

Share: I knew . . . so I . . .

➤ **Explore ways to interpret and evaluate algebraic expressions.**

A county fair has different ticket prices for adults and children. The expression $6a + 5c$ represents the total cost in dollars of tickets for a adults and c children.

The Patel family spends $38 on tickets. How many adult tickets and how many child tickets do they buy?

Analyze It

You can use the terms and coefficients of an expression to give you information about the situation.

The term $6a$ represents the cost of tickets for a adults and the term $5c$ represents the cost of tickets for c children. The coefficients of the terms tell you how much each type of ticket costs.

$$6a + 5c$$

An adult ticket costs $6.   A child ticket costs $5.

Model It

You can evaluate an algebraic expression by substituting values for the variables.

You can guess and check different combinations of tickets. Try to find a combination that gives a total cost of $38.

Evaluate the expression for $a = 2$ and $c = 3$.

$6a + 5c$

$6(2) + 5(3) = 12 + 15$

$\qquad\qquad = 27$

Because 27 is less than 38, try a greater value for one of the variables.

Evaluate the expression for $a = 5$ and $c = 3$.

$6a + 5c$

$6(5) + 5(3) = 30 + 15$

$\qquad\qquad = 45$

➤ **Use the problem from the previous page to help you understand how to interpret and evaluate an algebraic expression.**

1 Look at the algebraic expression in **Analyze It**. How do you know that the coefficient of the term 6*a* represents the cost of an adult ticket?

2 How does the order of operations help you interpret the expression 6*a* + 5*c* in **Model It**? Describe the order in which you perform the operations shown in the expression 6(2) + 5(3).

3 The choices for the variables in **Model It** do not give a total cost of $38. Show that the value of 6*a* + 5*c* is 38 when *a* = 3 and *c* = 4. What does this mean about the number of adult tickets and child tickets the Patel family buys?

4 How is evaluating an algebraic expression similar to evaluating a numerical expression? How is it different?

5 **Reflect** Think about all the models and strategies you have discussed today. Describe how one of them helped you better understand how to evaluate algebraic expressions.

Apply It

➤ **Use what you learned to solve these problems.**

6 A hot air balloon is rising. The expression $120 + 2t$ represents the height of the hot air balloon in meters after t seconds. Use the expression to find the height of the balloon after 15 s. Show your work.

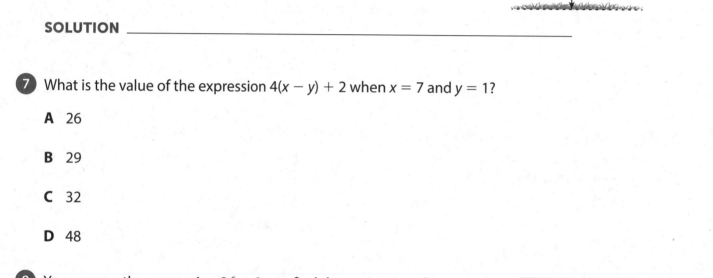

Rises 2 meters every second

120 m

SOLUTION _____

7 What is the value of the expression $4(x - y) + 2$ when $x = 7$ and $y = 1$?

A 26

B 29

C 32

D 48

8 You can use the expression $2\ell + 2w$ to find the perimeter of a rectangle where ℓ is the length and w is the width. Use the expression to find the perimeter of the rectangle. Show your work.

$\frac{1}{6}$ yd

$\frac{2}{3}$ yd

SOLUTION _____

Practice Evaluating Algebraic Expressions

➤ **Study the Example showing how to evaluate an algebraic expression. Then solve problems 1–5.**

Example

The expression $8s + 5m$ represents a student's score on a science test.

   s = the number of correct short answer items

   m = the number of correct multiple-choice items

Santo answers 4 short answer items correctly. He answers 10 multiple-choice items correctly. What is Santo's score?

Evaluate the expression $8s + 5m$ for $s = 4$ and $m = 10$.

$$8s + 5m = 8(4) + 5(10)$$
$$= 32 + 50$$
$$= 82$$

Santo's score is 82.

---

1 The expression $10s + 5m$ represents a student's score on a social studies test, where s = the number of correct short answer items and m = the number of correct multiple-choice items.

Noor answers 16 multiple-choice items correctly. She does not answer any short answer items correctly. What is Noor's score? Show your work.

SOLUTION _____

2 Evaluate the expression $300m + 240,000$ when $m = 21$. Show your work.

> **Vocabulary**
> **evaluate**
> to find the value of an expression.

SOLUTION _____

3) The surface area of a right rectangular prism is $2f + 2t + 2r$, where f is the area of the front face, t is the area of the top face, and r is the area of the right side face. Show how to use the expression to find the surface area of the right rectangular prism at the right. Show your work.

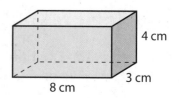

4 cm
3 cm
8 cm

SOLUTION _____

4) Rafael has a sheet with 100 stickers. He gives n stickers to each of his 6 cousins. Write an expression that represents the number of stickers Rafael has left. Then evaluate the expression for $n = 7$. Show your work.

SOLUTION _____

5) Jessica saves quarters and dimes in a jar. She uses the expression $0.25q + 0.1d$ to find the value of the coins. The variable q is the number of quarters and the d is the number of dimes. Find the value of the coins when Jessica has 18 quarters and 15 dimes. Show your work.

SOLUTION _____

Refine Working with Algebraic Expressions

➤ **Complete the Example below. Then solve problems 1–10.**

Example

Evaluate the algebraic expression $5[2(c - 1) + d]$ when $c = 8$ and $d = 6$.

Look at how you could show your work by substituting the given values for the variables and then following the order of operations.

$5[2(c - 1) + d]$

$5[2(8 - 1) + 6] = 5[2(7) + 6]$

$\qquad\qquad\qquad = 5[14 + 6]$

$\qquad\qquad\qquad = 5[20]$

SOLUTION _____

Apply It

1 You can use the expression $\frac{5}{9}(F - 32)$ to find a temperature in degrees Celsius when you know the temperature F in degrees Fahrenheit.

The temperature of a room is 77° Fahrenheit. What is the temperature of the room in degrees Celsius? Show your work.

SOLUTION _____

2 Carmen has a bag of *p* peaches. She adds 10 peaches to the bag. Then she shares all the peaches equally among 5 friends. Write an expression that represents the number of peaches each friend receives. Show your work.

CONSIDER THIS...
Is there a model that could help you see how the quantities are related?

PAIR/SHARE
How would your expression change if the peaches were shared equally among 3 friends?

SOLUTION _____

3 Which algebraic expression represents the statement below?

four less than two times a number

A $4 - 2x$

B $2x - 4$

C $2(x - 4)$

D $(4 - 2)x$

Katrina chose A as the correct answer. How might she have gotten that answer?

CONSIDER THIS...
The expression $9 - x$ can be read *nine minus x* or *x less than nine*. The first number in the algebraic expression is not always read first.

PAIR/SHARE
How can you decide whether or not the expression needs parentheses?

4 In a video game, players start with a score of 100 points. They earn 8 points for each gold coin and 25 points for each gem they find. Isaiah finds 3 gold coins and 2 gems. Write and evaluate an algebraic expression to find Isaiah's score. Use *c* for the number of gold coins found and *g* for the number of gems found. Show your work.

Level 1
8 points
25 points

SOLUTION _____

5 Elon writes an algebraic expression to represent *the product of 10 and the difference of 5y and 1*. The factors of his expression are _____ and _____ .

6 Demi starts a gardening project with 80 sunflower seeds. She plants 12 of the seeds. Then she gives 5 seeds each to some friends. Which expression represents the number of sunflower seeds Demi has left after she gives seeds to *f* friends?

A $80 - 12 - \frac{f}{5}$

B $80 - 12 - \frac{5}{f}$

C $80 - 12 - 5 - f$

D $80 - 12 - 5f$

7 Use the expression $11 + 9k + 6n$. Tell whether each statement is *True* or *False*.

	True	False
a. The expression has three terms.	○	○
b. In the expression, 11 is a coefficient.	○	○
c. In one of the terms, 6 is a factor.	○	○
d. The expression has two variables.	○	○

8 Enrico is going to a department store. T-shirts are on sale for $2 off the regular price, *p*. The expression 5(*p* − 2) represents the total cost of the T-shirts he buys. What are the factors in the expression? What does each factor tell you? Explain.

9 Evaluate the expression 3[*a*(4*b* − *c*)] for *a* = 2, *b* = 3, and *c* = 2.8.

10 **Math Journal** Write a real-world situation that matches the expression 10*y* − 3. Then evaluate the expression for *y* = 4. Explain the meaning of the result in terms of the real-world situation.

✔ **End of Lesson Checklist**

☐ **INTERACTIVE GLOSSARY** Review the entry for *expression*. Find the entry for *term*. Give an example of an algebraic expression with two terms.

☐ **SELF CHECK** Go back to the Unit 1 Opener and see what you can check off.

Dear Family,

This week your student is learning how to evaluate expressions with exponents.

Exponents are used to represent repeated multiplication. One way to show this is with a **power**. The **base** is the number you are multiplying. The **exponent** is the number of times the base is a factor.

base   exponent

$$5^4 = 5 \cdot 5 \cdot 5 \cdot 5$$

power   5 is a factor 4 times.

To evaluate expressions with exponents, use the order of operations. Exponents represent multiplication, so evaluate powers before you add or subtract.

Your student will be learning how to evaluate expressions like the one below.

Evaluate the expression $10 + 3^4$.

➤ **ONE WAY** to find the value of an expression with an exponent to rewrite the power as repeated multiplication. Then multiply from left to right.

$$10 + 3^4 = 10 + 3 \cdot 3 \cdot 3 \cdot 3$$
$$= 10 + 9 \cdot 3 \cdot 3$$
$$= 10 + 27 \cdot 3$$
$$= 10 + 81$$
$$= 91$$

➤ **ANOTHER WAY** is to group factors before you multiply.

$$10 + 3^4 = 10 + 3 \cdot 3 \cdot 3 \cdot 3$$
$$= 10 + (3 \cdot 3) \cdot (3 \cdot 3)$$
$$= 10 + 9 \cdot 9$$
$$= 10 + 81$$
$$= 91$$

Using either method, the value of the expression is 91.

 Use the next page to start a conversation about exponents.

Activity Thinking About Exponents

➤ **Do this activity together to look for patterns in evaluating expressions with exponents.**

Look at these three sets of powers.

What pattern do you notice in each set?

SET 1

$3^1 = 3$

$3^2 = 3 \cdot 3 = 9$

$3^3 = 3 \cdot 3 \cdot 3 = 27$

$3^4 = 3 \cdot 3 \cdot 3 \cdot 3 = 81$

SET 2

$0^2 = 0 \cdot 0 = 0$

$1^2 = 1 \cdot 1 = 1$

$2^2 = 2 \cdot 2 = 4$

$3^2 = 3 \cdot 3 = 9$

$4^2 = 4 \cdot 4 = 16$

SET 3

$\left(\frac{1}{2}\right)^2 = \frac{1}{2} \cdot \frac{1}{2} = \frac{1}{4}$

$\left(\frac{1}{3}\right)^2 = \frac{1}{3} \cdot \frac{1}{3} = \frac{1}{9}$

$\left(\frac{2}{3}\right)^2 = \frac{2}{3} \cdot \frac{2}{3} = \frac{4}{9}$

 Do you notice any patterns between two of the sets?

Explore Expressions with Exponents

Previously, you learned about using exponents to write powers of 10. In this lesson, you will learn about using exponents in both numerical and algebraic expressions.

➤ **Use what you know to try to solve the problem below.**

David builds a house for his cat using cubes with edges that are 1 foot long. He builds the house by making 4 layers of cubes. Each layer is made up of 4 rows and 4 columns of cubes. How many cubes does David use for the house?

TRY IT

Math Toolkit connecting cubes, grid paper, isometric dot paper, unit cubes

DISCUSS IT

Ask: What strategy did you use to find the number of cubes?

Share: I found the number of cubes by . . .

◎ **Learning Targets** SMP 1, SMP 2, SMP 3, SMP 4, SMP 5, SMP 6, SMP 8
• Write and evaluate numerical expressions involving whole-number exponents.
• Evaluate expressions at specific values of their variables. Include expressions that arise from formulas used in real-world problems. Perform arithmetic operations, including those involving whole-number exponents, in the conventional order when there are no parentheses to specify a particular order.

CONNECT IT

 Look Back How many cubes does David use for the house? How can you find the number of cubes?

 Look Ahead One way to solve the **Try It** problem is to use repeated addition. Another way is to use repeated multiplication.

   a. You can show repeated multiplication with an **exponent**. You have used exponents with powers of 10. Write the **power** 10^5 as repeated multiplication.

   b. You can also write powers with numbers other than 10 as the **base**. What are the base and exponent in the power 3^8? Write 3^8 as repeated multiplication.

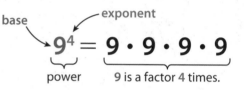

$$9^4 = 9 \cdot 9 \cdot 9 \cdot 9$$

base   exponent   power   9 is a factor 4 times.

   c. What are the base and exponent in the power 3^1? Write 3^1 without an exponent.

   d. You can also use exponents with variables. Use the variable s to represent the edge length of a cube. Then the volume formula $V = \ell w h$ becomes $V = s \cdot s \cdot s$, or $V = s^3$.

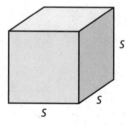

   The house that David builds for his cat is a cube with an edge length of 4 ft. Show how to use the volume formula $V = s^3$ to find the volume of the house.

 Reflect How are the expressions 2^7 and $2 \cdot 7$ alike? How are they different?

Prepare for Writing and Evaluating Expressions with Exponents

1   Think about what you know about powers of 10. Fill in each box. Use words, numbers, and pictures. Show as many ideas as you can.

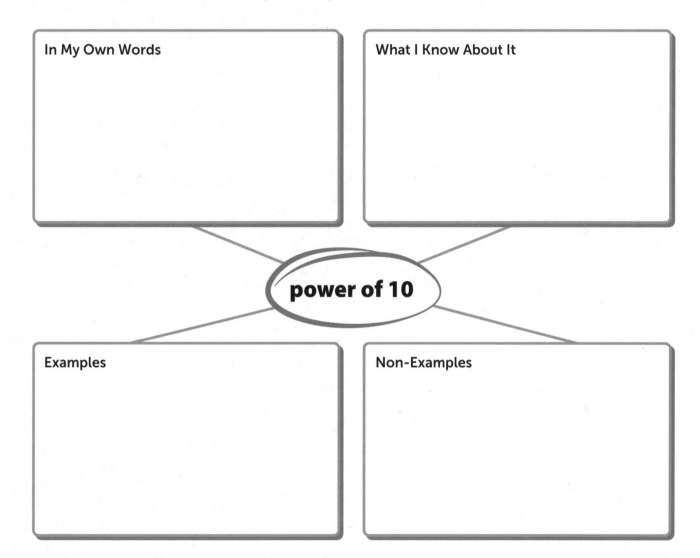

In My Own Words	What I Know About It

power of 10

Examples	Non-Examples

2   What power of 10 can you write to show the number of small cubes in the model? Explain.

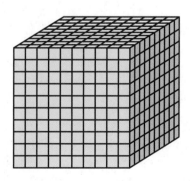

3 A restaurant keeps eggs in a rack that has 5 layers. Each layer has 5 rows, with 5 eggs in each row.

a. How many eggs does each 5-layer rack hold? Show your work.

SOLUTION _____

b. Check your answer to problem 3a. Show your work.

Develop Writing and Evaluating Expressions with Exponents

➤ **Read and try to solve the problem below.**

Kendra posts a photo on her social media account. In the first hour, 2 friends share the photo. In the second hour, each of those friends have 2 friends who share the photo. The pattern continues. How many people share the photo in the sixth hour?

TRY IT

Math Toolkit connecting cubes, counters, grid paper

DISCUSS IT

Ask: What did you do first to figure out how many people share the photo in the sixth hour?

Share: First I . . .

➤ **Explore different ways to write and evaluate expressions with exponents.**

Kendra posts a photo on her social media account. In the first hour, 2 friends share the photo. In the second hour, each of those friends have 2 friends who share the photo. The pattern continues. How many people share the photo in the sixth hour?

Picture It

You can use a tree diagram to find a pattern with repeated multiplication.

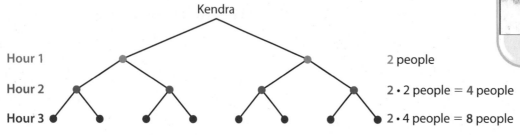

Kendra

Hour 1		2 people
Hour 2		2 · 2 people = 4 people
Hour 3		2 · 4 people = 8 people

Model It

You can use an exponent to represent repeated multiplication as a power.

Each hour, the number of people who share the photo increases by a factor of 2.

Hour	Number of People Who Share Photo	Written as a Power
1	2	2^1
2	2 · 2	2^2
3	2 · 2 · 2	2^3
4	2 · 2 · 2 · 2	2^4
5	2 · 2 · 2 · 2 · 2	2^5
6	2 · 2 · 2 · 2 · 2 · 2	?

➤ **Use the problem from the previous page to help you understand how to write and evaluate expressions with exponents.**

1 Look at the tree diagram in the **Picture It**. How many dots would there be in a row for Hour 4? Explain.

2 Explain how to use the number of people shown by one row of the tree diagram to find the number people in the next row of the tree diagram.

3 Look at the table in **Model It**. Write the number of people who share the photo in the sixth hour as a power of 2. How many people share the photo in the sixth hour?

4 Alexis finds the value of 2^6 by writing $4 \cdot 4 \cdot 4$. Xavier finds the value of 2^6 by writing $8 \cdot 8$. Why are both expressions ways to find 2^6?

5 Write the number of people who share the photo in Hour 9 as a power of 2. How do you know what number to use as the exponent?

6 **Reflect** Think about all the models and strategies you have discussed today. Describe how one of them helped you better understand how to solve the **Try It** problem.

Apply It

➤ **Use what you learned to solve these problems.**

7 Which expression is equivalent to $7 \times 7 \times 7 \times 3 \times 3$?

   A $3^7 \times 2^3$

   B $7^7 \times 3^3$

   C $7^3 \times 3^2$

   D $21^3 \times 6^2$

8 Evaluate n^3 when $n = \frac{2}{3}$. Show your work.

SOLUTION _____

9 On the Lucky Five game show, Troy wins $5 if he answers one question correctly. Each time he answers another question correctly without making a mistake, the amount of money he wins is multiplied by 5. Troy answers 6 questions correctly without making a mistake. His winnings are represented by the expression 5^6. How much money does Troy win? Show your work.

Lucky **5** *Game*

What is the capital of the state of California?

SOLUTION _____

Practice Writing and Evaluating Expressions with Exponents

➤ **Study the Example showing how to write and evaluate an expression with an exponent. Then solve problems 1–6.**

Example

On the first day, one person texts a compliment to 3 people. On the second day, each of these 3 people texts a compliment to 3 new people. The pattern continues. How many people receive a compliment on the eighth day?

Use a table to look for a pattern.

The number of people who receive a compliment each day is 3 times the number of people from the day before.

The pattern shows that 3^8 people receive a compliment on Day 8.

Day	Number of People Who Receive a Compliment	Written as a Power
1	3	3^1
2	$3 \cdot 3$	3^2
3	$3 \cdot 3 \cdot 3$	3^3
4	$3 \cdot 3 \cdot 3 \cdot 3$	3^4

$$3^8 = (3 \cdot 3) \cdot (3 \cdot 3) \cdot (3 \cdot 3) \cdot (3 \cdot 3)$$
$$= (9 \cdot 9) \cdot (9 \cdot 9)$$
$$= 81 \cdot 81$$
$$= 6,561$$

On the eighth day, 6,561 people receive a compliment.

1 Suppose the pattern in the Example continues. Write the number of people who receive a compliment on the ninth day as a power of 3. How many people receive a compliment on the ninth day? Show your work.

SOLUTION _____

2 Look at how 3^8 is evaluated in the Example. Write 3^8 as a power with a base of 81.

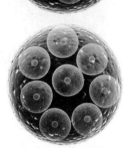

3 A scientist places a cell in a Petri dish. At the end of 1 hour, the cell divides so that there are 2 cells in the Petri dish. At the end of 2 hours, those cells divide so there are 4 cells in the Petri dish. The cells continue to divide this way every hour. Use the expression 2^{10} to find the number of cells in the Petri dish after 10 hours. Show your work.

SOLUTION _____

4 Write $7 \cdot 7 \cdot 7 \cdot 7 \cdot 7$ as a power. Then find the product. Show your work.

SOLUTION _____

5 Evaluate n^4 for $n = \frac{3}{4}$. Show your work.

SOLUTION _____

6 Paula says that $3^4 = 4^3$. Do you agree or disagree? Explain.

Develop Using Order of Operations with Expressions with Exponents

➤ **Read and try to solve the problem below.**

Puebla, Mexico has been known for its Talavera tiles since the 1500s. Today, artists in the United States use Talavera tiles on buildings and walkways.

Three stages of a pattern with tiles are shown below.
How many tiles are needed to make Stage 40 of the pattern?

Stage 1

Stage 2

Stage 3

TRY IT

Math Toolkit grid paper, unit tiles

DISCUSS IT

Ask: How does your strategy show or describe the tile pattern?

Share: My strategy shows . . .

➤ **Explore different ways to understand using order of operations when evaluating expressions with exponents.**

Puebla, Mexico has been known for its Talavera tiles since the 1500s. Today, artists in the United States use Talavera tiles on buildings and walkways.

Three stages of a pattern with tiles are shown below. How many tiles are needed to make Stage 40 of the pattern?

Stage 1

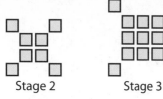
Stage 2

Stage 3

Model It

You can write numerical expressions with exponents to represent the pattern.

In every stage, the first and last row of tiles have a total of 4 tiles.

The other rows of tiles form a square.

Stage 1	Stage 2	Stage 3	Stage 4
$4 + 1$	$4 + 2 \cdot 2$	$4 + 3 \cdot 3$	$4 + 4 \cdot 4$
$4 + 1^2$	$4 + 2^2$	$4 + 3^2$	$4 + 4^2$

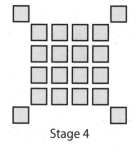
Stage 4

Model It

You can write an algebraic expression to represent the pattern.

Use the variable n to represent the stage number.

The number of tiles in the inner square is $n \cdot n$, or n^2.

There are 4 additional tiles at the corners.

So, the total number of tiles in Stage n is $4 + n^2$.

➤ **Use the problem from the previous page to help you understand using the order of operations when evaluating expressions with exponents.**

1 Look at the first **Model It**. Jayden evaluated the expression $4 + 3^2$ by adding first to get 7^2. Use the order of operations to explain Jayden's error.

2 Place parentheses in the expression $4 + 3^2$ so that the value of the expression is 7^2.

3 Evaluate $4 + n^2$ when $n = 40$. How many tiles are in Stage 40 of the pattern?

4 The expression $4 + n^2$ represents adding 4 to a power. Now think about multiplying a power by 4.

   a. Write $4 \cdot n^2$ and $(4 \cdot n)^2$ without exponents.

   b. Should you think of $4n^2$ as $4 \cdot n^2$ or as $(4n)^2$? Explain your reasoning.

5 Describe the order of operations you would use to evaluate $8 + 4(3^2)$.

6 How do exponents fit into the order of operations?

7 **Reflect** Think about all the models and strategies you have discussed today. Describe how one of them helped you better understand how to use order of operations to evaluate expressions with exponents.

Apply It

➤ **Use what you learned to solve these problems.**

8 Tamera is using rice paper to make Japanese lanterns. The expression $2s^2 + 40s$ represents the surface area of a lantern where the base edges are s inches long. What is the surface area of a lantern when s is 9 in.? Show your work.

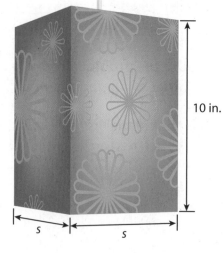

10 in.

s s

SOLUTION _____

9 What is the value of the expression $5(3^3 - 4)$? Show your work.

SOLUTION _____

10 What is the value of $m + 4n^2 - 5q + 4$ when $m = 5, n = 2$, and $q = 3$?

A 2

B 10

C 25

D 58

Practice Using Order of Operations with Expressions with Exponents

➤ **Study the Example showing how to evaluate an expression with exponents and parentheses. Then solve problems 1–6.**

Example

What is the value of the expression $4(5 - 2)^2 + 5^3$?

Use the order of operations to evaluate the expression.

Subtract inside the parentheses. $4(5 - 2)^2 + 5^3 = 4(3)^2 + 5^3$

Evaluate the powers. $= 4(9) + 125$

Multiply. $= 36 + 125$

Add. $= 161$

1 What is the value of the expression $5(2^3 - 3)$? Show your work.

SOLUTION _____

2 Miguel writes the expression $2n^4$. He says that when you double the value of n, you double the value of the expression. Do you agree or disagree? Explain.

3 Evaluate the expression $1^4 + 3(10 - 2)^2$. Show your work.

SOLUTION _____

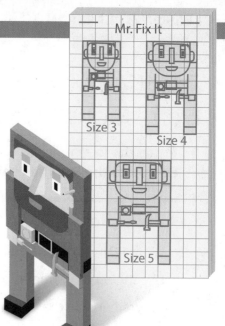

4 Zhen designs a character for a video game. He draws three sizes of the character on grid paper. Zhen use the expression $6 + s^2$ to find the number of grid squares in a character of any size s. Find the number of grid squares in a character of size 7. Show your work.

SOLUTION _____

5 Evaluate the expression $p^3 - q^4 + 3r \div 2$ for $p = 6$, $q = 2$, and $r = 4$. Show your work.

SOLUTION _____

6 You can use the formula $A = 6s^2$ to find the surface area of a cube with edge length s. A cube has edges that are 10 in. long. What is the surface area of the cube? Show your work.

SOLUTION _____

Refine Writing and Evaluating Expressions with Exponents

➤ **Complete the Example below. Then solve problems 1–10.**

Example

Write an expression that is equal to 36 using each number and symbol below exactly one time in the expression.

5   8   8 ^{2} ÷   +   (   )

Look at how you could use reasoning and the order of operations to make an expression whose value is 36.

I know that $6 \times 6 = 36$, and that $6^2 = 36$.

That means I can use 5, 8, 8, ÷, and + to write an expression with a value of 6. Then I can put parentheses around the expression and square it to make 36.

I know that $8 ÷ 8 = 1$ and $5 + 1 = 6$.

SOLUTION _____

CONSIDER THIS . . .
How can the order of operations help you write an expression that has the correct value?

PAIR/SHARE
How would the value of your expression change if you removed the parentheses?

Apply It

1 What is the value of the expression $(0.1)^3$? Show your work.

CONSIDER THIS . . .
Should the value of $(0.1)^3$ be greater than or less than 0.1?

PAIR/SHARE
How can you check your answer by writing 0.1^3 as $\left(\frac{1}{10}\right)^3$?

SOLUTION _____

2 An architect is trying different dimensions for the room shown below. Write an algebraic expression the architect can use to find the area of the room. Then find the area when x is 6 m. Show your work.

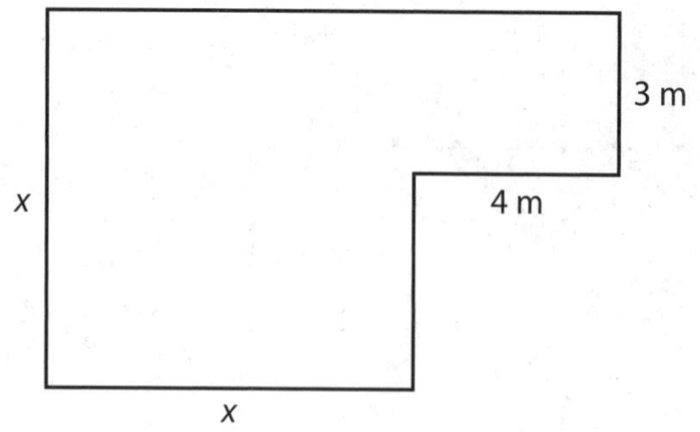

CONSIDER THIS...
How can you decompose the room into triangles, rectangles, or squares?

SOLUTION _____

PAIR/SHARE
How can you check that your answer is reasonable?

3 What is the value of $2 + b(a^2 + 4)$ when $a = 2$ and $b = 4$?

A 22

B 34

C 2

D 48

Zara chose D as the correct answer. How might she have gotten that answer?

CONSIDER THIS...
Which part of the expression would you evaluate first?

PAIR/SHARE
Where would you insert parentheses in the expression to make its value one of the other answer choices?

④ Which expressions have a value of 100 when $m = 5$? Select all that apply.

A $2m^2 + 50$

B $(2m)^2 + 50$

C $(m + 5)^2$

D $m^3 \div 5 \cdot 4$

E $4m^2$

F $(4m)^2$

⑤ Write 3^8 as a power with a base of 9. Show your work.

SOLUTION _____

⑥ What is the value of the expression $x^3 - 1,750$ when $x = 30$? Show your work.

SOLUTION _____

⑦ What is the value of the expression $3[4(3^2 - 7)] - 4^2$? Show your work.

SOLUTION _____

8 There are 32 teams in the first round of a basketball tournament. One half of the teams that play in each round of the tournament move on to play in the next round.

Smithtown
Basketball Tournament
....
32 Teams
Winner of each game moves forward to next round.
....

Cheer your team to the finals!

a. Explain why the expression $32 \times \left(\frac{1}{2}\right)^3$ represents the number of teams that play in the fourth round.

b. How many teams play in the fourth round? Show your work.

SOLUTION _____

9 The value of 2^{14} is how many times as great as the value of 2^{11}? Explain.

10 **Math Journal** Write an expression that is equal to 8 using each number and symbol below exactly one time in the expression. Explain your thinking.

    1   2   3 ^{3} +   −   ( )

✓ **End of Lesson Checklist**

☐ **INTERACTIVE GLOSSARY** Find the entry for *power*. Add another example and label the exponent and base in your example.

☐ **SELF CHECK** Go back to the Unit 1 Opener and see what you can check off.

Dear Family,

This week your student is learning about the greatest common factor and the least common multiple of two whole numbers.

The **greatest common factor (GCF)** of two numbers is the greatest factor the two numbers have in common. For example, the GCF of 12 and 18 is 6.

Factors of 12: 1, **2**, **3**, 4, **6**, 12

Factors of 18: 1, **2**, **3**, **6**, 9, 18

The **least common multiple (LCM)** of two numbers is the least multiple that the two numbers share. For example, the LCM of 12 and 18 is 36.

Multiples of 12: 12, 24, **36**, 48, . . .

Multiples of 18: 18, **36**, 54, . . .

Your student will be learning to use the greatest common factor to solve problems like the one below.

> A teacher gives out 30 markers and 40 colored pencils. He gives an equal number of markers and an equal number of colored pencils to each student. What is the greatest number of students the teacher can give markers and colored pencils to?

➤ **ONE WAY** to find the greatest common factor of two whole numbers is to list all the factors of each number.

Factors of 30: 1, **2**, 3, **5**, 6, ⑩, 15, 30

Factors of 40: 1, **2**, 4, **5**, 8, ⑩, 40

The common factors of 30 and 40 are 1, 2, 5, and 10. The greatest common factor is 10.

➤ **ANOTHER WAY** is to write each number as a product of prime factors. Then multiply the common prime factors.

$30 = 3 \cdot 2 \cdot 5$ $\qquad$ $40 = 2 \cdot 2 \cdot 2 \cdot 5$

Greatest common factor: $2 \cdot 5 = 10$

Using either method, the greatest number of students the teacher can give an equal number of markers and an equal number of colored pencils to is 10.

▶ Use the next page to start a conversation about factors.

Activity Exploring Common Factors

➤ **Do this activity together to explore common factors.**

You are helping with the 6th grade spirit day at school. There will be games with prize bags for winners. Your teacher asks you to use these supplies to make prize bags. All the prize bags must contain the same items.

Different combinations of supplies will result in different numbers of prize bags. Which combination would you choose and why?

42 puzzles
48 bouncy balls
30 sets of paint
36 markers

COMBINATION 1	
30 prize bags **Items in each bag**	**Leftover supplies**
1 puzzle	12 puzzles
1 bouncy ball	18 bouncy balls
1 set of paint	6 markers
1 marker	

COMBINATION 2	
15 prize bags **Items in each bag**	**Leftover supplies**
2 puzzles	12 puzzles
3 bouncy balls	3 bouncy balls
2 sets of paint	6 markers
2 markers	

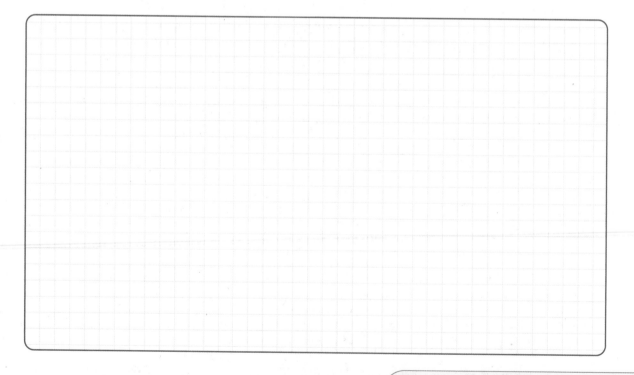

? What combination of prizes would result in zero leftover supplies?

Explore Common Factors and Multiples

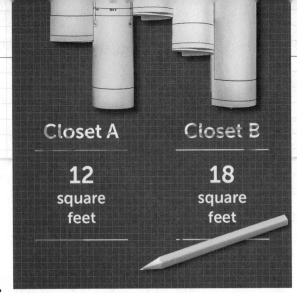

Closet A   Closet B

12 square feet   **18** square feet

Previously, you learned how to find factors and multiples of a whole number. In this lesson, you will learn how to find the greatest common factor and the least common multiple of two whole numbers.

➤ **Use what you know to try to solve the problem below.**

A floor plan for a new house shows a linen closet with an area of 12 ft² and a clothes closet with an area of 18 ft². The two closets will share one wall. What are all the possible whole-number lengths for the shared wall?

TRY IT

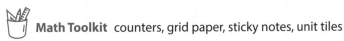 **Math Toolkit** counters, grid paper, sticky notes, unit tiles

DISCUSS IT

Ask: How would you explain what the problem is asking in your own words?

Share: The problem is asking . . .

◎ **Learning Target** SMP 1, SMP 2, SMP 3, SMP 4, SMP 5, SMP 6, SMP 7, SMP 8
Find the greatest common factor of two whole numbers less than or equal to 100 and the least common multiple of two whole numbers less than or equal to 12. Use the distributive property to express a sum of two whole numbers 1–100 with a common factor as a multiple of a sum of two whole numbers with no common factor.

CONNECT IT

1 **Look Back** Is there more than one possible side length for the wall shared by the two closets? Explain how you know.

2 **Look Ahead** The length of the shared wall is a common factor of 12 and 18 because it divides both 12 and 18 without a remainder. You can use common factors in situations that involve dividing objects into equal groups.

Suppose Malik wants to share a bag of connecting cubes with some friends. He has 6 blue cubes and 15 red cubes. He wants each friend to get the same number of blue cubes and the same number of red cubes.

a. List all the ways Malik can put the blue cubes into equal groups.

b. List all the ways Malik can put the red cubes into equal groups.

c. Malik wants to share all the cubes. How many friends can Malik give cubes to? Explain how you know.

d. How is your answer to problem 2c related to factors of the numbers 6 and 15?

3 **Reflect** Hugo says that some whole numbers have no common factors. Jasmine says any two whole numbers will always have at least one common factor. Who is correct? Explain.

Prepare for Finding Greatest Common Factor and Least Common Multiple

1 Think about what you know about factors and multiples. Fill in each box.
Use words, numbers, and pictures. Show as many ideas as you can.

What Is It?	What I Know About It

multiple

Examples	Examples

2 Any multiple of 12 is also a multiple of 4. Explain why this is true.

3 Rectangular paintings hang on the wall of an art gallery. One painting has an area of 24 ft^2. Another painting has an area of 32 ft^2. The paintings have whole-number side lengths and have one pair of side lengths in common.

a. What could the common side length be? Show your work.

SOLUTION _____

b. Check your answer to problem 3a. Show your work.

Develop Finding the Greatest Common Factor of Two Whole Numbers

➤ **Read and try to solve the problem below.**

Akio has 27 blankets and 18 flashlights to use in emergency relief kits for communities in need. He will put the same number of blankets and the same number of flashlights in each kit. He wants to use all the blankets and flashlights. What is the greatest number of emergency relief kits Akio can make?

27 Blankets
18 Flashlights

 TRY IT

Math Toolkit counters, multiplication tables, number lines, unit tiles

DISCUSS IT

Ask: How does your strategy show the greatest number of kits?

Share: In my solution, . . . represents . . .

➤ **Explore different ways to find the greatest common factor of two whole numbers.**

Akio has 27 blankets and 18 flashlights to use in emergency relief kits for communities in need. He will put the same number of blankets and the same number of flashlights in each kit. He wants to use all the blankets and flashlights. What is the greatest number of kits Akio can make?

Analyze It

You can list all the factors of each number to find the factors that divide both numbers without a remainder.

Factors of 27: 1, 3, 9, 27

Factors of 18: 1, 2, 3, 6, 9, 18

The common factors of 27 and 18 are 1, 3, and 9.

The **greatest common factor (GCF)** of 27 and 18 is 9.

Model It

You can use the prime factors of two numbers to find their greatest common factor.

One way to show all the prime factors of a number is with a factor tree.

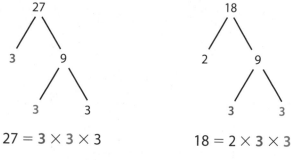

$27 = 3 \times 3 \times 3$ $18 = 2 \times 3 \times 3$

The numbers 27 and 18 share two factors of 3.

$$GCF = 3 \times 3$$
$$= 9$$

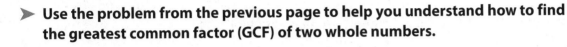

CONNECT IT

➤ **Use the problem from the previous page to help you understand how to find the greatest common factor (GCF) of two whole numbers.**

1 Look at **Analyze It**. How are the factors of 27 and 18 related to the number of kits Akio can make?

2 Look at **Analyze It** and **Model It**. They both show that 9 is the greatest common factor (GCF) of 27 and 18. What does the GCF represent in this situation?

3 How many blankets and how many flashlights will be in each kit if Akio uses the GCF as the number of kits? Where do you see these amounts in the equations under the factor trees?

4 Jada writes the equations under the factor trees using exponents.

$27 = 3^3$ and $18 = 2 \times 3^2$

How could using exponents help you find the GCF of 18 and 27?

5 **Reflect** Think about all the models and strategies you have discussed today. Describe how one of them helped you better understand how to find the greatest common factor of two whole numbers.

Apply It

➤ **Use what you learned to solve these problems.**

6　Find the greatest common factor (GCF) of 56 and 96. Show your work.

SOLUTION _____

7　Reth says the greatest common factor of 36 and 60 is 6. Is Reth correct? Explain.

8　Luis buys 16 bellflowers and 20 roses. He wants to plant an equal number of bellflowers and an equal number of roses in each of his flower boxes. What is the greatest number of flower boxes Luis can plant using all the bellflowers and roses? Show your work.

SOLUTION _____

Practice Finding the Greatest Common Factor of Two Whole Numbers

➤ **Study the Example showing how to find the greatest common factor of two whole numbers. Then solve problems 1–4.**

Example

Kennedy plans to completely cover the wall behind her kitchen sink with square tiles. The wall is a rectangle that is 15 in. high and 24 in. long. Each square tile will have whole-number side lengths. What is the side length of the largest square tile that Kennedy can use?

The side length of the tile must divide both 15 in. and 24 in.

List the factors of 15: 1, 3, 5, 15

List the factors of 24: 1, 2, 3, 4, 6, 8, 12, 24

The only whole numbers that divide into both 15 and 24 are 1 and 3. The greatest common factor of 15 and 24 is 3.

The side length of the largest tile Kennedy can use is 3 in.

1 Suppose the wall in the Example is 16 in. high and 28 in. long.

   a. What is the side length of the largest square tile that Kennedy can use? Show your work.

   SOLUTION _____

   b. How many tiles does Kennedy need to completely fill the wall? Show your work.

   SOLUTION _____

2 Avery says the greatest common factor of 12 and 15 is 60. Is Avery correct? Explain how you know.

3 What is the GCF of 60 and 100? Show your work.

SOLUTION _____

4 An art teacher is making packages of paintbrushes and paint for his students. He has 24 brushes and 40 tubes of paint. Each package will have the same number of brushes and the same number of tubes of paint.

   a. What is the greatest number of packages that the art teacher can make using all the paintbrushes and paint? Show your work.

SOLUTION _____

   b. How many paintbrushes and tubes of paint are in each package?

Develop Finding the Least Common Multiple of Two Whole Numbers

NORTH COUNTRY SHEEP FARM

Morgan — Shear every **6** months

Anne — Shear every **8** months

➤ **Read and try to solve the problem below.**

Morgan and Anne own North Country Sheep Farm. Morgan shears one herd of sheep every 6 months. Anne decides to shear another herd of sheep every 8 months to see if waiting longer results in higher quality wool.

Both herds are sheared this month. In how many months will Morgan and Anne shear their herds in the same month again?

TRY IT

Math Toolkit counters, grid paper, hundred chart, number lines

LESSON 6 Find Greatest Common Factor and Least Common Multiple   **119**

➤ **Explore different ways to find the least common multiple of two whole numbers.**

Morgan and Anne own North Country Sheep Farm. Morgan shears one herd of sheep every 6 months. Anne decides to shear another herd of sheep every 8 months to see if waiting longer results in higher quality wool.

Both herds are sheared this month. In how many months will Morgan and Anne shear their herds in the same month again?

Model It

You can list multiples of 6 and 8 to show the numbers of months until the sheep from each herd will have their wool sheared.

Multiples of 6: 6, 12, 18, **24**, 30, 36, 42, **48**, . . .

Multiples of 8: 8, 16, **24**, 32, 40, **48**, 56, 64, . . .

The numbers **24** and **48** that appear in both lists are common multiples of 6 and 8.

The **least common multiple (LCM)** of 6 and 8 is 24.

Model It

You can use the prime factors of two numbers to find their least common multiple.

$6 = 2 \times 3$ $\qquad\qquad\qquad\qquad$ $8 = 2 \times 2 \times 2$

6 and 8 have one common factor of **2**.

$6 = 2 \times 3$
$8 = 2 \times 2 \times 2$

Multiply the factors of the numbers. Use the common factor only once.

$LCM = 2 \times 2 \times 2 \times 3$
$ = 24$

➤ **Use the problem from the previous page to help you understand how to find the least common multiple of two whole numbers.**

1 The numbers 24 and 48 are common multiples of 6 and 8. What do these numbers represent in this situation?

2 Both **Model Its** show that the least common multiple (LCM) of 6 and 8 is 24. What does the LCM represent in this situation?

3 Why is the common factor of 2 used only once in the LCM of 6 and 8?

4 The product of 6 and 8 is a common multiple of 6 and 8, but it is not the least common multiple of 6 and 8. Look at these statements about least common multiples. Underline the LCMs that are the product of the two numbers.

The LCM of 4 and 5 is 20.   The LCM of 4 and 6 is 12.

The LCM of 4 and 3 is 12.   The LCM of 4 and 8 is 8.

When can you multiply two numbers to find their LCM?

5 **Reflect** Think about all the models and strategies you have discussed today. Describe how one of them helped you better understand how to find the least common multiple of two whole numbers.

Apply It

➤ **Use what you learned to solve these problems.**

6 Ria is buying plates and cups for a party. She wants the same number of each. Plates are sold in packs of 8. Cups are sold in packs of 12. What is the least number of plates and cups that Ria can buy?

  A 12

  B 24

  C 48

  D 96

7 In problem 6, suppose that Ria wants at least 40 plates and 40 cups. Could Ria buy exactly 40 plates and 40 cups? Explain.

8 When Carlos goes to his favorite restaurant for lunch, he gets a sandwich and a smoothie. The restaurant has two rewards programs.

  • Buy 10 sandwiches, get one free sandwich.

  • Buy 4 smoothies, get one free smoothie.

  How many times does Carlos need to buy a sandwich and a smoothie to get both of them for free on the same visit? Show your work.

SOLUTION _____

Practice Finding the Least Common Multiple of Two Whole Numbers

➤ **Study the Example showing how to find the least common multiple of two whole numbers. Then solve problems 1–5.**

Example

At a train station, trains stop on track A and track B at 8:00 AM. A train stops on track A every 9 minutes. A train stops on track B every 12 minutes. When will trains stop on both tracks at the same time again?

Find the least common multiple (LCM) of 9 minutes and 12 minutes.

    Multiples of 9: 9, 18, 27, **36**, 45, 54, **60**, ...

    Multiples of 12: 12, 24, **36**, 48, **60**, 72, ...

The numbers **36** and **60** are common multiples of 9 and 12. The LCM is 36.

It will be 36 minutes until a train stops on each track at the same time again. So, trains will stop on both tracks again at 8:36 AM.

1 A train stops on track C every 10 minutes. A train stops on track D every 6 minutes. Trains stop on track C and track D at 10:30 AM. When will trains stop on both tracks at the same time again? Show your work.

SOLUTION _____

2 Find the LCM of 6 and 9. Show your work.

SOLUTION _____

③ What is the least common multiple (LCM) of 7 and 10? Show your work.

SOLUTION _____

④ The LCM of two numbers is 18. One of the numbers is 9. The other number is less than 9. What could the other number be? Show your work.

SOLUTION _____

⑤ Pilar swims every 4 days and jogs every 6 days. She did both activities today. How many days from now will she both swim and jog again? Show your work.

SOLUTION _____

Refine Finding Greatest Common Factor and Least Common Multiple

➤ **Complete the Example below. Then solve problems 1–9.**

Example

What is the least common multiple (LCM) of 5, 8, and 10?

Look at how you could show your work using lists of multiples.

Multiples of 5: 5, 10, 15, 20, 25, 30, 35, (40,) 45

Multiples of 8: 8, 16, 24, 32, (40,) 48, 56, 64, 72

Multiples of 10: 10, 20, 30, (40,) 50, 60, 70, 80, 90

The first number to appear in all three lists is 40.

SOLUTION _____

CONSIDER THIS . . .
You can use the same strategies to find the LCM of three numbers that you use to find the LCM of two numbers.

PAIR/SHARE
If you continue listing multiples of 5, 8, and 10, what will be the next number to appear in all three lists?

Apply It

1. Solve the puzzle from the clues. Show your work.

    Clue 1: We are two whole numbers less than or equal to 12.

    Clue 2: Our least common multiple is 36.

    Clue 3: Our greatest common factor is 1.

    What two whole numbers are we?

CONSIDER THIS . . .
If the GCF of two numbers is 1, it means they share no other common factors.

PAIR/SHARE
Which clue did you start with? Why?

SOLUTION _____

2 Chantel has 45 green balloons and 54 purple balloons to make into bunches for a school celebration. She wants each bunch to have the same number of each color balloon. What is the greatest number of bunches Chantel can make if she wants to use all of her balloons? How many purple balloons will she put in each bunch? Show your work.

CONSIDER THIS...
Do you need to find the greatest common factor or the least common multiple?

SOLUTION _____

_____

PAIR/SHARE
Would the number of bunches be different if Chantal had 27 purple balloons instead of 54?

3 What is the least common multiple of 5 and 10?

A 1

B 5

C 10

D 50

Alyssa chose B as the correct answer. How might she have gotten that answer?

CONSIDER THIS...
Can the least common multiple of two numbers be less than one of the numbers?

PAIR/SHARE
When is the product of two numbers also the LCM of the two numbers?

4 Ignacio buys three types of fish. He buys 12 guppies,
9 mollies, and 15 swordtails. He plans to divide the fish
between more than one fish tank. He wants to put
the same number of each type of fish into each tank.
How many tanks should Ignacio use? How many of
each type of fish will be in each tank? Show your work.

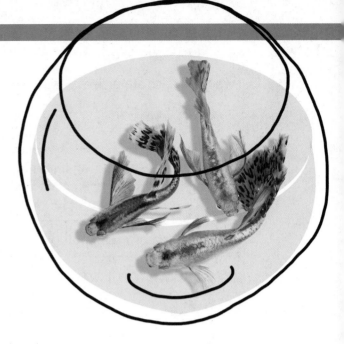

SOLUTION _____

_____

5 The GCF of 20 and another number is 4. Which of these could be the other
number? Select all that apply.

A 4

B 8

C 10

D 20

E 80

6 Inés finds the greatest common factor and the least common multiple of
10 and 12. She then subtracts to find the difference between the GCF and the
LCM. What is the difference? Show your work.

SOLUTION _____

7 Tell whether each statement about 20 and 30 is *True* or *False*.

	True	False
a. The greatest common factor is 5.	○	○
b. 10 is a common multiple.	○	○
c. The least common multiple is 60.	○	○
d. 2 is a common factor.	○	○

8 **a.** Find the GCF of 8 and 12. Show that $\frac{8}{12} = \frac{2}{3}$ by dividing the numerator and denominator of $\frac{8}{12}$ by the GCF.

b. Show how to add the fractions $\frac{1}{8}$ and $\frac{1}{12}$ by using the LCM of 8 and 12 as the common denominator.

9 **Math Journal** Write two different whole numbers that have 6 as their greatest common factor. Explain how you found your two numbers. Then find the least common multiple of your numbers.

✓ **End of Lesson Checklist**

☐ **INTERACTIVE GLOSSARY** Find the entries for *greatest common factor* and *least common multiple*. Tell how greatest common factor and least common multiple are different.

☐ **SELF CHECK** Go back to the Unit 1 Opener and see what you can check off.

Math in Action | **SESSION 1** ■ ☐

Area, Surface Area, and Algebraic Expressions

Math IN Action

SMP 1 Make sense of problems and persevere in solving them.

Study an Example Problem and Solution

➤ **Read this problem involving surface area and common factors. Then look at one student's solution to this problem on the following pages.**

Buying Hens

Juan's agriculture class will be raising hens. The school already has coops for the hens, but the class will need to build pens so that the hens have a place to roam around in the fresh air. Read the requirements from Juan's teacher, and help him respond to the email.

🗑 Delete	🗑 Archive		✉ Reply	✉ Reply All	✉ Forward

To: Juan
Subject: Building Pens for Hens

Hi Juan,

You will be in charge of purchasing new hens and building pens for all the hens.

Hens: Right now, we have 12 hens (4 leghorns and 8 orpingtons).
Your class will raise a total of 20–25 hens.
Here are prices for different quantities of each type of hen.

LEGHORN HENS		ORPINGTON HENS	
Quantity	Price (Each)	Quantity	Price (Each)
1–5 Hens	$4.00	1–5 Hens	$4.75
6–15 Hens	$3.75	6–15 Hens	$4.25

Pens: You can build at most 8 pens. Each pen will contain only one type of hen. All pens will be the same size and hold the same number of hens. Each pen should be at least 4 feet high, and there should be at least 8 square feet of floor space per hen. Chicken wire will cover the top and sides of each pen.

PLEASE PROVIDE:
• the number of and type(s) of hens you plan to buy.
• the number of pens you plan to build.
• the amount of chicken wire you will need to build all the pens.

Thanks!

Mr. McClary

Chickens can remember over 100 different faces of animals or people.

One Student's Solution

NOTICE THAT...
When choosing how many hens to buy, think about whether the total numbers of each type of hen will have any common factors.

First, I will decide how many hens to buy.

I know Juan needs to have between 20 and 25 total hens. He already has 4 leghorns and 8 orpingtons. I will suggest that he buy 6 leghorns and 7 orpingtons. Because $4 + 6 = 10$ and $8 + 7 = 15$, Juan will then have 10 leghorns and 15 orpingtons, for a total of 25 hens.

Next, I need to determine the number of hens Juan can keep in each pen.

I want to have as many hens as possible in each pen, so I will find the GCF of 10 and 15.

Factors of 10: 1, 2, ⑤ 10

Factors of 15: 1, 3, ⑤ 15   Each pen can hold 5 hens.

NOTICE THAT...
The number of leghorns and orpingtons needs to be considered to determine the number of pens needed. Remember that each pen will contain only one type of hen.

Then, I will calculate how many pens are needed.

There are 5 hens in each pen. That means 2 pens will be for leghorns and 3 pens will be for orpingtons. Because $2 + 3 = 5$, Juan needs 5 pens in all.

Now, I can design the pens.

I know that each pen needs to be at least 4 feet high. I can make each pen in the shape of a rectangular prism with a height of 4 feet.

I also know that each hen needs at least 8 square feet of floor space, so each pen needs a floor area of $8 \cdot 5$, or 40 square feet. I can make the floor of each pen a rectangle with dimensions 8 feet by 5 feet.

I can show my work by drawing a sketch of a pen.

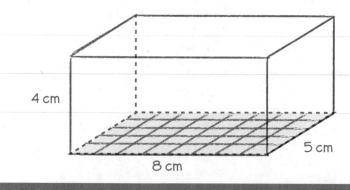

☑ **Problem-Solving Checklist**

- ☐ Tell what is known.
- ☐ Tell what the problem is asking.
- ☐ Show all your work.
- ☐ Show that the solution works.

Finally, I will use surface area to find how much chicken wire is needed.

I can find the areas of the top and side faces, and then add these areas together. I can draw a net to help find the areas.

NOTICE THAT . . .
Because the chicken wire only goes on the top and side faces, do not include the area of the bottom face.

	long face		
short face	top face	short face	bottom face
	long face		

Area of the **top face**: 8 feet • 5 feet = **40** square feet

Area of each **short face**: 5 feet • 4 feet = **20** square feet

Area of each **long face**: 8 feet • 4 feet = **32** square feet

40 + **20** + **20** + **32** + **32** = 144

So, the total area for 1 pen is 144 square feet.

NOTICE THAT . . .
There are 2 long faces, 2 short faces, and 1 top face that will be covered in chicken wire.

I can calculate the total amount of chicken wire by multiplying the amount needed for 1 pen by the total number of pens. Because 5 • 144 = 720, Juan needs 720 square feet of chicken wire.

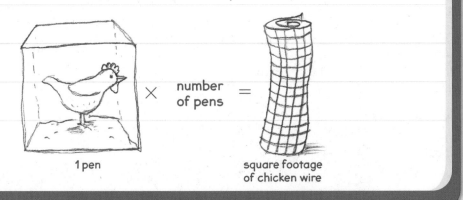

1 pen   ×   number of pens   =   square footage of chicken wire

Try Another Approach

➤ **There are many ways to solve problems. Think about how you might solve the Buying Hens problem in a different way.**

Buying Hens

Juan's agriculture class will be raising hens. The school already has coops for the hens, but the class will need to build pens so that the hens have a place to roam around in the fresh air. Read the requirements from Juan's teacher, and help him respond to the email.

🗑 Delete   🗑 Archive   ✉ Reply   ✉ Reply All   ✉ Forward

To: Juan
Subject: Building Pens for Hens

Hi Juan,

You will be in charge of purchasing new hens and building pens for all the hens.

Hens: Right now, we have 12 hens (4 leghorns and 8 orpingtons).
Your class will raise a total of 20–25 hens.
Here are prices for different quantities of each type of hen.

LEGHORN HENS		ORPINGTON HENS	
Quantity	Price (Each)	Quantity	Price (Each)
1–5 Hens	$4.00	1–5 Hens	$4.75
6–15 Hens	$3.75	6–15 Hens	$4.25

Pens: You can build at most 8 pens. Each pen will contain only one type of hen. All pens will be the same size and hold the same number of hens. Each pen should be at least 4 feet high, and there should be at least 8 square feet of floor space per hen. Chicken wire will cover the top and sides of each pen.

PLEASE PROVIDE:
- the number of and type(s) of hens you plan to buy.
- the number of pens you plan to build.
- the amount of chicken wire you will need to build all the pens.

Thanks!

Mr. McClary

Plan It

➤ **Answer these questions to help you start thinking about a plan.**

  a. What are some pairs of numbers with sums between 20 and 25? Which of these pairs have common factors other than 1?

  b. How tall will you suggest that Juan make his pens?

Solve It

➤ **Find a different solution for the Buying Hens problem. Show all your work on a separate sheet of paper. You may want to use the Problem-Solving Tips to get started.**

PROBLEM-SOLVING TIPS

Math Toolkit grid paper, unit cubes, unit tiles

Models You may want to use . . .

- tables to show the factor pairs for different numbers of hens.

- prime factorization or factor trees to find the common factors of two numbers.

- a net to find the surface area of each pen.

Questions

- How can you calculate the number of hens in each pen after you decide which hens to buy?

- How can you determine the dimensions of the floor space for a pen once you know the area it should cover?

Reflect

Use Mathematical Practices As you work through the problem, discuss these questions with a partner.

- **Use a Model** How can drawing a net help you calculate the amount of chicken wire Juan will need?

- **Critique Reasoning** Do the pens your partner described meet the requirements from Juan's teacher? Explain.

Discuss Models and Strategies

➤ **Read the problem. Write a solution on a separate sheet of paper. Remember, there can be lots of ways to solve a problem.**

Outdoor Classroom

The school board holds a contest to design an outdoor classroom for the agriculture department at Juan's school. Read the requirements, and help Juan come up with a design.

Design an Outdoor Classroom!

The school board is pleased to announce a contest to design an outdoor classroom. The winning classroom design will be built in an unused space around the shed and used by the agriculture department.

Classroom plans should include a **vegetable garden**, a **flower garden**, and a **seating space**.

- The area of the **vegetable garden**, v, must be at least 80 square feet.

- The area of the **flower garden**, f, must be no more than 50 square feet.

- The area of the **seating space**, s, must be 75 square feet.

- There may be space left unused.

- Use the diagram of the design location to plan your design.

- Use the expression $0.5v + 8f + 12s$ to estimate the total cost to install your design, in dollars.

ALL ENTRIES MUST INCLUDE:

- a drawing of your plan that shows each section of the outdoor classroom labeled with its area.

- the estimated cost to install your design.

□ = 1 square foot

School Building

18 ft

Shed

Plan It and Solve It

➤ **Find a solution to the Outdoor Classroom problem.**

Write a detailed plan and support your answer. Be sure to include:

- a drawing that shows the dimensions of each section of the outdoor classroom.

- the area of each section of the outdoor classroom.

- the estimated cost to install the design you drew.

PROBLEM-SOLVING TIPS

Math Toolkit colored pencils, grid paper, unit cubes, unit tiles

Key Terms

term	coefficient	expression
substitute	evaluate	variable
value	parallelogram	area

Questions

- What shapes could you use for the different sections of the outdoor garden?

- What are different ways you can find the area of a shape that is not a rectangle?

Reflect

Use Mathematical Practices As you work through the problem, discuss these questions with a partner.

- **Make Sense of Problems** What will you do first? Why?

- **Reason Mathematically** What do the coefficients in the expression represent? How do you know?

Durable outdoor furniture can be made with recycled plastic.

Persevere On Your Own

➤ **Read the problem. Write a solution on a separate sheet of paper.**

Buying Supplies

Juan wants to limit the number of trips he takes to the store to buy supplies for the hens. Read more about what Juan needs to buy and the supplies that are available at the store. Juan has storage for a maximum of 500 pounds of grain and 300 pounds of straw.

How often do you recommend that Juan shop for supplies? What will he buy on each trip? Write an expression to show how much money Juan spends on grain mix and straw each time he visits the store.

HORIZONS FARM SUPPLY

~since 1890~

SUMMER SPECIALS for all your farm needs!

GRANNY'S GRAIN MIX
60 lb

GRANNY'S GRAIN MIX
40 lb

90 lb

36 lb

Weekly Supplies (for all hens):

Feed: 10 lb grain mix

Bedding: 9 lb straw

Solve It

➤ **Find a solution to the Buying Supplies problem.**

- Decide how frequently Juan should go to the store.

- Suggest which items to purchase if he shops as frequently as you suggest.

- Give an expression that represents the total cost of grain mix and straw on each visit. (Remember to define your variables!)

Reflect

Use Mathematical Practices After you complete the problem, choose one of these questions to discuss with a partner.

- **Persevere** Did you try different combinations of numbers before deciding on a final answer? Explain.

- **Make an Argument** How can you justify the number of trips you suggested?

Some hen breeds can produce 300 eggs per year.

In this unit you learned to . . .

Skill	Lesson
Find the area of parallelograms.	1
Find the area of triangles and other polygons.	2
Identify and draw a net for a three-dimensional figure.	3
Find the surface area of a three-dimensional figure.	3
Write and evaluate algebraic expressions.	4
Write and evaluate numerical and algebraic expressions, including those with whole-number exponents.	4, 5
Find the greatest common factor (GCF) and least common multiple (LCM) of two whole numbers to solve real-world problems.	6
Actively participate in discussions by asking questions and rephrasing or building on classmates' ideas.	1, 2, 4–6

Think about what you have learned.

➤ **Use words, numbers, and drawings.**

 Three examples of what I learned are . . .

 Something I know well is . . .

 A question I still have is . . .

Vocabulary Review

➤ **Review the unit vocabulary. Put a check mark by items you can use in speaking and writing. Look up the meaning of any terms you do not know.**

Math Vocabulary

Academic Vocabulary

☐ base
(of a power)

☐ coefficient

☐ exponent

☐ net

☐ power

☐ prism

☐ pyramid

☐ surface area

☐ term

☐ variable

☐ constant

☐ corresponds to

☐ relate to

☐ represent

☐ vertical

➤ **Use the unit vocabulary to complete the problems.**

1 Use arrows to label parts of the expression with at least five math or academic vocabulary terms.

$$11m + 5 + 3b + 15 + e^3$$

2 What are some similarities and differences between Figure *A* and Figure *B*? What does *x* represent in each figure? Use at least four math or academic vocabulary terms in your answer. Underline each term you use.

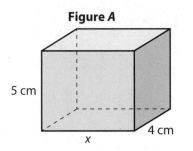

Figure A

5 cm

x

4 cm

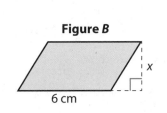

Figure B

6 cm

x

➤ **Use what you have learned to complete these problems.**

1 Find the area of the triangle.

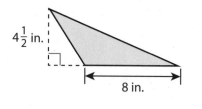

$4\frac{1}{2}$ in.

8 in.

A 16 in.^{2}

B 18 in.^{2}

C 32 in.^{2}

D 36 in.^{2}

2 Draw a line to match each statement on the left with the algebraic expression that represents the same value.

a. three more than the difference of five and a number

b. five divided by the product of three and a number

c. a number times the difference of five and three

$f(5 - 3)$

$(5 - f) + 3$

$5 \div 3f$

$(3 + 5) - f$

3 Micah has a first aid kit shaped like a square prism. The expression $32x + 2x^2$ represents the surface area of the first aid kit where the base edges are x inches long. Complete the equation to find the surface area of the first aid kit when x is 12 inches. Write your answers in the blanks.

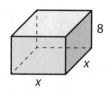

8

x

x

32(_____) + 2(_____)——— = _____ in.^{2}

4 What is the value of the expression $3[12 + (4^3 - 25)] + 2^3$? Show your work.

SOLUTION _____

What is the surface area of the right triangular prism? Show your work.

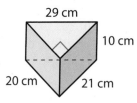

29 cm

10 cm

20 cm   21 cm

SOLUTION _____

 Pascal sells fruit from a fruit stand. He starts the day with 80 pounds of fruit. In the morning, 5 customers each buy *w* pounds of fruit. In the afternoon, Pascal feeds $\frac{2}{3}$ of his remaining fruit to birds in the park. Write an algebraic expression that represents the weight of the fruit that Pascal still has after feeding the birds. Show your work.

SOLUTION _____

7 Find the greatest common factor (GCF) for 54 and 90. Show your work.

SOLUTION _____

Performance Task

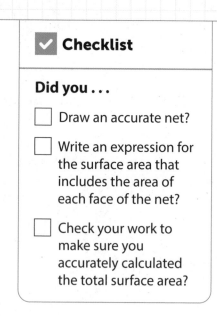
➤ **Answer the questions and show all your work on separate paper.**

A carpenter makes a model of a plywood ramp she plans to build as part of the set for the school play. The length must be 2.4 times the height, x, so that the ramp is not too steep. Once the ramp is built, she will completely coat it with sealant to protect it. The ramp is in the shape of a right triangular prism. An incomplete net for the model is shown.

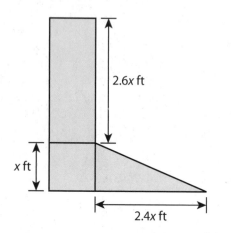

2.6x ft

x ft

2.4x ft

Help the carpenter finish her plans for the ramp.

• Draw and label a complete net for the model.

• Write an expression that represents the surface area.

• Evaluate your expression to find the surface area when the height, x, is 5 ft.

Explain how you completed the net, how you used the net to write the expression representing surface area, and how you used the expression to find surface area.

Reflect

Use Mathematical Practices After you complete the task, choose one of the following questions to answer.

• **Make Sense of the Problem** What was your plan to accurately draw and label the faces that are missing from the net?

• **Be Precise** How did you make sure your expression represents the entire surface area of the model?

Unit 2

Decimals and Fractions

Base-Ten Operations, Division with Fractions, and Volume

✓ Self Check	Before starting this unit, check off the skills you know below. As you complete each lesson, see how many more skills you can check off!

I can . . .	Before	After
Add, subtract, and multiply multi-digit decimals using standard algorithms.	☐	☐
Divide multi-digit whole numbers and multi-digit decimals using standard algorithms.	☐	☐
Divide fractions.	☐	☐
Solve real-world problems that involve dividing fractions.	☐	☐
Find the volume of a right rectangular prism with fractional edge lengths.	☐	☐
Use math vocabulary and precise language to describe a strategy and how that strategy is used to solve a problem.	☐	☐

➤ **You have learned to use reasoning to add, subtract, multiply, and divide decimals and fractions. Without evaluating the expressions, place each expression in the correct category. Then write your own expression in each category.**

a. 98×0.01 **e.** $5.4 \div 0.5$ **i.** $0.6 + 0.54$

b. $5.8 \times \frac{1}{2}$ **f.** $5 \div \frac{1}{4}$ **j.** $\frac{1}{2} \times \frac{7}{8}$

c. 10×0.25 **g.** $0.75 - 0.5$ **k.** $2.2 - 1.18$

d. $\frac{1}{4} \div 2$ **h.** 9.9×1.35 **l.** $0.09 + 0.89$

Less than 1	Between 1 and 10	Greater than 10

Without performing any calculations, write $<$, $>$, or $=$ in each circle to make a true statement.

a. 152×0.76 ◯ 152

b. $28.4 \div 0.5$ ◯ 28.4

c. 68.3×1.04 ◯ 68.3

d. $0.8 + 0.07$ ◯ 0

Dear Family,

This week your student is learning how to add, subtract, and multiply decimals up to the thousandths place.

Previously, your student learned how to add, subtract, and multiply whole numbers using a variety of methods. Similar strategies can be used to perform these same operations with decimals.

$$
\begin{array}{r}
2{,}135 \\
+\ 3{,}402 \\
\hline
5{,}537
\end{array}
\qquad
\begin{array}{r}
2.135 \\
+\ 3.402 \\
\hline
5.537
\end{array}
$$

Your student will be learning to solve problems like the one below.

Find the product of 0.23 and 2.14.

➤ **ONE WAY** to find the product is to write the decimals as fractions.

$0.23 = 23$ hundredths $= \dfrac{23}{100}$

$2.14 = 214$ hundredths $= \dfrac{214}{100}$

Then multiply the fractions.

$$
\frac{23}{100} \times \frac{214}{100} = \frac{23 \times 214}{100 \times 100}
$$

$$
= \frac{4{,}922}{10{,}000} = 0.4922
$$

➤ **ANOTHER WAY** is to use the standard algorithm for multiplication.

Multiply as with whole numbers. Then place the decimal point.

$$
\begin{array}{r}
0.23 \quad \leftarrow \text{hundredths} \\
\times \quad 2.14 \quad \leftarrow \text{hundredths} \\
\hline
92 \\
230 \\
+\ 4600 \\
\hline
0.4922 \quad \leftarrow \text{hundredths} \times \text{hundredths} = \text{ten-thousandths}
\end{array}
$$

Using either method, the product is 0.4922.

 Use the next page to start a conversation about decimals.

Activity Thinking About Decimals Around You

yearly **FRUIT & VEGETABLE CONSUMPTION***

383.25 cups of fruit

135.05 cups of potatoes

51.1 cups of dark green vegetables

*Average adult American, 2007–2010

➤ **Do this activity together to investigate decimals in the real world.**

Have you ever noticed that some foods are more popular than others? Each year between 2007–2010, the average adult American ate 135.05 cups of potatoes, 51.1 cups of dark green vegetables, and 383.25 cups of fruit. That is 248.2 more cups of fruit than potatoes and 83.95 more cups of potatoes than dark green vegetables!

? **Where else do you see decimals in the world around you?**

Explore Adding and Subtracting Multi-Digit Decimals

Previously, you learned about decimal operations to the hundredths. In this lesson, you will learn about adding, subtracting, and multiplying decimals to the thousandths.

➤ **Use what you know to try to solve the problem below.**

Mateo is training to swim the 100-meter freestyle event in the Youth Olympic Games. During practice, he swims two laps. What is his total time for the two laps?

Mateo's times

Lap 1 24.138 s

Lap 2 25.393 s

 TRY IT

Math Toolkit base-ten blocks, base-ten grid paper, grid paper, number lines, place-value charts

 **DISCUSS IT**

Ask: What did you do first to find the total time?

Share: I started by . . .

Learning Target SMP 1, SMP 2, SMP 3, SMP 4, SMP 5, SMP 6, SMP 7
Fluently add, subtract, multiply, and divide multi-digit decimals using the standard algorithm for each operation.

CONNECT IT

1 **Look Back** What is Mateo's total time for the two laps? Explain how you could find the answer.

2 **Look Ahead** Place value can help you add or subtract decimals. You add 25.393 and 24.138 to find Mateo's total time. You can subtract 24.138 from 25.393 to find how much faster Mateo swims the first lap than the second lap.

a. How could it help you to line up the decimals on their decimal points?

b. What do you need to do before you can subtract the digits in the thousandths place in this problem? Explain.

$$\begin{array}{r} 25.393 \\ -\ 24.138 \\ \hline \end{array}$$

c. Complete the equation.

9 hundredths + 3 thousandths = 8 hundredths + _____ thousandths

d. How much faster is Mateo's time for the first lap than the second lap? How did you find your answer?

3 **Reflect** How do you use place value when adding and subtracting decimals?

Prepare for Adding, Subtracting, and Multiplying Multi-Digit Decimals

1 Think about what you know about decimals and place value. Fill in each box.
Use words, numbers, and pictures. Show as many ideas as you can.

What Is It?	What I Know About It

place value

Examples	Examples	Examples

2 Wyatt says that 0.6 has the same value as 0.600. Do you agree? Explain.

3 In science class, Layla mixes 0.165 L of a blue liquid and 0.185 L of a green liquid.

   a. What is the total volume of Layla's mixture? Show your work.

SOLUTION _____

   b. Check your answer to problem 3a. Show your work.

Develop Using the Standard Algorithm to Add and Subtract Decimals

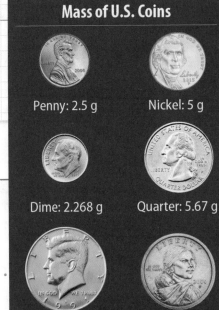

Mass of U.S. Coins

Penny: 2.5 g

Nickel: 5 g

Dime: 2.268 g

Quarter: 5.67 g

Half-Dollar: 11.34 g

Dollar: 8.1 g

➤ **Read and try to solve the problem below.**

How much greater is the mass of a dollar coin than the combined masses of a dime and a quarter?

TRY IT

Math Toolkit base-ten blocks, base-ten grid paper, grid paper, number lines, place-value charts

DISCUSS IT

Ask: How is your model similar to mine? How is it different?

Share: My model shows . . .

➤ **Explore different ways to understand how to add and subtract decimals.**

How much greater is the mass of a dollar coin than the combined masses of a dime and a quarter?

Coin	Penny	Nickel	Dime	Quarter	Half-Dollar	Dollar
Mass	2.5 g	5 g	2.268 g	5.67 g	11.34 g	8.1 g

Model It

You can use place-value charts to add or subtract decimals.

Add the masses of the dime and the quarter.

1

Tens	Ones	•	Tenths	Hundredths	Thousandths
	2	•	2	6	8
+	5	•	6	7	
	7	•	9	3	8

Subtract the combined mass from the mass of a dollar coin.

Tens	Ones	•	Tenths	Hundredths	Thousandths
	8	•	1		
−	7	•	9	3	8
		•			

Model It

You can use an algorithm to add or subtract decimals.

Line up the decimals by place value.

```
   1
  2.268            8.100
+ 5.670          − 7.938
 ------           ------
  7.938
```

LESSON 7 Add, Subtract, and Multiply Multi-Digit Decimals

➤ **Use the problem from the previous page to help you understand how to add and subtract decimals.**

1 Look at the first **Model It**. In the first place-value chart, why is the thousandths column for the decimal 5.67 empty?

2 Look at the second **Model It**. In the addition step, 5.67 is written as 5.670. Does this change the value of 5.67? Explain your reasoning.

3 Look at the subtraction step in the second **Model It**. Why is 8.1 rewritten as 8.100?

4 How much greater is the mass of a dollar coin than the combined masses of a dime and a quarter? How can you check that your answer is reasonable?

5 How are algorithms for adding or subtracting decimals similar to algorithms for adding or subtracting whole numbers? How are they different?

6 **Reflect** Think about all the models and strategies you have discussed today. Describe how one of them helped you better understand how to add and subtract decimals.

Apply It

➤ **Use what you learned to solve these problems.**

7 Noe makes a mistake when he finds $8.196 - 2.4$. Describe his mistake and show the correct subtraction.

Noe

$$
\begin{array}{r}
8.196 \\
-\ 2.004 \\
\hline
6.192
\end{array}
$$

8 Evaluate $m - 7.432$ when $m = 15.45$. Show your work.

SOLUTION _____

9 A city receives 0.063 m of rain in April and 0.15 m of rain in May. What is the total amount of rain the city receives for both months? Show your work.

Rainfall Totals

April	May
0.063 m	0.15 m

SOLUTION _____

Practice Using the Standard Algorithm to Add and Subtract Decimals

➤ **Study the Example showing how to use the standard algorithm to add decimals. Then solve problems 1–5.**

Example

Tara's house is 1.94 km from the library. The library is 0.347 km from the park. Tara walks from her house to the library and then from the library to the park. What is the total distance Tara walks?

Line up the decimals by place value. Write each decimal with the same number of decimal places. Then regroup as needed to add.

$$
\begin{array}{r}
\overset{1}{1}.940 \\
+\ 0.347 \\
\hline
2.287
\end{array}
$$

Tara walks a total distance of 2.287 km.

1 In the Example, how much farther is it from Tara's house to the library than it is from the library to the park? Show your work.

SOLUTION _____

2 A day on Venus is about 224.7 Earth days. A day on Mercury is about 58.646 Earth days. How much longer is a day on Venus than a day on Mercury?

A about 165.361 Earth days

B about 166.054 Earth days

C about 166.146 Earth days

D about 166.641 Earth days

3 Evaluate the expression $4^2 - d$ when $d = 3.643$. Show your work.

SOLUTION _____

4 Anders adds 8.84 and 62.5, but he makes an error in his work. Describe his mistake and show the correct addition.

Anders

$$
\begin{array}{r}
\overset{1}{}8.84 \\
+\ 62.5 \\
\hline
150.9
\end{array}
$$

5 The length of a lap on a running track depends on the lane. Greg runs one lap in lane 4, one lap in lane 5, and one lap in lane 6. What is the total distance Greg runs? Show your work.

Lane Number	Lap Length (m)
1	407.67
2	415.33
3	423
4	430.66
5	433.38
6	446

SOLUTION _____

Develop Using the Standard Algorithm to Multiply Decimals

➤ **Read and try to solve the problem below.**

Jabari's cat has a mass of 4.2 kg. The cat needs 0.224 mg of medicine for each kilogram of its mass. What is the total amount of medicine the cat needs?

Jabari's cat: **4.2 kg**

For each kilogram of mass:
0.224 mg of medicine

 TRY IT

Math Toolkit base-ten grid paper, grid paper, place-value charts

 **DISCUSS IT**

Ask: How is your strategy similar to mine? How is it different?

Share: My strategy is similar to yours . . . It is different . . .

LESSON 7 Add, Subtract, and Multiply Multi-Digit Decimals   **157**

➤ **Explore different ways to understand how to multiply decimals.**

Jabari's cat has a mass of 4.2 kg. The cat needs 0.224 mg of medicine for each kilogram of its mass. What is the total amount of medicine the cat needs?

Model It

You can use what you know about fractions to multiply decimals.

Use place value to write each decimal as a fraction.

$$0.224 = 224 \text{ thousandths} = \frac{224}{1,000}$$

$$4.2 = 42 \text{ tenths} = \frac{42}{10}$$

Then multiply the fractions.

$$\frac{224}{1,000} \times \frac{42}{10} = \frac{224 \times 42}{1,000 \times 10}$$

$$= \frac{9,408}{10,000}$$

Model It

You can use an algorithm to multiply decimals.

Multiply as with whole numbers. Then place the decimal point.

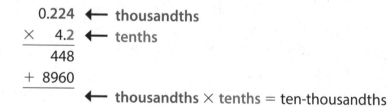

```
    0.224  ← thousandths
  ×   4.2  ← tenths
    ─────
     448
  + 8960
```
← thousandths × tenths = ten-thousandths

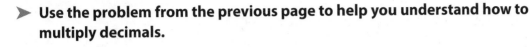

CONNECT IT

➤ **Use the problem from the previous page to help you understand how to multiply decimals.**

1 Look at the first **Model It**. How are products of whole numbers used to find the product of 0.224 and 4.2?

2 Look at the second **Model It**. What is the sum of the partial products 448 and 8,960? Where do you see this sum in the fraction form of the product?

3 Why does multiplying a decimal in the thousandths by a decimal in the tenths give a product in the ten-thousandths?

4 What is the total amount of medicine the cat needs, written as a decimal? How do you know where to place the decimal point in the product?

5 How can you use the algorithm for multiplying whole numbers when you multiply decimals?

6 **Reflect** Think about all the models and strategies you have discussed today. Describe how one of them helped you better understand how to multiply decimals.

Apply It

➤ **Use what you learned to solve these problems.**

7 Fiona earns $7.25 for each hour that she walks her neighbor's dog. This month, she walks the dog for a total of 4.5 h.

   a. How much does Fiona earn this month? Show your work.

   SOLUTION _____

   b. Did you round your answer to problem 7a? Why or why not?

8 What is the value of the expression x^2y when $x = 0.8$ and $y = 3.15$?

   A 0.2016

   B 0.504

   C 2.016

   D 5.04

9 Find the product 8.524×0.71. Show your work.

   SOLUTION _____

Practice Using the Standard Algorithm to Multiply Decimals

➤ **Study the Example showing how to use the standard algorithm to multiply decimals. Then solve problems 1–5.**

Example

A store sells ropes for rock climbing. A blue rope is 35.5 m long. Each meter of the rope has a mass of 0.064 kg. What is the total mass of the blue rope?

You can multiply decimals as you would with whole numbers. Then use what you know about place value to place the decimal point in the product.

$$
\begin{array}{r}
35.5 \quad \longleftarrow \text{ tenths} \\
\times \ 0.064 \quad \longleftarrow \text{ thousandths} \\
\hline
1420 \\
+\ 21300 \\
\hline
2.2720 \quad \longleftarrow \text{ tenths} \times \text{thousandths} = \text{ten-thousandths}
\end{array}
$$

The total mass of the blue rope is 2.272 kg.

1 A green rope is 60.5 m long. Each meter of the rope has a mass of 0.052 kg. What is the total mass of the green rope? Show your work.

SOLUTION _____

2 Find 0.102 × 7.3. Show your work.

SOLUTION _____

3 What is the area of the parallelogram? Show your work.

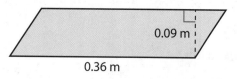

0.09 m

0.36 m

SOLUTION _____

4 At a grocery store, each pound of apples costs $1.77. Lian weighs a bag of apples on the store's scale. The scale shows that the apples weigh 1.32 lb. How much do Lian's apples cost? Show your work.

SOLUTION _____

5 Ethan and Anica both multiply 3.045 and 1.3. Who finds the correct product? How do you know?

Ethan

$$\begin{array}{r} 3.045 \\ \times \quad 1.3 \\ \hline 9135 \\ + \quad 30450 \\ \hline 3.9585 \end{array}$$

Anica

$$\begin{array}{r} 3.045 \\ \times \quad 1.3 \\ \hline 9135 \\ + \quad 30450 \\ \hline 39.585 \end{array}$$

Refine Adding, Subtracting, and Multiplying Multi-Digit Decimals

➤ **Complete the Example below. Then solve problems 1–9.**

Example

An online store charges a fee of $4.50 for shipping. There is an additional charge of $0.50 for each pound the item weighs. How much does the store charge to ship a hammock that weighs 10.54 lb?

Look at how you could show your work using an expression and algorithms for multiplying and adding decimals.

4.50 + (10.54 × 0.50)

$$
\begin{array}{r}
10.54 \\
\times \quad 0.50 \\
\hline
5.2700
\end{array}
\qquad
\begin{array}{r}
5.27 \\
+ \ 4.50 \\
\hline
9.77
\end{array}
$$

4.50 + (10.54 × 0.50) = 9.77

SOLUTION _____

CONSIDER THIS ...
How does the expression show the additional charge for the hammock's weight?

PAIR/SHARE
Why can 5.2700 be written as 5.27?

Apply It

1 Claudia is playing a game on her phone. She finishes Level One in 20.341 s. She finishes Level Two 1.283 s faster than she finishes Level One. How many seconds does it take Claudia to finish Level One and Level Two? Show your work.

CONSIDER THIS ...
Which level does it take Claudia longer to finish?

PAIR/SHARE
How would the problem change if Claudia finished Level Two more slowly than Level One?

SOLUTION _____

Find 0.42 × 8.27. Show your work.

CONSIDER THIS . . .
How does the place value of the product relate to the place value of the factors?

SOLUTION _____

PAIR/SHARE
How can you use fractions to check your work?

3 Each day, Caleb feeds his horse 2.25 lb of oats. He also feeds it hay. The weight of hay is 6.5 times the weight of oats. What is the combined weight of oats and hay Caleb feeds his horse in one week?

CONSIDER THIS . . .
There are 7 days in 1 week.

A 61.250 lb

B 102.375 lb

C 118.125 lb

D 259.875 lb

Naomi chose C as the correct answer. How might she have gotten that answer?

PAIR/SHARE
How could Naomi check whether her answer is reasonable?

4 What is the value of the expression $3ab + c$ when $a = 0.32$, $b = 0.45$, and $c = 7.2$?

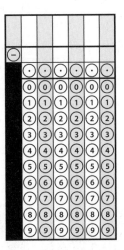

5 What is the surface area of the tissue box? Show your work.

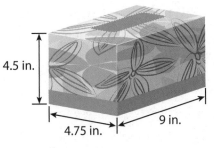

4.5 in.

4.75 in.

9 in.

SOLUTION _____

6 Jennifer knows that $3{,}312 \times 15 = 49{,}680$. Based on this fact, Jennifer claims that $33.12 \times 0.15 = 0.4968$. She says that the product has four digits after the decimal point because a product of two decimals in the hundredths should be a decimal in the ten-thousandths. Describe Jennifer's error.

7 Which expressions have the same product as 0.056 × 0.34? Select all that apply.

A $\frac{56 \times 34}{100,000}$

B 0.56 × 3.4

C 56 × 34 × 0.001

D 56 × 34 × $\frac{1}{100}$ × $\frac{1}{100}$

E 56 thousandths × 34 hundredths

8 Rani's family walks the Lower Trail three times. Elijah's family walks the Ridge Trail one time and the Panther Trail one time. Whose family walks farther? How much farther does that family walk? Show your work.

Trail Name	Length (km)
Lower Trail	2.225
Ridge Trail	3.45
Panther Trail	3.375

SOLUTION _____

9 **Math Journal** Write a multiplication problem involving decimals. Both decimals must include hundredths. Show how to solve your problem.

✓ **End of Lesson Checklist**

☐ **INTERACTIVE GLOSSARY** Write a new entry for *combine*. Tell what you do when you *combine* two quantities.

☐ **SELF CHECK** Go back to the Unit 2 Opener and see what you can check off.

Dear Family,

This week your student is learning how to use an algorithm to divide with whole numbers and decimals.

When dividing with whole numbers, a remainder can be expressed as a decimal.

Dividing 34 by 4 shows that a runner who completes a 4-mile course in 34 min needs 8.5 min to run each mile.

$$
\begin{array}{r}
8.5 \\
4\overline{)34.0} \\
-32\downarrow \\
\hline
20 \\
-20 \\
\hline
0
\end{array}
$$

← 20 tenths

← 5 tenths × 4 = 20 tenths

Your student will be learning to solve problems like the one below.

Find 27.5 ÷ 2.5.

➤ **ONE WAY** to divide by a decimal is to use equivalent fractions.

First, write the division problem as a fraction.

$$27.5 \div 2.5 = \frac{27.5}{2.5}$$

Multiply the numerator and denominator by **10** to get an equivalent fraction with a whole-number denominator.

$$\frac{27.5 \times 10}{2.5 \times 10} = \frac{275}{25}$$

27.5 ÷ 2.5 is equivalent to 275 ÷ 25, which equals 11.

➤ **ANOTHER WAY** is to use an algorithm.

First, multiply 2.5 and 27.5 by **10** to write an equivalent division problem with a whole-number divisor.

Then, divide 275 by 25.

Using either method, the answer is 11.

$$
2.5\overline{)27.5} \longrightarrow
\begin{array}{r}
11 \\
25\overline{)275} \\
-25\downarrow \\
\hline
25 \\
-25 \\
\hline
0
\end{array}
$$

× 10   × 10

Use the next page to start a conversation about division.

Divide Whole Numbers and Multi-Digit Decimals

Activity Thinking About Division Around You

➤ **Do this activity together to investigate division in the real world.**

Have you ever seen dogs with police officers at an airport or train station? These dogs have an important job to help keep communities safe, but first they must go through a lot of training!

Training for three pairs of dogs and officers costs $90,000. Since 90,000 ÷ 3 = 30,000, a community should budget $30,000 to train each pair!

? Where else do you see division in the world around you?

Explore The Standard Algorithm for Division with Whole Numbers

25,650 game pieces
6 pieces in each package

Previously, you used area models and partial quotients to divide. In this lesson, you will learn about an algorithm for division.

➤ **Use what you know to try to solve the problem below.**

On Monday, a board game factory makes 25,650 game pieces. The game pieces are put into packages of 6 pieces each. How many packages of game pieces does the factory make on Monday?

TRY IT

 Math Toolkit base-ten blocks, base-ten grid paper, grid paper

DISCUSS IT

Ask: How is your solution similar to mine? How is it different?

Share: My solution is similar to yours . . . It is different . . .

◎ **Learning Targets** SMP 1, SMP 2, SMP 3, SMP 4, SMP 5, SMP 6, SMP 7, SMP 8
• Fluently divide multi-digit numbers using the standard algorithm.
• Fluently add, subtract, multiply, and divide multi-digit decimals using the standard algorithm for each operation.

CONNECT IT

1 Look Back How many packages of game pieces does the factory make on Monday? Explain how you know.

2 Look Ahead One way to divide whole numbers is to use partial quotients. Another way is to use a shortened form of the partial quotients strategy, sometimes called the standard algorithm. You can use these two division strategies to find $384 \div 4$.

Partial Quotients

$$
\begin{array}{r}
96 \\
\overline{6} \\
90 \\
4\overline{)384} \\
-360 \\
\overline{24} \\
-24 \\
\overline{0}
\end{array}
$$

Standard Algorithm

$$
\begin{array}{r}
96 \\
4\overline{)384} \\
-36\downarrow \\
\overline{24} \\
-24 \\
\overline{0}
\end{array}
$$

a. Look at the partial quotients strategy. What are the partial quotients? How do you use the them to find the total quotient?

b. Look at the standard algorithm division strategy. The digit 9 is written in the tens place of the quotient. What partial quotient does this digit represent? How do you know?

3 Reflect How is using the standard algorithm similar to using partial quotients to divide a three-digit number by a one-digit number? How is it different?

Name: _____

Prepare for Dividing Whole Numbers and Multi-Digit Decimals

1 Think about what you know about dividing with partial quotients. Fill in each box. Use words, numbers, and pictures. Show as many ideas as you can.

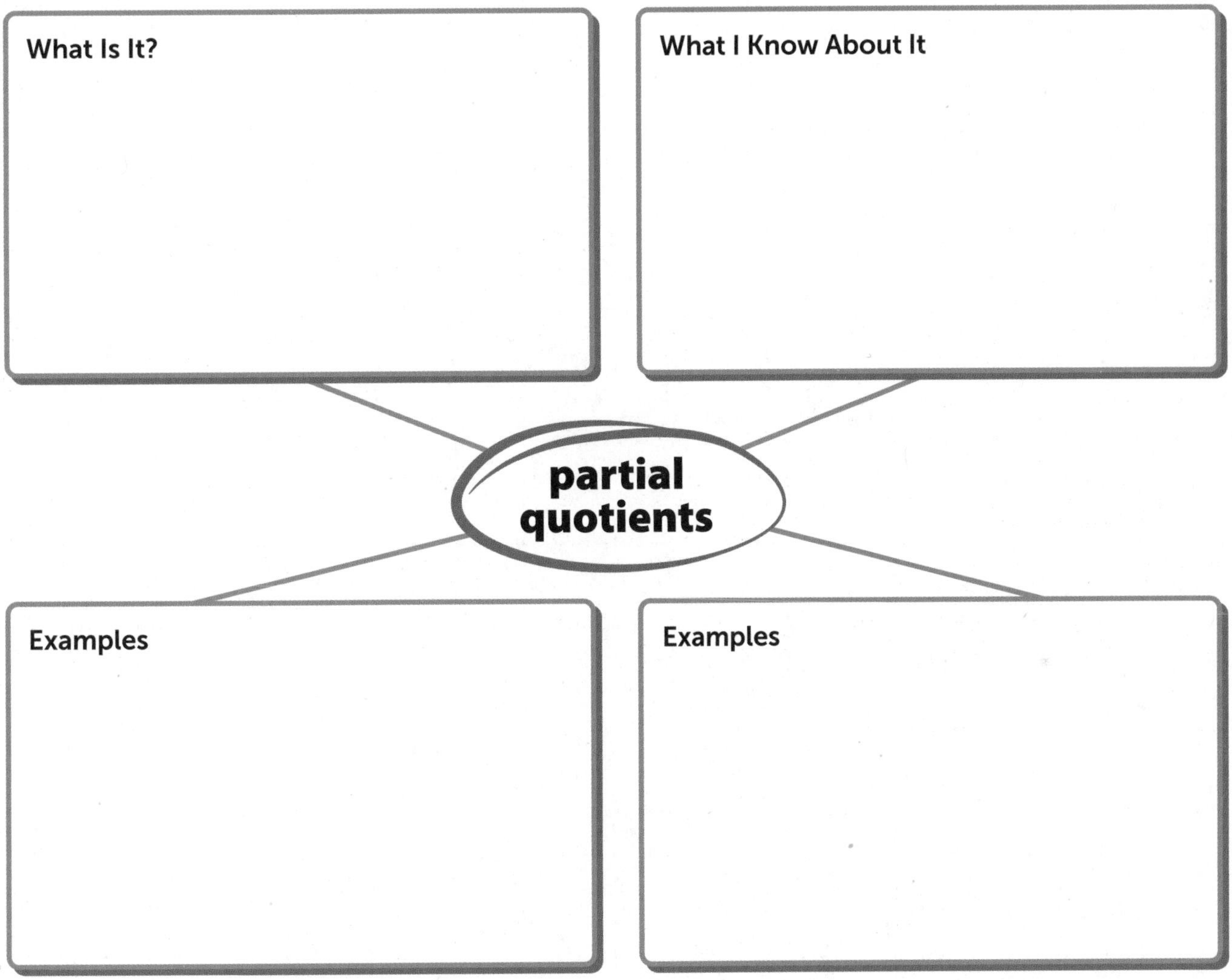

What Is It?	What I Know About It

partial quotients

Examples	Examples

2 Erik finds 516 ÷ 12. The partial quotients he finds are 40 and 3. What is the quotient? Explain.

3 A factory receives an order for 94,500 tennis balls for a major U.S. tournament. Three tennis balls are packed into each can.

a. How many cans of tennis balls does the factory pack for the order? Show your work.

SOLUTION _____

b. Check your answer to problem 3a. Show your work.

Develop Using the Standard Algorithm for Division

➤ **Read and try to solve the problem below.**

The librarians at a new city library order 11,328 books. They estimate that 32 books can fit on each shelf. Based on this estimate, how many shelves does the library need to hold all the books?

TRY IT

Math Toolkit base-ten blocks, base-ten grid paper, grid paper

---

DISCUSS IT

Ask: How is your strategy similar to mine? How is it different?

Share: My model shows . . .

➤ **Explore different ways to understand using an algorithm to divide whole numbers.**

The librarians at a new city library order 11,328 books. They estimate that 32 books can fit on each shelf. Based on this estimate, how many shelves does the library need to hold all the books?

Model It

You can divide using partial quotients.

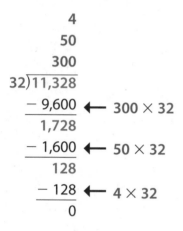

```
       4
      50
     300
32)11,328
   − 9,600  ← 300 × 32
    1,728
   − 1,600  ← 50 × 32
      128
    − 128   ← 4 × 32
        0
```

Model It

You can divide using the standard algorithm for division.

Many of the zeros shown in the partial quotients strategy are not written when you use the standard algorithm.

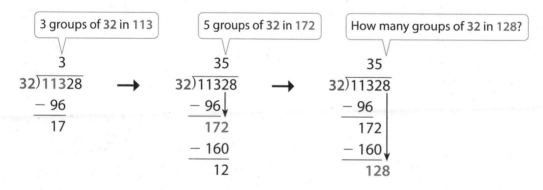

```
  3 groups of 32 in 113        5 groups of 32 in 172        How many groups of 32 in 128?

        3                            35                           35
32)11328          →          32)11328          →          32)11328
  − 96                          − 96↓                         − 96
    17                           172                          172
                               − 160                        − 160↓
                                  12                          128
```

➤ **Use the problem from the previous page to help you understand how to use an algorithm to divide whole numbers.**

1 Look at the second **Model It**. The first digit to be written in the quotient is 3. Explain how this 3 represents the partial quotient 300 in the first **Model It**.

2 What is the value of the number 96 in the second **Model It**? How do you know?

3 Why is the digit 2 from the dividend brought down to make 172?

4 How many shelves does the library need to hold all the books? How could you use estimation to check your answer?

5 When you use the standard algorithm for division, how do you know where to write each digit of the quotient?

6 **Reflect** Think about all the models and strategies you have discussed today. Describe how one of them helped you better understand how to use the standard algorithm for division to divide whole numbers.

Apply It

➤ **Use what you learned to solve these problems.**

7 Members of a school band sell 1,680 bags of popcorn to raise money. There are 112 band members. Each band member sells the same number of bags. How many bags of popcorn does each band member sell? Show your work.

SOLUTION _____

8 Nathan incorrectly divides 33,947 by 83. Describe his mistake.

Nathan

$$
\begin{array}{r}
49 \\
83\overline{)33947} \\
-332 \\
\hline
747 \\
-747 \\
\hline
0
\end{array}
$$

9 Find 62,208 ÷ 36. Show your work.

SOLUTION _____

Name:

Practice Using the Standard Algorithm for Division

➤ **Study the Example showing how to divide whole numbers using the standard algorithm. Then solve problems 1–4.**

Example

A restaurant uses 450,000 eggs in a year. One week, the cook needs to place an order for 8,640 eggs. The eggs come to the restaurant in boxes of 180 eggs each. How many boxes of eggs should the cook order for the week?

You can use the standard algorithm to divide 8,640 by 180.

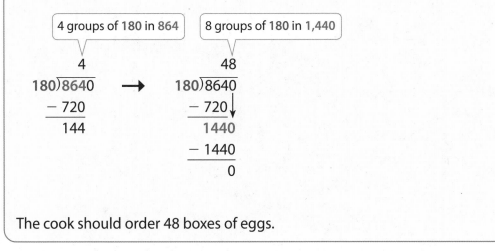

4 groups of 180 in 864   8 groups of 180 in 1,440

The cook should order 48 boxes of eggs.

---

1 The cook in the Example needs 11,160 eggs during a holiday week. How many boxes of eggs should the cook order for the holiday week? Show your work.

SOLUTION _____

LESSON 8 Divide Whole Numbers and Multi-Digit Decimals   **177**

2 Platon's mom buys a car using a loan. She repays the loan by paying $22,032 in 48 equal monthly payments. How much is each payment? Show your work.

Total to repay loan:
$22,032

Length of loan:
48 months

SOLUTION _____

3 Find the quotient 40,936 ÷ 34. Show your work.

SOLUTION _____

4 Francisca incorrectly divides 31,104 by 18. Describe her mistake.

Francisca

```
        1 7 3
18)31,104
   − 18
     13 1
    − 12 6
         5 4
       − 5 4
           0
```

Develop Expressing Remainders as Decimals

➤ **Read and try to solve the problem below.**

Serafina is taking ballet folklórico lessons at the local dance school. A semester of lessons costs $318. There are 24 lessons in a semester and each lesson costs the same amount. How much does each lesson cost?

TRY IT

Math Toolkit base-ten blocks, base-ten grid paper, grid paper

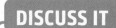

DISCUSS IT

Ask: How did you get started?

Share: At first I . . .

➤ **Explore different ways to express remainders as decimals.**

Serafina is taking ballet folklórico lessons at the local dance school. A semester of lessons costs $318. There are 24 lessons in a semester and each lesson costs the same amount. How much does each lesson cost?

Model It

You can use an area model to divide.

If there is a remainder, you can express it as a decimal by adding more parts to the model.

	?
24	318

➡️ 24

10	+	3	+	0.2	+	0.05
(24 × 10 = 240)		(24 × 3 = 72)		(24 × 0.2 = 4.8)		(24 × 0.05 =1.20)
318		78		6.0		1.20
−240		−72		−4.8		−1.20
78		6		1.2		0

Model It

You can use the standard algorithm to divide and write a remainder as a decimal.

```
      13
  24)318
   − 24↓
      78
    − 72
       6
```
➡️
```
      13.2
  24)318.0
   − 24
      78
    − 72↓
         60
       − 48
         12
```
➡️
```
      13.2
  24)318.00
   − 24
      78
    − 72
         6 0
       − 4 8↓
         1 20
```

➤ **Use the problem from the previous page to help you understand how to express remainders as decimals.**

1 Look at the area model in the first **Model It**. The first two partial quotients are 10 and 3. Why is the next partial quotient less than 1?

2 Look at the second **Model It**. The dividend is written first as 318, then as 318.0, and then as 318.00. Why are 0s shown in the tenths and hundredths places?

3 How much does each lesson cost? How can you check your answer?

4 The division at the right shows dividing the decimal 318.6 by a whole number. How is this division like the one shown in the second **Model It**? How is it different?

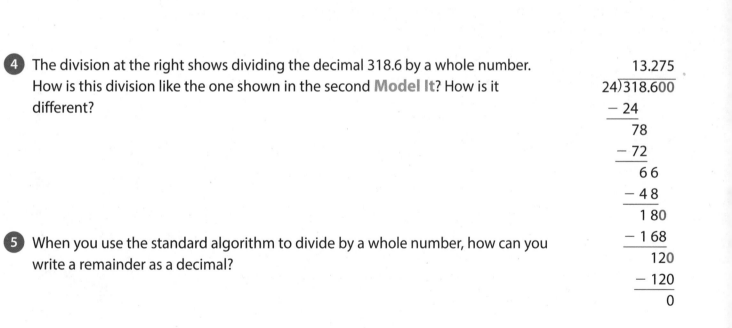

```
        13.275
  24)318.600
    - 24
      ‾‾‾‾
       78
     - 72
       ‾‾‾
        6 6
      - 4 8
        ‾‾‾‾
        1 80
      - 1 68
        ‾‾‾‾
          120
        - 120
          ‾‾‾‾
            0
```

5 When you use the standard algorithm to divide by a whole number, how can you write a remainder as a decimal?

6 **Reflect** Think about all the models and strategies you have discussed today. Describe how one of them helped you better understand how to express a remainder as a decimal.

Apply It

➤ **Use what you learned to solve these problems.**

7 What is the value of 8.25 ÷ 66? Show your work.

SOLUTION _____

8 Jason says that 1,330 ÷ 28 is equal to 47.14. Do you agree? If so, show how
Jason could have gotten his answer. If not, explain the mistake that Jason
made and show how to find the correct quotient.

9 Bianca is making necklaces for her friends. She has 6.3 m of leather cord.
Bianca cuts the cord into 14 equal pieces, one for each necklace. How long
is each piece? Show your work.

SOLUTION _____

Practice Expressing Remainders as Decimals

➤ **Study the Example showing how to express remainders as decimals. Then solve problems 1–5.**

Example

Fadil is making a batch of 18 rolls. The dough for the rolls weighs 29.7 oz. Fadil wants to make each roll the same size. How much should each roll weigh?

You can use an algorithm to divide 29.7 by 18.

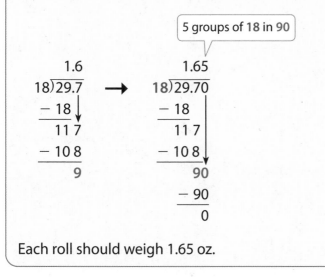

5 groups of 18 in 90

Each roll should weigh 1.65 oz.

1. Look at the Example. Suppose Fadil decides to use the dough to make 12 rolls instead of 18 rolls. How much should each roll weigh? Show your work.

SOLUTION _____

2. Insert a decimal point in the number 3625 to show the correct quotient.

$29 \div 8 = 3625$

3 A stack of 50 cards is 1.9 cm thick. All cards in the stack have the same thickness. How thick is one card? Show your work.

SOLUTION _____

4 Find the quotient 9.43 ÷ 82. Show your work.

SOLUTION _____

5 A school receives gifts of $600 and $800. The money is split equally among the school's 16 clubs. How much money does each club receive? Show your work.

SOLUTION _____

Develop Dividing Multi-Digit Decimals

Bananas
$0.48 for each pound
$2.64 spent

➤ **Read and try to solve the problem below.**

A soccer coach buys bananas for her team. The total cost is $2.64.
How many pounds of bananas does the coach buy?

TRY IT

Math Toolkit base-ten blocks, base-ten grid paper, grid paper

DISCUSS IT

Ask: How does your work show the total cost of the bananas?

Share: In my work . . . represents . . .

➤ **Explore different ways to divide multi-digit decimals.**

A soccer coach buys bananas for her team. The total cost is $2.64. Each pound of bananas costs $0.48. How many pounds of bananas does the coach buy?

Model It

You can use what you know about place value to help you divide with decimals.

2.64 ÷ 0.48 = ?

264 hundredths ÷ 48 hundredths = ?

264 ÷ 48 = ?

Divide the hundredths as you would with whole numbers.

$48\overline{)264}$

Model It

You can use what you know about equivalent fractions to help you divide with decimals.

First, write the division problem as a fraction.

$2.64 ÷ 0.48 = \dfrac{2.64}{0.48}$

Next, multiply the numerator and denominator by the same power of 10 to write an equivalent fraction with a whole-number denominator.

$\dfrac{2.64 \times 100}{0.48 \times 100} = \dfrac{264}{48}$

$2.64 ÷ 0.48 = 264 ÷ 48$

$0.48\overline{)2.64}$ ⟶ $48\overline{)264}$
× 100 × 100

©Curriculum Associates, LLC Copying is not permitted.

➤ **Use the problem from the previous page to help you understand how to divide multi-digit decimals.**

1 Look at the first **Model It**. Why can you use 264 ÷ 48 to find 2.64 ÷ 0.48?

2 Look at the pattern in the division problems. How could you use this pattern to help you divide two decimals?

$$4{,}200 \div 600 = 7$$
$$420 \div 60 = 7$$
$$42 \div 6 = 7$$
$$4.2 \div 0.6 = 7$$
$$0.42 \div 0.06 = 7$$

3 Look at the arrows in the second **Model It**. Multiplying by 100 moves each digit in a number two places to the left. Why do you need to multiply both the dividend and the divisor by the same power of 10?

4 How many pounds of bananas does the coach buy? How do you know that your answer is reasonable?

5 How do you rewrite a division problem involving a decimal divisor in order to use the standard algorithm to find the quotient?

6 **Reflect** Think about all the models and strategies you have discussed today. Describe how one of them helped you better understand how to divide multi-digit decimals.

Apply It

➤ **Use what you learned to solve these problems.**

7 Find the value of 54.08 ÷ 6.4. Show your work.

SOLUTION _____

8 Muna incorrectly divides 48.6 by 0.75. Describe her mistake.

$$0.75\overline{)48.6} \longrightarrow \begin{array}{r} 6.48 \\ 75\overline{)486.00} \\ -450 \\ \hline 36\,0 \\ -30\,0 \\ \hline 6\,00 \\ -6\,00 \\ \hline 0 \end{array}$$

9 A pile of soil has a volume of 67.5 ft³. A worker's wheelbarrow holds 2.25 ft³ of soil when full. How many times does the worker need to fill the wheelbarrow to move all of the soil to a vegetable garden? Show your work.

SOLUTION _____

Practice Dividing Multi-Digit Decimals

➤ **Study the Example showing how to divide multi-digit decimals. Then solve problems 1–5.**

Example

A lake is 8.75 mi long. Yukio and his stepdad are paddling a canoe on the lake. They travel 2.5 mi each hour. At this speed, how many hours does it take them to travel the length of the lake?

You can divide decimals by writing an equivalent problem with a whole number divisor. Multiply the dividend and the divisor by the same power of 10.

$$
2.5\overline{)8.75} \quad \longrightarrow \quad 25\overline{)87.5}
$$

$$
\times 10 \quad \times 10
$$

$$
\begin{array}{r}
3.5 \\
25\overline{)87.5} \\
-\ 75 \\
\hline
12\ 5 \\
-\ 12\ 5 \\
\hline
0
\end{array}
$$

It takes Yukio and his stepdad 3.5 h to travel the length of the lake.

---

1 Show how to use a power of 10 to write 42.66 ÷ 2.97 as an equivalent expression with a whole number divisor.

2 Find the quotient 27.47 ÷ 4.1. Show your work.

SOLUTION _____

3 Ellie earns money by raking leaves. She earns $2.25 for each bag she fills with leaves. This week, she earns $24.75. How many bags of leaves does Ellie fill this week? Show your work.

SOLUTION _____

4 Which expression is equivalent to 8.508 ÷ 70.9?

A 8.508 ÷ 709

B 85.08 ÷ 709

C 850.8 ÷ 709

D 8,508 ÷ 709

5 What is the value of 0.5 ÷ 0.8? Show your work.

SOLUTION _____

Refine Dividing Whole Numbers and Multi-Digit Decimals

➤ **Complete the Example below. Then solve problems 1–9.**

Example

A bag of peanuts costs $2.16 and a granola bar costs $1.08. A group of 4 friends buys 3 bags of peanuts and 1 granola bar to share. They decide to split the cost equally. How much does each friend pay?

Look at how you could show your work using algorithms.

Cost of Peanuts:
$$\begin{array}{r} \overset{1}{2.16} \\ \times3 \\ \hline 6.48 \end{array}$$

Total cost:
$$\begin{array}{r} \overset{1\ 1}{6.48} \\ +1.08 \\ \hline 7.56 \end{array}$$

One share:
$$\begin{array}{r} 1.89 \\ 4\overline{)7.56} \\ -\ 4 \\ \hline 35 \\ -\ 32 \\ \hline 36 \\ -\ 36 \\ \hline 0 \end{array}$$

SOLUTION _____

> **CONSIDER THIS . . .**
> Splitting the cost equally is the same as dividing the total cost by the number of people.

> **PAIR/SHARE**
> What is a different sequence of operations you could use to find how much each friend pays?

Apply It

1 To find a softball player's batting average, divide the player's number of hits by the player's number of turns at bat. Kazuko has 26 hits in 125 turns at bat. Savanna has 11 hits in 50 turns at bat. Who has a greater batting average? Show your work.

> **CONSIDER THIS . . .**
> A batting average is written as a decimal rounded to three decimal places.

> **PAIR/SHARE**
> Would your answer change if Savanna has 15 hits in 50 turns at bat? Explain.

SOLUTION _____

2 The area of the parallelogram is 29.4 cm². What is the parallelogram's height? Show your work.

b = 5.25 cm

CONSIDER THIS...
The formula for the area of a parallelogram is $A = bh$.

SOLUTION _____

PAIR/SHARE
How could you check that you found the height correctly?

3 A football stadium has a total of 22,392 seats. Of these seats, 1,920 are VIP seats. The rest of the seats are divided into 24 equal sections of standard seats. How many seats are in each section of standard seats?

A 933

B 853

C 80

D 11

Chase chose A as the correct answer. How might he have gotten that answer?

CONSIDER THIS...
How many of the 22,392 seats are standard seats?

PAIR/SHARE
What steps did you use to solve this problem?

4 A middle school has a bridge-building contest. Teams of students try to build the strongest bridge using craft sticks and glue. Each team is given 75 craft sticks. There are 1,635 craft sticks available. Tell whether each statement is *True* or *False*.

	True	False
a. There are enough craft sticks for 23 teams.	○	○
b. If there are 20 teams, there will be 135 craft sticks left over.	○	○
c. If each team is given 60 craft sticks, there will be enough for 28 teams.	○	○
d. The teachers need 15 more craft sticks to have enough craft sticks for 22 teams.	○	○

5 Elon and Rachel want to find 28.25 ÷ 0.7. Elon says you should multiply the dividend and the divisor by 10 before dividing. Rachel says you should multiply the dividend and the divisor by 100 before dividing. Who is correct? Explain.

6 An adventure race is 9.75 mi long. The race is divided into equal sections. Each section is 0.75 mi long. The race organizer needs 4 volunteers in each section. How many volunteers does the race organizer need? Show your work.

SOLUTION _____

LESSON 8 Divide Whole Numbers and Multi-Digit Decimals

7 Fernando is playing a video game. He has 13,782 coins. He buys 2 dance moves. What is the greatest number of costumes Fernando can buy with the coins he has left? Show your work.

Item	Coins Needed
Dance move	175
Costume	850

SOLUTION _____

8 Based on the equation $287 \div 8.2 = 35$, which equations are true? Select all that apply.

A $2.87 \div 3.5 = 0.082$

B $287 \div 35 = 8.2$

C $2,870 \div 350 = 8.2$

D $2.87 \div 0.82 = 0.35$

E $28.7 \div 82 = 0.35$

9 **Math Journal** Choose a decimal with a 7 in the tenths place. Divide your decimal by 0.25. Explain how you found the quotient.

✓ **End of Lesson Checklist**

☐ **INTERACTIVE GLOSSARY** Write a new entry for *standard*. Write at least one synonym for *standard*.

☐ **SELF CHECK** Go back to the Unit 2 Opener and see what you can check off.

Dear Family,

This week your student is exploring division with fractions.

You can think of the division expression $2 \div \frac{1}{4}$ as asking the question *How many parts of size $\frac{1}{4}$ are there in 2?* Using a bar model, you can divide each of 2 wholes into fourths and count to see that there are 8 parts of size $\frac{1}{4}$ in 2.

| $\frac{1}{4}$ | $\frac{1}{4}$ | $\frac{1}{4}$ | $\frac{1}{4}$ | $\frac{1}{4}$ | $\frac{1}{4}$ | $\frac{1}{4}$ | $\frac{1}{4}$ |

$2 \div \frac{1}{4} = 8$

2

Your student will be learning to model division situations like the one below.

> How many pieces of yarn that are $\frac{2}{3}$ foot long can be cut from a piece of yarn that is $\frac{8}{3}$ feet long?

➤ **ONE WAY** to show how many $\frac{2}{3}$s are in $\frac{8}{3}$ is to use a bar model.

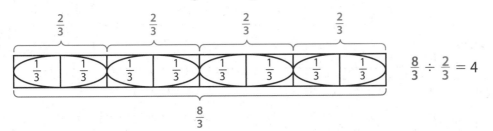

$\frac{8}{3} \div \frac{2}{3} = 4$

➤ **ANOTHER WAY** is to use a number line.

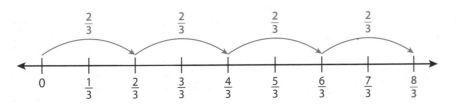

Both models show that a piece of yarn that is $\frac{8}{3}$ feet long can be cut into 4 pieces that are each $\frac{2}{3}$ foot long.

> ▶ Use the next page to start a conversation about dividing with fractions.

Activity Exploring Division with Fractions

➤ **Do this activity together to look for patterns in division with fractions.**

What patterns do you notice in each set?

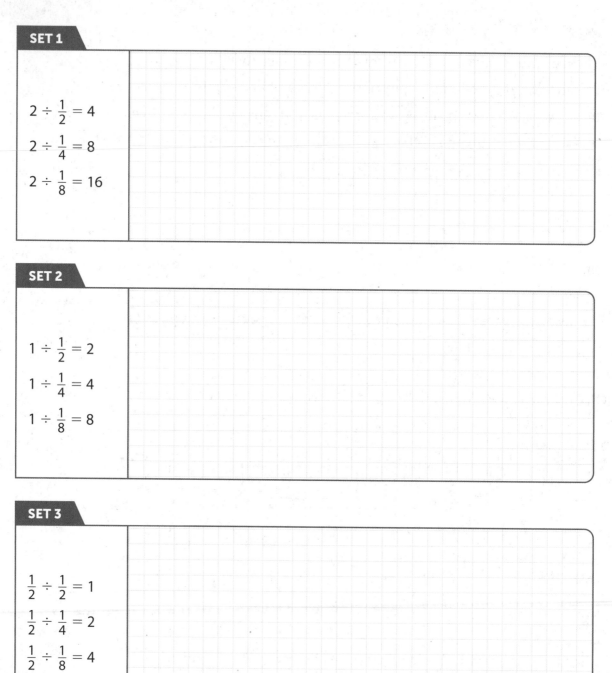

SET 1

$2 \div \frac{1}{2} = 4$

$2 \div \frac{1}{4} = 8$

$2 \div \frac{1}{8} = 16$

SET 2

$1 \div \frac{1}{2} = 2$

$1 \div \frac{1}{4} = 4$

$1 \div \frac{1}{8} = 8$

SET 3

$\frac{1}{2} \div \frac{1}{2} = 1$

$\frac{1}{2} \div \frac{1}{4} = 2$

$\frac{1}{2} \div \frac{1}{8} = 4$

? Do you notice any patterns between two of the sets?

Explore Division with Fractions

Model It

➤ **Complete the problems about dividing a whole number by a fraction.**

Wooden stacking game

1 In carpentry class, students are making wooden stacking games. Brett cuts a board that is 3 feet long into pieces that are each $\frac{1}{4}$ foot long to make his game.

a. Complete the model to show $3 \div \frac{1}{4}$.

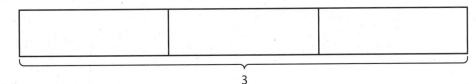

3

b. Brett cuts his board into _____ equal-size pieces.

2 Madison cuts a board that is 3 feet long into pieces that are each $\frac{3}{4}$ foot long for her stacking game.

a. Complete the model to show $3 \div \frac{3}{4}$.

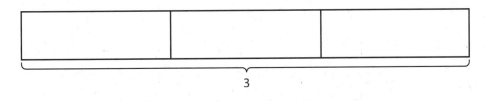

3

b. Madison cuts her board into _____ equal-size pieces.

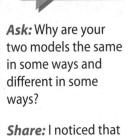

DISCUSS IT

Ask: Why are your two models the same in some ways and different in some ways?

Share: I noticed that when the divisor changes from $\frac{1}{4}$ to $\frac{3}{4}$ . . .

◎ Learning Target SMP 2, SMP 3, SMP 7
Interpret and compute quotients of fractions, and solve word problems involving division of fractions by fractions.

Model It

➤ **Complete the problems about dividing a fraction by a fraction.**

3 Lin starts with a board that is $\frac{3}{2}$ feet long. She cuts it into pieces that are each $\frac{1}{4}$ foot long for her stacking game.

a. Complete the model to show how many pieces Lin cuts her board into.

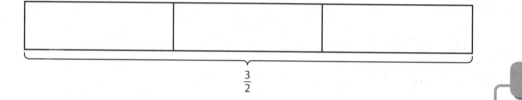

$$\frac{3}{2}$$

b. Write a division equation that represents your model and shows how many pieces Lin cuts her board into. What related multiplication equation does your model represent?

c. Lin cuts her board into _____ equal-size pieces.

4 **Reflect** How are models for dividing with fractions similar to models for dividing with whole numbers? How are they different?

Name:

Prepare for Division with Fractions

1 Think about what you know about division. Fill in each box. Use words, numbers, and pictures. Show as many ideas as you can.

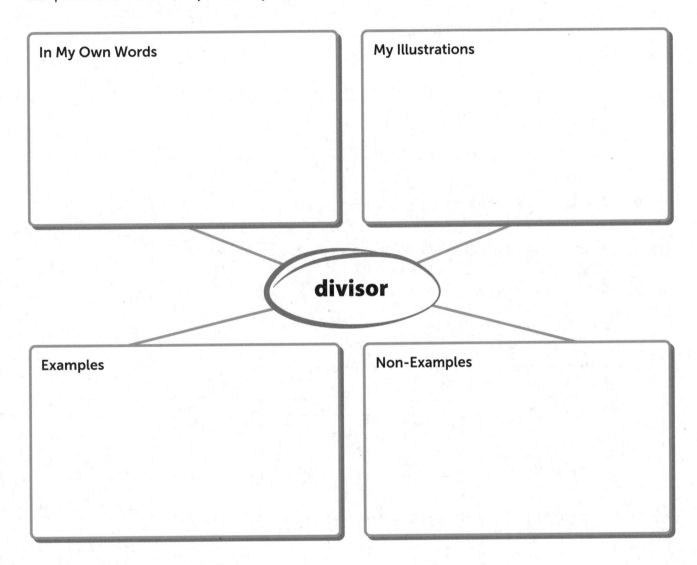

In My Own Words

My Illustrations

divisor

Examples

Non-Examples

2 Circle the equation that shows a divisor of 6.

$6 \div \frac{1}{2} = 12$ $\qquad$ $12 \div 6 = 2$ $\qquad$ $12 \div 2 = 6$

LESSON 9 Understand Division with Fractions   **199**

➤ **Complete problems 3–5.**

3 Lola cuts a string that is 4 feet long into pieces that are each $\frac{1}{6}$ foot long.

a. Complete the model to show $4 \div \frac{1}{6}$.

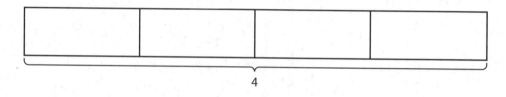

4

b. Lola cuts her string into _____ equal-size pieces.

4 Robert cuts a string that is 4 feet long into pieces that are each $\frac{2}{6}$ foot long.

a. Complete the model to show $4 \div \frac{2}{6}$.

4

b. Robert cuts his string into _____ equal-size pieces.

5 Hiroko cuts a string that is 4 feet long into pieces that are each $\frac{4}{6}$ foot long.

a. Complete the model to show $4 \div \frac{4}{6}$.

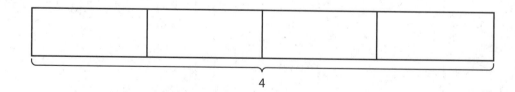

4

b. Hiroko cuts her string into _____ equal-size pieces.

Develop Understanding of Division with Fractions

Model It: Bar Models

➤ **Try these two problems about dividing a fraction by a fraction.**

1 Uma lives near a path that is $\frac{1}{2}$ mile long. She wants to know how many times she needs to run the path in order to run $\frac{6}{4}$ miles.

Path: $\frac{1}{2}$ mile

a. Complete the model to show how many $\frac{1}{2}$s make $\frac{6}{4}$.

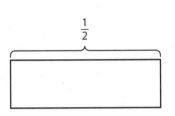

b. How many $\frac{1}{2}$s make $\frac{6}{4}$?

c. Use your model to write a division equation that represents this situation. What related multiplication equation represents your model?

d. Uma needs to run the $\frac{1}{2}$-mile path _____ times to run $\frac{6}{4}$ miles.

2 **a.** Complete the model to show how many $\frac{3}{4}$s make $\frac{6}{4}$.

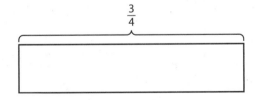

b. Write a division equation and a related multiplication equation that represent your model.

Model It: Number Lines

➤ **Try this problem about dividing with fractions.**

3 **a.** Use the number line to show $\frac{4}{6} \div \frac{1}{6}$.

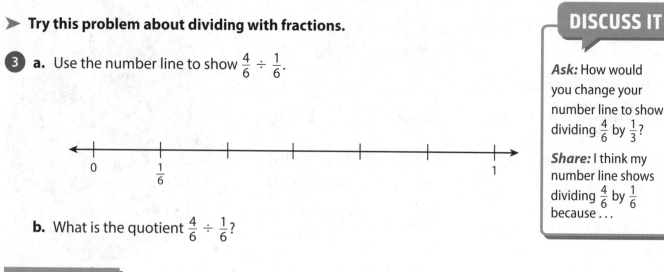

0    $\frac{1}{6}$ 1

b. What is the quotient $\frac{4}{6} \div \frac{1}{6}$?

DISCUSS IT

Ask: How would you change your number line to show dividing $\frac{4}{6}$ by $\frac{1}{3}$?

Share: I think my number line shows dividing $\frac{4}{6}$ by $\frac{1}{6}$ because . . .

CONNECT IT

➤ **Complete the problems below.**

4 How can you show the quotient $\frac{4}{6} \div \frac{1}{6}$ with a bar model? How is using a bar model similar to showing the quotient with a number line? How is it different?

5 Draw a model to show $\frac{10}{8} \div \frac{1}{4}$. How many $\frac{1}{4}$s are in $\frac{10}{8}$?

Practice Division with Fractions

➤ **Study how the Example shows division of a fraction by a fraction. Then solve problems 1–4.**

Example

Mr. Díaz has $\frac{3}{4}$ yard of ribbon to make badges for the science fair. He uses $\frac{1}{8}$ yard of ribbon for each badge. How many badges can Mr. Díaz make?

Find the number of $\frac{1}{8}$s in $\frac{3}{4}$.

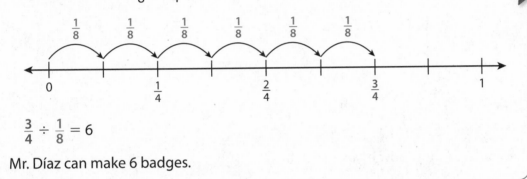

$$\frac{3}{4} \div \frac{1}{8} = 6$$

Mr. Díaz can make 6 badges.

1 **a.** How does the model in the Example show how much ribbon Mr. Díaz starts with?

b. How does the model show how much ribbon Mr. Díaz uses for each badge?

c. How many $\frac{1}{8}$s are in $\frac{3}{4}$?

2 Another day, Mr. Díaz makes badges using $\frac{3}{8}$ yard of ribbon for each badge. He starts with another $\frac{3}{4}$ yard of ribbon. Describe how you can change the model in the Example to show $\frac{3}{4} \div \frac{3}{8}$.

3 Rosa is filling tortillas. She puts $\frac{2}{3}$ cup of vegetables in each tortilla. She has 6 cups of vegetables.

a. Rosa says that to find how many tortillas she can fill, she can first find how many $\frac{1}{3}$ cups are in 6 cups. What else does Rosa need to do to find how many tortillas she can fill?

b. Do you expect the number of tortillas Rosa can fill to be *less than* or *greater than* 6? Explain.

c. Complete the model to show how many $\frac{2}{3}$s are in 6.

d. Complete the division equation to show how many tortillas Rosa can fill.

$6 \div \frac{2}{3} = $ _____

Rosa can fill _____ tortillas.

4 Michael has $\frac{12}{8}$ cups of orange juice in a jar. He pours the juice into glasses that each hold $\frac{3}{4}$ cup. How many glasses can he fill? Draw a model to show your work.

SOLUTION _____

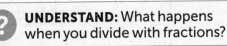

Refine Ideas About Division with Fractions

Apply It **Math Toolkit** fraction bars, fraction tiles, grid paper, number lines

➤ **Complete problems 1–5.**

1 **Interpret** Look at the model below. Write a division equation that the model can represent. Explain how to find the quotient using the model.

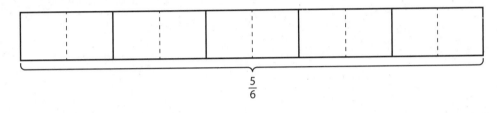

$$\frac{5}{6}$$

2 **Analyze** Nikia says that $\frac{3}{2} \div \frac{1}{4}$ equals $\frac{3}{8}$. Draw a model and use words to explain why Nikia's statement is not reasonable.

3 **Justify** Look at problem 2. Explain why the quotient is greater than the dividend when you divide by $\frac{1}{4}$.

4 Aiyana needs $\frac{3}{8}$ pound of sweet potatoes for each serving of sweet

potato fries. She wants to know how many servings of sweet

potato fries she can make with $1\frac{1}{2}$ pounds of sweet potatoes.

PART A Write a division expression and draw a model to
represent the situation.

PART B Use your model to explain how to find the quotient and what the
quotient means.

5 **Math Journal** What does it mean to divide with fractions? Use models and

words to describe how to divide with fractions. Use $\frac{3}{4} \div \frac{3}{8}$ in your response.

✓ **End of Lesson Checklist**

☐ **INTERACTIVE GLOSSARY** Write a new entry for *reasonable*. Tell what you do when you
determine whether a statement is *reasonable*.

Dear Family,

This week your student is learning how to divide fractions.

When dividing fractions, it is helpful to think about the relationship between multiplication and division. Just as the equations $2 \times 4 = 8$ and $8 \div 4 = 2$ tell you there are **two** 4s in 8, the equations below tell you there is only **half** of $\frac{1}{4}$ in $\frac{1}{8}$.

$$\frac{1}{2} \times \frac{1}{4} = \frac{1}{8} \qquad \frac{1}{8} \div \frac{1}{4} = \frac{1}{2}$$

Your student will be learning to solve problems like the one below.

> A recipe calls for $1\frac{1}{2}$ cups of rice. You only have a $\frac{1}{3}$-cup measure. How many scoops of the $\frac{1}{3}$-cup measure should you use?

➤ **ONE WAY** to find how many $\frac{1}{3}$s are in $1\frac{1}{2}$ is to use the common denominator 6.

Split 1 whole into parts of size $\frac{1}{6}$. Now you can see that $1\frac{1}{2} = \frac{9}{6}$ and $\frac{1}{3} = \frac{2}{6}$.

$$\frac{1}{3} = \frac{2}{6}$$

There are 4 full groups of $\frac{1}{3}$ plus $\frac{1}{2}$ of a group of $\frac{1}{3}$.

$$1\frac{1}{2} = \frac{9}{6}$$

$$1\frac{1}{2} \div \frac{1}{3} = \frac{9}{6} \div \frac{2}{6} = 4\frac{1}{2}$$

➤ **ANOTHER WAY** is to use multiplication.

Multiply $1\frac{1}{2}$ by 3 to find how many $\frac{1}{3}$s are in $1\frac{1}{2}$ wholes.

$$1\frac{1}{2} \div \frac{1}{3} = 1\frac{1}{2} \times 3 \quad \longleftarrow \text{The numbers } \frac{1}{3} \text{ and 3 are called \textbf{reciprocals}.}$$

$$= \frac{3}{2} \times 3$$

$$= \frac{9}{2}, \text{ or } 4\frac{1}{2}$$

Using either method, you need $4\frac{1}{2}$ scoops of the $\frac{1}{3}$-cup measure to have $1\frac{1}{2}$ cups of rice.

> ▶ Use the next page to start a conversation about fraction division.

Activity Thinking About Fraction Division Around You

➤ **Do this activity together to investigate division with fractions in the real world.**

Cities and towns often have rules for how land is used for housing. A town might require that a group of townhouses is built on at least $1\frac{1}{2}$ acres of land. The town might also require that each townhouse in the group has $\frac{1}{6}$ acre of land.

The division expression $1\frac{1}{2} \div \frac{1}{6}$ tells how many $\frac{1}{6}$-acre lots fit into $1\frac{1}{2}$ acres of land. Because $1\frac{1}{2} \div \frac{1}{6} = 9$, a builder knows that 9 townhouses can be built on $1\frac{1}{2}$ acres of land.

? What would the division expression be if the builder has $5\frac{2}{3}$ acres and each house needs $\frac{1}{4}$ acre?

Explore Dividing Fractions

Previously, you learned what it means to divide with fractions. In this lesson, you will learn more about dividing fractions.

➤ **Use what you know to try to solve the problem below.**

Ramona is making clay animals with her friends. She has $\frac{3}{4}$ lb of clay. She shares the clay equally among herself and 3 friends. How much clay does each person have?

Math Toolkit fraction bars, fractions circles, grid paper, number lines

DISCUSS IT

Ask: How does your model show that Ramona shares the clay equally among herself and 3 friends?

Share: My model shows . . .

◎ **Learning Target**   SMP 1, SMP 2, SMP 3, SMP 4, SMP 5, SMP 6, SMP 7
Interpret and compute quotients of fractions, and solve word problems involving division of fractions by fractions.

CONNECT IT

1 **Look Back** How much clay does each person have when Ramona shares her clay? Explain how you know.

2 **Look Ahead** Dividing $\frac{3}{4}$ lb of clay equally among several people is a division situation that involves fractions. As when you divide with whole numbers, it can be helpful to estimate a quotient before you divide.

a. Estimate whether $\frac{3}{4} \div 6$ is *greater than* or *less than* the dividend, $\frac{3}{4}$. Use an example of dividing $\frac{3}{4}$ lb of clay into 6 equal portions to explain your thinking.

b. Estimate whether $2\frac{1}{2} \div \frac{1}{4}$ is *greater than* or *less than* the dividend, $2\frac{1}{2}$. Use an example of dividing $2\frac{1}{2}$ lb of clay into $\frac{1}{4}$-lb portions to explain your thinking.

c. Yolanda estimates that $3\frac{1}{4} \div \frac{1}{8}$ is about 24. Show how to use multiplication to check whether Yolanda's estimate is reasonable.

3 **Reflect** What division equation can you write to show that when $\frac{3}{4}$ lb of clay is divided equally among 6 people, each person gets $\frac{1}{8}$ lb of clay? How would you use multiplication to check that the quotient is correct?

Prepare for Dividing Fractions

1 Think about what you know about fractions. Fill in each box. Use words, numbers, and pictures. Show as many ideas as you can.

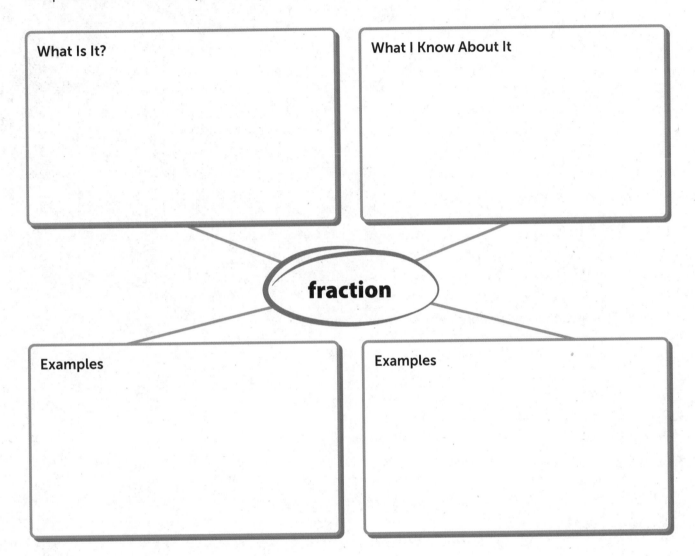

What Is It?

What I Know About It

fraction

Examples

Examples

2 A fraction of the model is shaded. What are the numerator and the denominator of the fraction? Explain how you know.

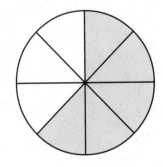

3 Patrick is using layers of colored sand in an art project. He divides $\frac{2}{3}$ lb of blue sand into 3 equal parts in order to make 3 layers.

a. What is the weight of the sand in each layer of blue sand? Show your work.

SOLUTION _____

b. Check your answer to problem 3a. Show your work.

Develop Dividing Fractions

➤ **Read and try to solve the problem below.**

Imani is planning her city's Juneteenth festival. There will be $3\frac{1}{2}$ hours of performances on the main stage. Each performer's time slot lasts $\frac{3}{4}$ hour. How many time slots can Imani plan to have?

 TRY IT

🖊 **Math Toolkit** fraction bars, fraction circles, grid paper, number lines

---

DISCUSS IT

Ask: How is your strategy similar to mine? How is it different?

Share: My strategy is similar to yours because . . . It is different because . . .

➤ **Explore different ways to divide fractions, including when the quotient is not a whole number.**

Imani is planning her city's Juneteenth festival. There will be $3\frac{1}{2}$ hours of performances on the main stage. Each performer's time slot lasts $\frac{3}{4}$ hour. How many time slots can Imani plan to have?

Dance performers at a Juneteenth festival

Model It

You can use the relationship between multiplication and division to represent a division situation with equations.

How many $\frac{3}{4}$-hour time slots are in $3\frac{1}{2}$ hours? $? \times \frac{3}{4} = 3\frac{1}{2}$

Use division to find the unknown factor. $3\frac{1}{2} \div \frac{3}{4} = ?$

Model It

You can use a bar model to divide fractions.

Show 3 wholes and $\frac{1}{2}$ of another whole. Split each whole into 2 halves. Then divide each half into 2 fourths and separate the fourths into groups of 3.

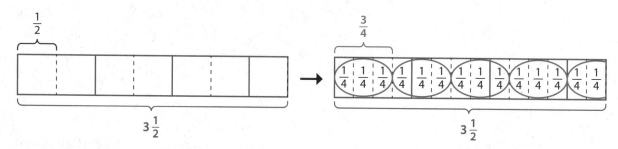

Analyze It

You can use a common denominator to divide fractions.

$$3\frac{1}{2} \div \frac{3}{4} = \frac{7}{2} \div \frac{3}{4}$$

$$= \frac{14}{4} \div \frac{3}{4}$$

Now you can think of dividing **14** fourths by **3** fourths, which is the same as **14 ÷ 3**.

➤ **Use the problem from the previous page to help you understand how to divide fractions when the quotient is not a whole number.**

 1 Look at the second **Model It**. How many full $\frac{3}{4}$-hour time slots does Imani have for performances? How does the second bar model show this?

2 The second bar model shows one group that has only 2 parts of size $\frac{1}{4}$. Explain why this group is $\frac{2}{3}$ of a full time slot.

3 Look at **Analyze It** and the second **Model It**. How does the bar model show that you can use the quotient $14 \div 3$ to find the quotient $\frac{14}{4} \div \frac{3}{4}$?

4 When you divide 14 by 3, the result is 4 with a remainder of 2. When you divide $\frac{14}{4}$ by $\frac{3}{4}$, the remainder is $\frac{2}{4}$. Where do you see this remainder in the bar model? What fraction of the divisor, $\frac{3}{4}$, does this remainder represent?

5 How many times does $\frac{3}{4}$ fit into $3\frac{1}{2}$? Use multiplication to check your answer.

6 **Reflect** Think about all the models and strategies you have discussed today. Describe how one of them helped you better understand how to divide fractions when the quotient is not a whole number.

Apply It

➤ **Use what you learned to solve these problems.**

7 Mr. Lincoln is making slime for his kindergarten class. He has 3 cups of glue. Each batch of slime uses $\frac{2}{3}$ cup of glue. How many batches of slime can Mr. Lincoln make? Show your work.

SOLUTION _____

8 Sofia has pitchers that each hold $1\frac{2}{5}$ L. She has $4\frac{1}{5}$ L of iced tea. Which division expression can you use to find the number of pitchers Sofia can fill with iced tea: $1\frac{2}{5} \div 4\frac{1}{5}$ or $4\frac{1}{5} \div 1\frac{2}{5}$? How many pitchers can Sofia fill? Show your work.

SOLUTION _____

9 What is $2\frac{3}{4} \div \frac{3}{8}$? Show your work.

SOLUTION _____

Practice Dividing Fractions

➤ **Study the Example showing how to divide fractions when the quotient is not a whole number. Then solve problems 1–5.**

Example

The jogging loop at Lake Park is $1\frac{1}{3}$ mi long. Brianna wants to jog $3\frac{1}{3}$ mi.

How many times should she jog around the loop?

You can use a number line to show dividing $3\frac{1}{3}$ mi into lengths of $1\frac{1}{3}$ mi.

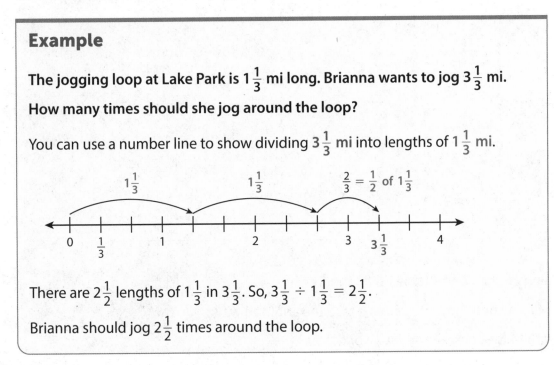

There are $2\frac{1}{2}$ lengths of $1\frac{1}{3}$ in $3\frac{1}{3}$. So, $3\frac{1}{3} \div 1\frac{1}{3} = 2\frac{1}{2}$.

Brianna should jog $2\frac{1}{2}$ times around the loop.

1　The number line model in the Example shows that $1\frac{1}{3}$ fits into $3\frac{1}{3}$ two times, with a remainder of $\frac{2}{3}$.

  a. How is the remainder $\frac{2}{3}$ shown in the number line model?

  b. How do you know that the remainder represents $\frac{1}{2}$ of the jogging loop?

2　Show that there is no remainder when you divide $2\frac{1}{2}$ by $\frac{5}{8}$.

Vocabulary

remainder
the amount left over when one number does not divide another number a whole number of times.

quotient
the result of division.

3 Andre is comparing the weights of his pets. His gerbil weighs $\frac{1}{4}$ lb. His kitten weighs $\frac{7}{8}$ lb. How many times the gerbil's weight is the kitten's weight? Show your work.

SOLUTION _____

4 An ant walks along a stick. The stick is $1\frac{1}{2}$ ft long. The ant travels $\frac{3}{10}$ ft every second. How long does it take the ant to to walk the whole length of the stick? Show your work.

SOLUTION _____

5 A serving of dried fruit is $\frac{1}{5}$ cup. A bag contains $\frac{9}{10}$ cup of dried fruit. Which division expression can you use to find the number of servings in the bag: $\frac{1}{5} \div \frac{9}{10}$ or $\frac{9}{10} \div \frac{1}{5}$? Explain your reasoning.

Develop Using Multiplication to Divide by a Fraction

Feed for 1 meal
Paulo: $\frac{1}{2}$ cup | Aimee: $\frac{3}{2}$ cups

➤ **Read and try to solve the problem below.**

Paulo and Aimee each have $\frac{3}{4}$ cup of feed left in their bags of chicken feed. Paulo uses $\frac{1}{2}$ cup of feed each time he gives his chickens a meal. Aimee uses $\frac{3}{2}$ cups of feed each time she gives her chickens a meal. How many meals can Paulo give his chickens? How many meals can Aimee give her chickens?

TRY IT

Math Toolkit fraction bars, fraction circles, grid paper, number lines

DISCUSS IT

Ask: How does your model show the relationship between $\frac{3}{4}$ and $\frac{1}{2}$? Between $\frac{3}{4}$ and $\frac{3}{2}$?

Share: In my model, ... represents ...

➤ **Explore different ways to solve problems that involve dividing by a fraction.**

Paulo and Aimee each have $\frac{3}{4}$ cup of feed left in their bags of chicken feed.

Paulo uses $\frac{1}{2}$ cup of feed each time he gives his chickens a meal. Aimee uses

$\frac{3}{2}$ cups of feed each time she gives her chickens a meal. How many meals can

Paulo give his chickens? How many meals can Aimee give her chickens?

Model It

You can use a diagram and words to help you represent a division situation.

Shade $\frac{3}{4}$ of a square to represent the amount of feed Paulo and Aimee have.

Paulo   **Aimee**

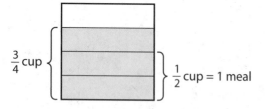 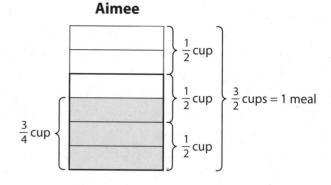

How many $\frac{1}{2}$ cups are in $\frac{3}{4}$ cup of feed?   How many $\frac{3}{2}$ cups are in $\frac{3}{4}$ cup of feed?

$$\frac{3}{4} \div \frac{1}{2} = ?$$ $$\frac{3}{4} \div \frac{3}{2} = ?$$

Analyze It

You can use multiplication to divide by a fraction.

To find how many $\frac{3}{2}$s are in a number, you can use two multiplication steps. $\frac{3}{4} \div \frac{3}{2}$

First find how many $\frac{1}{2}$s are in the number.

To do this, **multiply by 2**. $\frac{3}{4} \times 2 = \frac{6}{4}$

Then separate the **number of $\frac{1}{2}$s** into 3 equal parts.

To divide by 3, **multiply by $\frac{1}{3}$**. $\frac{6}{4} \times \frac{1}{3} = \frac{6}{12}$, or $\frac{1}{2}$

➤ **Use the problem from the previous page to help you understand how to use multiplication to divide by a fraction.**

1 How many meals can Paulo give his chickens? How many meals can Aimee give her chickens? Explain how you know.

2 Look at **Analyze It**. Why does multiplying by 2 tell you how many $\frac{1}{2}$s are in a number? Why does multiplying the number of $\frac{1}{2}$s by $\frac{1}{3}$ tell you how many $\frac{3}{2}$s are in the number?

3 The fraction $\frac{2}{3}$ is called the **reciprocal** of $\frac{3}{2}$. Explain why dividing by $\frac{3}{2}$ gives the same result as multiplying by its reciprocal, $\frac{2}{3}$.

4 Explain why dividing by any fraction gives the same result as multiplying by that fraction's reciprocal. Use the example $4 \div \frac{2}{5}$.

5 Complete the equations to show how to divide any fraction $\frac{a}{b}$ by any fraction $\frac{c}{d}$.

$$\frac{a}{b} \div \frac{c}{d} = \frac{a}{b} \times \boxed{} \times \frac{1}{\boxed{}} \quad \longrightarrow \quad \frac{a}{b} \div \frac{c}{d} = \frac{a}{b} \times \frac{\boxed{}}{\boxed{}}$$

6 **Reflect** Think about all the models and strategies you have discussed today. Describe how one of them helped you better understand how solve problems that involve dividing by a fraction.

Apply It

➤ **Use what you learned to solve these problems.**

7 Find the quotient $\frac{2}{3} \div \frac{2}{5}$. Show your work.

SOLUTION _____

8 The parallelogram has an area of $1\frac{1}{8}$ yd². Use the formula $A = bh$ to find the length of the base, b. Show your work.

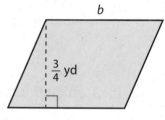

b

$\frac{3}{4}$ yd

SOLUTION _____

9 It takes Francisco $\frac{5}{6}$ minute to upload a video to his blog. How much of one video can he upload in $\frac{1}{2}$ minute? Show your work.

SOLUTION _____

Name:

Practice Using Multiplication to Divide by a Fraction

➤ **Study the Example showing how to use multiplication to divide by a fraction. Then solve problems 1–4.**

Example

Tyrone has $1\frac{1}{2}$ quarts of honey. He is pouring the honey into jars that each hold $\frac{3}{8}$ quart. How many jars can Tyrone fill?

You can divide the total quarts of honey, $1\frac{1}{2}$, by the number of quarts each jar can hold, $\frac{3}{8}$.

$1\frac{1}{2} \div \frac{3}{8} = 1\frac{1}{2} \times \frac{8}{3}$ ← To divide by $\frac{3}{8}$, multiply by its reciprocal, $\frac{8}{3}$.

$= \frac{3}{2} \times \frac{8}{3}$

$= \frac{24}{6} = 4$

Tyrone can fill 4 jars of honey.

1 The Example shows finding the quotient $1\frac{1}{2} \div \frac{3}{8}$ by multiplying $1\frac{1}{2}$ by the reciprocal of $\frac{3}{8}$, or $\frac{8}{3}$. You can relate multiplying by the reciprocal to a bar model that represents the division equation $1\frac{1}{2} \div \frac{3}{8} = 4$.

a. Explain why multiplying by $\frac{8}{3}$ gives the same result as first multiplying by 8 and then multiplying by $\frac{1}{3}$.

b. What is the value of the expression $\left(1\frac{1}{2} \times 8\right) \times \frac{1}{3}$? Explain how finding the value of the expression is related to the bar model.

Vocabulary

reciprocal

for any nonzero number a, the reciprocal is $\frac{1}{a}$. The reciprocal of any fraction $\frac{a}{b}$ is $\frac{b}{a}$.

2 A rectangular city park is $\frac{6}{8}$ mi long. The park has an area of $\frac{1}{4}$ mi². What is the width of the park? Show your work.

SOLUTION _____

3 Find the value of $6 \div 3\frac{3}{4}$. Show your work.

SOLUTION _____

4 During a community service day, 6 teams of students clean a beach by picking up trash. The beach is $1\frac{4}{5}$ mi long. Each team cleans the same length of beach. What is the length of beach that each team cleans? Show your work.

SOLUTION _____

Refine Dividing Fractions

➤ **Complete the Example below. Then solve problems 1–9.**

Example

Sarah uses this recipe to make trail mix. She puts the trail mix in small bags. Each bag holds $1\frac{1}{4}$ cups. How many bags does Sarah fill?

Look at how you could show your work using operations with fractions.

First, find the total amount of trail mix.

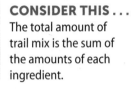

Trail Mix

$2\frac{1}{2}$ cups almonds

$\frac{3}{4}$ cup dried cherries

$2\frac{1}{4}$ cups walnuts

$\frac{3}{4}$ cup raisins

$$2\frac{1}{2} + \frac{3}{4} + 2\frac{1}{4} + \frac{3}{4} = 2\frac{1}{2} + 3 + \frac{3}{4}$$
$$= 5\frac{1}{2} + \frac{3}{4} = 6\frac{1}{4}$$

Then divide the total amount by the amount for 1 bag.

$$6\frac{1}{4} \div 1\frac{1}{4} = \frac{25}{4} \div \frac{5}{4} = 25 \div 5$$

SOLUTION _____

CONSIDER THIS ...
The total amount of trail mix is the sum of the amounts of each ingredient.

PAIR/SHARE
What is another way you could find the value of $6\frac{1}{4} \div 1\frac{1}{4}$?

Apply It

1 Hiroaki buys $3\frac{1}{2}$ gal of paint. He uses $1\frac{1}{2}$ gal of paint. What fraction of the paint that Hiroaki buys does he use? Show your work.

CONSIDER THIS ...
How could you use a multiplication equation with an unknown factor to represent the question?

PAIR/SHARE
How could you use estimation to help you check your answer?

SOLUTION _____

2 Tiana uses $1\frac{3}{5}$ oz of detergent for each full load of laundry. How many full loads of laundry can she do with 100 oz of detergent? Show your work.

CONSIDER THIS ...
What would a remainder represent in this division situation?

PAIR/SHARE
How do you know that your answer is reasonable?

SOLUTION _____

3 Which expression can be used to determine the number of $\frac{3}{4}$-cup servings in $\frac{1}{2}$ cup of pasta salad?

A $\frac{1}{2} \times \frac{3}{4}$

B $\frac{1}{2} \times \frac{4}{3}$

C $\frac{3}{4} \times \frac{2}{1}$

D $\frac{4}{3} \times \frac{2}{1}$

Lillie chose C as the correct answer. How might she have gotten that answer?

CONSIDER THIS ...
How can you rewrite a division expression as a multiplication expression?

PAIR/SHARE
Is there *more than* one full serving of pasta salad or *less than* one full serving? How do you know?

4　A new nature trail is $\frac{8}{10}$ mi long. A park ranger divides the trail into 4 equal sections. How long is each section of the trail? Show your work.

SOLUTION _____

5　Estela has 10 ft³ of soil. She uses $3\frac{1}{2}$ ft³ in her garden. She uses the rest of the soil for tomato plants. She needs $\frac{3}{4}$ ft³ of the soil for each tomato plant. How many tomato plants can she plant? Show your work.

SOLUTION _____

6　Without dividing, tell whether each quotient is *less than 1, greater than 1,* or *equal to 1.*

	Less Than 1	Greater Than 1	Equal to 1
a. $\frac{2}{9} \div \frac{1}{27}$	○	○	○
b. $\frac{1}{2} \div \frac{3}{4}$	○	○	○
c. $\frac{4}{3} \div \frac{3}{5}$	○	○	○
d. $\frac{20}{8} \div 2\frac{1}{2}$	○	○	○

7 Sierra spreads grass seed on her lawn. She needs $\frac{5}{6}$ lb of grass seed to cover her whole lawn. She has $\frac{1}{3}$ lb of grass seed. How much of her lawn can she cover? Show your work.

SOLUTION _____

8 What is $4\frac{1}{7} \div 2\frac{1}{14}$?

A $\frac{1}{98}$ **B** $\frac{1}{2}$

C 2   **D** 98

9 **Math Journal** Write a word problem that you can use the division expression $\frac{3}{4} \div \frac{3}{8}$ to solve. Then solve the problem.

✓ **End of Lesson Checklist**

☐ **INTERACTIVE GLOSSARY** Find the entry for *reciprocal*. Give examples of three numbers and their reciprocals.

☐ **SELF CHECK** Go back to the Unit 2 Opener and see what you can check off.

Dear Family,

This week your student is learning how to find the volume of right rectangular prisms with fractional edge lengths.

Previously, your student found volumes of prisms with whole-number edge lengths using the formulas below. These same formulas can be used to find volumes of prisms with fractional edge lengths.

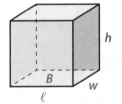

$V = \ell wh$ and $V = Bh$

Your student will be learning to solve problems like the one below.

The right rectangular prism is filled with identical cubes. What is the volume of the prism?

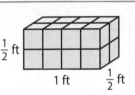

➤ **ONE WAY** to find the volume is to use the volume of the cubes that fill the prism.

Four cubes fill the 1-ft length of the prism, so the edge length of each cube is $\frac{1}{4}$ ft.

Volume of each cube $= \ell wh$

$$= \frac{1}{4} \cdot \frac{1}{4} \cdot \frac{1}{4} = \frac{1}{64}$$

The bottom layer of the prism has 8 cubes. There are 2 layers, so the total number of cubes is 8 • 2, or **16.**

Multiply the **volume of one cube** by the **total number of cubes** inside the prism.

$16 \cdot \frac{1}{64} = \frac{1}{4}$

➤ **ANOTHER WAY** is to use the dimensions of the prism in a volume formula.

$V = \ell wh$

$$= 1 \cdot \frac{1}{2} \cdot \frac{1}{2}$$

$$= \frac{1}{4}$$

Using either method, the volume is $\frac{1}{4}$ ft³.

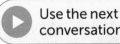 Use the next page to start a conversation about volume.

Activity Exploring Volume of Right Rectangular Prisms

➤ **Do this activity together to explore volume.**

You can find the volume of a right rectangular prism using the number of identical cubes that you can pack inside of it.

What do you notice about these prisms?

PRISM 1

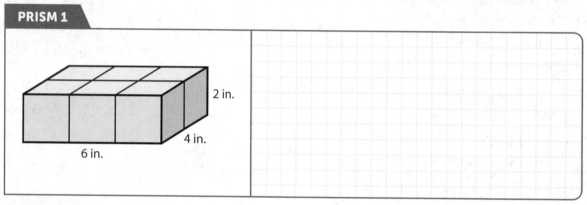

2 in.
4 in.
6 in.

PRISM 2

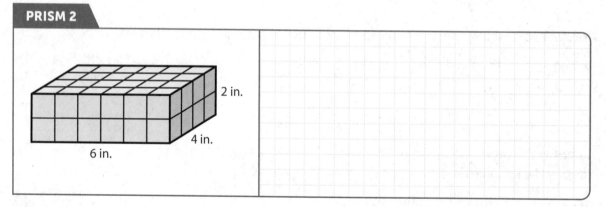

2 in.
4 in.
6 in.

PRISM 3

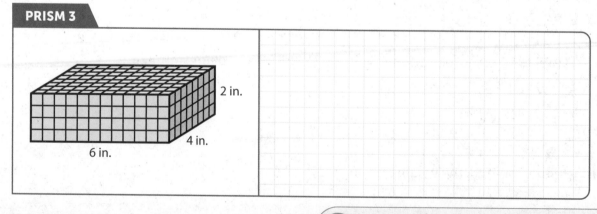

2 in.
4 in.
6 in.

? How does the size of the cube relate to the number of cubes needed to fill the prism?

Explore Volume Problems with Fractions

Previously, you learned about the volume of right rectangular prisms with whole-number edge lengths. In this lesson, you will learn about the volume of right rectangular prisms with fractional edge lengths.

➤ **Use what you know to try to solve the problem below.**

Jiro has some small cubes. He puts them together to make a large cube, as shown. What is the volume of each small cube?

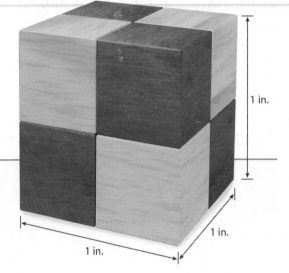

1 in.

1 in.

1 in.

TRY IT

Math Toolkit grid paper, isometric dot paper, unit cubes

DISCUSS IT

Ask: How do you know the volume you found is reasonable?

Share: The volume makes sense because . . .

⊙ **Learning Target**   SMP 1, SMP 2, SMP 3, SMP 4, SMP 5, SMP 6, SMP 8
Find the volume of a right rectangular prism with fractional edge lengths by packing it with unit cubes of the appropriate unit fraction edge lengths, and show that the volume is the same as would be found by multiplying the edge lengths of the prism. Apply the formulas $V = \ell wh$ and $V = bh$ to find volumes of right rectangular prisms with fractional edge lengths in the context of solving real-world and mathematical problems.

LESSON 11 Solve Volume Problems with Fractions   **231**

CONNECT IT

1 **Look Back** What is the volume of each small cube in Jiro's large cube? Explain.

2 **Look Ahead** You can use the volume of a unit cube to find the volume of a small cube with unit fraction edge lengths.

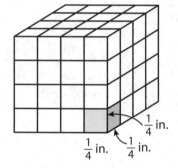

$\frac{1}{4}$ in.

$\frac{1}{4}$ in. $\frac{1}{4}$ in.

   a. What is the edge length of the large cube shown here? Explain.

   b. What is the volume of the large cube? How do you know?

   c. How many small cubes make up the large cube? How do you know?

   d. What does this tell you about the volume of one small cube? Why?

   e. The formula $V = s^3$ gives the volume of a cube, where s is the edge length of the cube. Use the formula $V = s^3$ to find the volume of one small cube. Compare your answer here to your answer to problem 1d.

3 **Reflect** How is finding the volume of a cube with a fractional edge length similar to finding the volume of a cube with a whole-number edge length?

Prepare for Solving Volume Problems with Fractions

1 Think about what you know about three-dimensional figures and volume. Fill in each box. Use words, numbers, and pictures. Show as many ideas as you can.

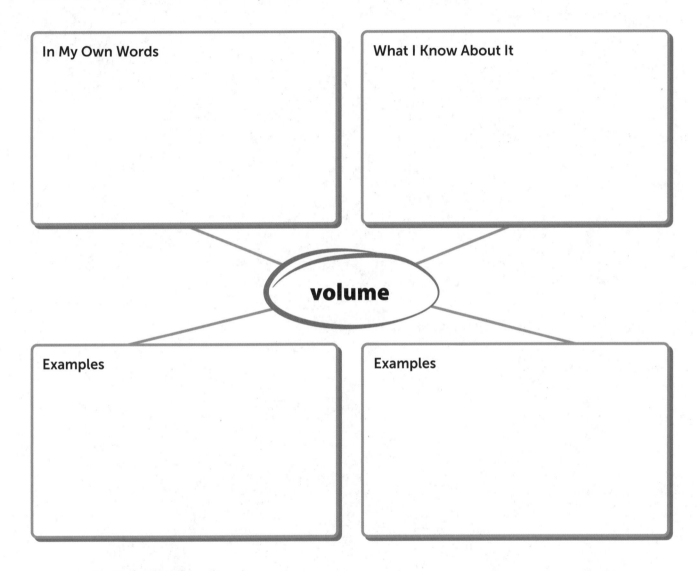

In My Own Words

What I Know About It

volume

Examples

Examples

2 Prisms *A* and *B* are made of centimeter cubes. Which prism has a greater volume? Why?

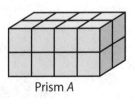

Prism *A*

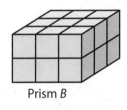

Prism *B*

3 Isabella is playing a video game. Players use blocks to build objects. Isabella chooses blocks that are small cubes to build a large cube, as shown.

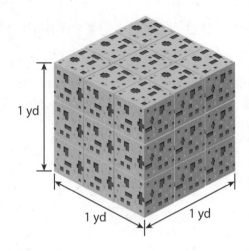

1 yd

1 yd   1 yd

a. In the game, the edge length of the large cube is 1 yd. What is the volume of each small cube? Show your work.

SOLUTION _____

b. Check your answer to problem 3a. Show your work.

Develop Finding the Volume of a Prism with Fractional Edge Lengths

➤ **Read and try to solve the problem below.**

A reptile tank is a right rectangular prism. The tank is 1 ft long, $\frac{3}{4}$ ft wide, and $1\frac{1}{2}$ ft tall. What is the volume of the tank?

TRY IT   **Math Toolkit** grid paper, isometric dot paper, unit cubes

➤ **Explore different ways to find the volume of a right rectangular prism with fractional edge lengths.**

A reptile tank is a right rectangular prism. The tank is 1 ft long, $\frac{3}{4}$ ft wide, and $1\frac{1}{2}$ ft tall. What is the volume of the tank?

Model It

You can fill the prism with cubes with fractional edge lengths.

Find a fraction that divides 1, $\frac{3}{4}$, and $1\frac{1}{2}$ without a remainder. The edge length of each cube can be $\frac{1}{4}$ ft.

Cubes along length: $1 \div \frac{1}{4} = 4$

Cubes along width: $\frac{3}{4} \div \frac{1}{4} = 3$

Cubes along height: $1\frac{1}{2} \div \frac{1}{4} = 6$

Build a prism that is 4 cubes across, 3 cubes wide, and 6 cubes tall. The total number of cubes is $4 \times 3 \times 6 = 72$.

The volume of each cube is $\frac{1}{64}$ ft³.

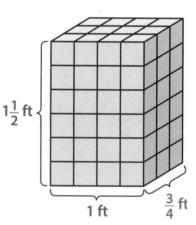

Model It

You can use a volume formula.

The volume V of a right rectangular prism is $V = \ell wh$.

$$V = (1)\left(\frac{3}{4}\right)\left(1\frac{1}{2}\right)$$

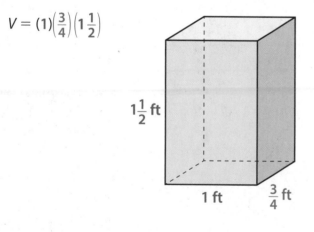

➤ **Use the problem from the previous page to help you understand how to find the volume of a right rectangular prism with fractional edge lengths.**

 Look at the prism filled with cubes in the first **Model It**. Could you fill the prism with cubes that have edges that are $\frac{1}{2}$ ft long or $\frac{1}{3}$ ft long? Explain.

2 Why could you fill the prism with cubes that have edges that are $\frac{1}{8}$ ft long? How many cubes would fit along each edge of the prism?

3 Explain how to find the volume of a prism once you know the number of cubes that fill the prism. What is the volume of the reptile tank?

4 What is the volume of the tank using the formula $V = \ell wh$? How does it compare to the volume you get by filling the prism with cubes?

5 Describe two different ways to find the volume of a right rectangular prism with fractional edge lengths.

6 **Reflect** Think about all the models and strategies you have discussed today. Describe how one of them helped you better understand the volume of a right rectangular prism with fractional edge lengths.

LESSON 11 Solve Volume Problems with Fractions   **237**

Apply It

➤ **Use what you learned to solve these problems.**

7 Miyako is building a raised garden bed. The garden bed is a
right rectangular prism with the dimensions shown. How many
cubic feet of soil does Miyako need to fill the garden bed?
Show your work.

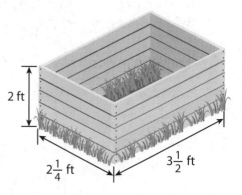

2 ft

$2\frac{1}{4}$ ft $3\frac{1}{2}$ ft

SOLUTION _____

8 A right rectangular prism is completely filled with small cubes. Each small cube
has edges that are $\frac{1}{4}$ in. long. The volume of the prism is 5 in.^{3}. How many cubes
does it take to fill the prism?

A 20   **B** 64

C 125   **D** 320

9 Each of the small cubes in this larger cube has edges that are $\frac{1}{6}$ yd long.
What is the volume of the larger cube? Show your work.

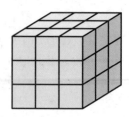

SOLUTION _____

Practice Finding the Volume of a Prism with Fractional Edge Lengths

➤ **Study the Example showing how to find the number of cubes it takes to fill a prism. Then solve problems 1–4.**

Example

Geraldo has a collection of baseballs. He keeps each baseball in a cube-shaped box with edges that are $\frac{1}{3}$ ft long. Geraldo keeps the boxes in a rectangular bin, as shown. How many boxes can Geraldo keep in the bin?

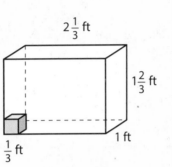

Divide to find the number of cube-shaped boxes that fit along the length, width, and height of the bin.

Length: $2\frac{1}{3} \div \frac{1}{3} = \frac{7}{3} \div \frac{1}{3} = 7$

Width: $1 \div \frac{1}{3} = 3$

Height: $1\frac{2}{3} \div \frac{1}{3} = \frac{5}{3} \div \frac{1}{3} = 5$

Since $7 \times 3 \times 5 = 105$, Geraldo can keep 105 boxes in the bin.

1 **a.** What is the volume of each cube-shaped box in the Example?

b. Use your answer to problem 1a to find the volume of the bin.

c. Show how you can use a formula to check the volume you found.

Vocabulary

cube
a rectangular prism in which each face of the prism is a square.

right rectangular prism
a right prism where the bases and other faces are rectangles.

2 A fish pond at a park is in the shape of a right rectangular prism. The pond has a length of $3\frac{1}{2}$ yd, a width of $3\frac{1}{2}$ yd, and a height of $\frac{1}{4}$ yd. What is the volume of the pond? Show your work.

SOLUTION _____

3 A right rectangular prism has edge lengths of $3\frac{1}{2}$ ft, $2\frac{1}{4}$ ft, and $4\frac{1}{3}$ ft. Safara wants to completely fill the prism with cubes. The cubes must have edge lengths that are unit fractions. What is the greatest edge length of the cubes that Safara should use? Explain.

4 The right rectangular prism is filled with cubes. The edge length of each cube is $\frac{1}{2}$ in. What is the volume of the prism? Show your work.

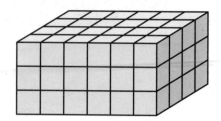

SOLUTION _____

Develop Solving Problems with Volume Formulas

➤ **Read and try to solve the problem below.**

Dalila bakes cornbread for family barbecues. The cornbread batter has a volume of 134 in.³. She needs at least $1\frac{1}{4}$ in. of space between the top of the batter and the top of the pan. Will the batter fit in a rectangular pan that is 8 in. long, $12\frac{1}{2}$ in. wide, and 3 in. high?

TRY IT

Math Toolkit grid paper, isometric dot paper, unit cubes

DISCUSS IT

Ask: How is your strategy similar to mine? How is it different?

Share: My strategy is similar to yours because . . . It is different because . . .

➤ **Explore different ways to solve problems with volume formulas.**

Dalila bakes cornbread for family barbecues. The cornbread batter has a volume of 134 in.³. She needs at least $1\frac{1}{4}$ in. of space between the top of the batter and the top of the pan. Will the batter fit in a rectangular pan that is 8 in. long, $12\frac{1}{2}$ in. wide, and 3 in. high?

Picture It

You can draw a diagram to help you understand the problem.

Label the diagram with the length, width, and height of the pan.

The dashed line shows that Dalila needs at least $1\frac{1}{4}$ in. of space above the batter.

Because $3 - 1\frac{1}{4} = 1\frac{3}{4}$, the height of the batter can be no more than $1\frac{3}{4}$ in.

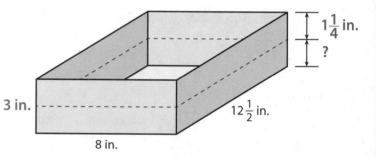

Model It

You can use a volume formula to help you solve the problem.

Find the volume of the space available for batter in the pan.

$V = \ell wh$

$\quad = (8)\left(12\frac{1}{2}\right)\left(1\frac{3}{4}\right)$

$\quad = 175$

➤ **Use the problem from the previous page to help you understand how to solve problems with volume formulas.**

1 Look at the diagram in **Picture It**. You can think of the dashed line as dividing the right rectangular prism of the pan into two smaller prisms. Describe what these two prisms represent in the context of the problem.

2 How does the diagram help you find the dimensions of the prism that represents the space available for the batter?

3 Will the batter fit in the pan with enough space left at the top? Explain.

4 Another prism represents the actual batter after it is poured into the pan. What is the volume of this prism? What dimensions of this prism do you know? Explain how you could find any missing dimensions.

5 Describe how you can approach solving a problem that involves the volume of one or more right rectangular prisms.

6 **Reflect** Think about all the models and strategies you have discussed today. Describe how one of them helped you better understand how to solve the **Try It** problem.

Apply It

➤ **Use what you learned to solve these problems.**

7 Roberto buys a package of three identical food containers, as shown. The total volume of the containers is 210 in.³. How many of these containers could Roberto set side by side on a shelf that is 24 in. long? Show your work.

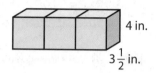

4 in.

$3\frac{1}{2}$ in.

SOLUTION _____

8 What is the volume of the solid figure shown at the right?

A $12\frac{3}{8}$ cm³

B $13\frac{1}{2}$ cm³

C $22\frac{1}{2}$ cm³

D $25\frac{7}{8}$ cm³

$1\frac{1}{2}$ cm $1\frac{1}{2}$ cm

6 cm

$1\frac{1}{2}$ cm

$1\frac{1}{2}$ cm

$5\frac{1}{2}$ cm

9 A fountain is a right rectangular prism that is $2\frac{1}{3}$ yd long, 3 yd wide, and $1\frac{1}{2}$ yd high. The fountain is $\frac{1}{3}$ full of water. What is the volume of the water in the fountain? Show your work.

SOLUTION _____

Practice Solving Problems with Volume Formulas

➤ **Study the Example showing how to solve a problem with volume formulas. Then solve problems 1–4.**

Example

A fish tank is a right rectangular prism that is 2 ft long and $1\frac{1}{2}$ ft wide. The tank can hold $3\frac{3}{4}$ ft³ of water when it is full. Tameka fills the tank $\frac{2}{5}$ full of water. What is the height of the water in the tank?

Find the area of the base of the tank.

$$B = (2)\left(1\frac{1}{2}\right) = 3$$

Since $V = Bh$, you can divide the volume by B to find h.

$$h = 3\frac{3}{4} \div 3 = 1\frac{1}{4}$$

The height of the water when the tank is $\frac{2}{5}$ full is $\frac{2}{5}$ of h.

$$\frac{2}{5} \cdot 1\frac{1}{4} = \frac{2}{5} \cdot \frac{5}{4} = \frac{10}{20} = \frac{1}{2}$$

The height of the water in the tank is $\frac{1}{2}$ ft.

(diagram: right rectangular prism labeled h, $1\frac{1}{2}$ ft, and 2 ft)

---

1. **a.** What is the volume of the water that Tameka puts in the fish tank in the Example? Explain how you can use the fact that the tank is $\frac{2}{5}$ full to find the volume of the water without finding the height of the fish tank.

b. How can you use your answer to problem 1a to find the height of the water? What is the height of the water?

Vocabulary

base (of a three-dimensional figure)

a face of a three-dimensional figure from which the height is measured.

2 Kevin designs the pasta box shown. His box holds exactly the required amount of pasta. Kevin's boss says there must be at least $\frac{1}{2}$ in. of space between the top of the pasta and the top of the box. Kevin changes his design so that the height of the box is 9 in. and the area of the base is 9 in.². Will the pasta fit in the new box with enough space at the top? Explain.

OLD WORLD PASTA

PENNE RIGATE

$6\frac{1}{2}$ in.

5 in.

$2\frac{1}{4}$ in.

3 A solid metal sculpture is made up of three identical right rectangular prisms. What is the volume of the metal? Show your work.

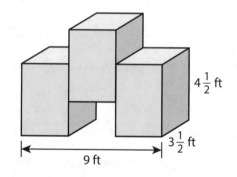

$4\frac{1}{2}$ ft

$3\frac{1}{2}$ ft

9 ft

SOLUTION

4 A trash bin is a right rectangular prism with a width of $2\frac{1}{8}$ ft, a length of $1\frac{7}{8}$ ft, and a volume of $16\frac{1}{8}$ ft³. Can a 3-ft board fit completely in the bin? Explain how to use estimation to solve the problem.

Refine Solving Volume Problems with Fractions

➤ **Complete the Example below. Then solve problems 1–9.**

Example

A teacher stores number cubes in a rectangular box. The number cubes have edge lengths of 1.5 cm. The inside edge lengths of the box are 9 cm by 5.4 cm by 7.8 cm. What is the maximum number of cubes that can be stored in the box?

Look at how you could show your work using division of decimals.

Divide to find the maximum number of cubes that fit along the length, width, and height of the box.

Length: 9 ÷ 1.5 = 6 ➡ Exactly 6 cubes fit along the length.

Width: 5.4 ÷ 1.5 = 3.6 ➡ At most, 3 cubes fit along the width.

Height: 7.8 ÷ 1.5 = 5.2 ➡ At most, 5 cubes fit along the height.

Total number of cubes: 6 × 3 × 5

SOLUTION _____

CONSIDER THIS . . .
Can these cubes be used to fill the prism completely?

PAIR/SHARE
Could you solve the problem by finding the volume of the prism and dividing by the volume of a cube? Why or why not?

Apply It

1 Javier glues together small cubes to make a large cube, as shown. The large cube has edges that are $1\frac{1}{4}$ ft long. What is the volume of a small cube? Show your work.

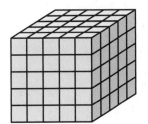

CONSIDER THIS . . .
How is the edge length of a small cube related to the edge length of the large cube?

PAIR/SHARE
How can you solve the problem a different way to check your answer?

SOLUTION _____

2 Ummi is setting up an aquarium in the shape shown here. She fills it partially with water. The volume of the water is 15 ft³. Then she adds more water to the aquarium. Now the volume of the water is $22\frac{1}{2}$ ft³. How much does the level of the water rise when Ummi adds more water? Show your work.

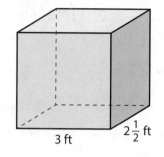

3 ft $2\frac{1}{2}$ ft

SOLUTION _____

3 In the figure, each small cube has edges that are $\frac{1}{3}$ yd long. Which expression can you use to find the volume of the rectangular prism in cubic yards?

A $2 \times 4 \times 5$

B $2 \times 4 \times 5 \times \frac{1}{3} \times \frac{1}{3} \times \frac{1}{3}$

C $\frac{1}{3} \times \frac{1}{3} \times \frac{1}{3}$

D $2 \times 4 \times 5 \div \left(\frac{1}{3} \times \frac{1}{3} \times \frac{1}{3} \right)$

Cody chose D as the correct answer. How might he have gotten that answer?

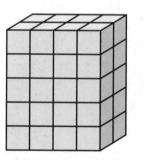

4 The figure shows the dimensions of a rectangular storage room. Darnell has boxes that are cubes with edges $1\frac{1}{2}$ ft long. What is the maximum number of boxes that Darnell can fit in the storage room? Explain.

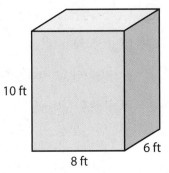

10 ft

8 ft

6 ft

5 What is the volume of the solid figure in cubic inches?

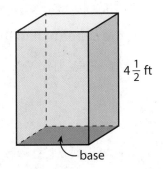

3 in.

5 in.

6.5 in.

5.5 in.

12 in.

6 It takes 144 cubes that have edge lengths $\frac{1}{2}$ ft to completely fill this cardboard box. What is the area of the base of the box?

A 4 ft²

B 16 ft²

C 18 ft²

D 32 ft²

$4\frac{1}{2}$ ft

base

7 Dolores has a block of wax that is $2\frac{1}{2}$ in. long, 2 in. wide, and $4\frac{1}{2}$ in. high. She melts the wax and pours it into a candle mold. The mold is a right rectangular prism with a base area of $3\frac{3}{4}$ in.^{2}. What is the height of the wax in the mold? Show your work.

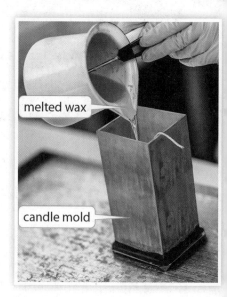

melted wax

candle mold

SOLUTION _____

8 What is the volume of the right rectangular prism shown by the net? Show your work.

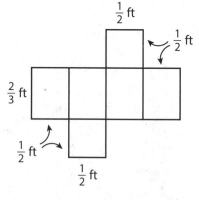

$\frac{1}{2}$ ft

$\frac{1}{2}$ ft

$\frac{2}{3}$ ft

$\frac{1}{2}$ ft

$\frac{1}{2}$ ft

SOLUTION _____

9 **Math Journal** Give the dimensions of a right rectangular prism that can be filled completely with cubes that have edge lengths of $\frac{1}{2}$ in. Explain how to use the cubes to find the volume of the prism.

✓ **End of Lesson Checklist**

☐ **INTERACTIVE GLOSSARY** Write a new entry for *diagram*. Write at least one synonym for *diagram*.

☐ **SELF CHECK** Go back to the Unit 2 Opener and see what you can check off.

Study an Example Problem and Solution

➤ **Read this problem involving volume and decimal operations. Then look at one student's solution to this problem on the following pages.**

Growing Salt Crystals

In science club, Alberto looks at table salt under a microscope. Later, he mixes table salt with water to grow salt crystals. Read through Alberto's notes, and help him answer his question.

LAB NOTES

Table Salt Observations:

- The grains of salt are approximately cube-shaped.

- The edge lengths of the grains range from 0.2 mm to 0.4 mm.

Salt Crystal Observations:

salt crystal

- I grew 3 salt crystals. Each crystal is approximately a cube.

- The edge length of the smallest cube is 4.5 mm.

- The edge length of the middle cube is 5.7 mm.

- The edge length of the largest cube is 6.3 mm.

? **About how many grains of salt did it take to grow one of my salt crystals?**

Salt crystals magnified

One Student's Solution

First, I need to choose one of Alberto's three salt crystals.

I will choose the crystal with edge length 5.7 mm, since it is not the largest or the smallest.

> **NOTICE THAT...**
> Because the salt crystal is a cube, the length, width, and height are all 5.7 mm.

Next, I will draw a picture to help me think about the problem.

I can sketch a cube to represent the crystal and label its edge lengths.

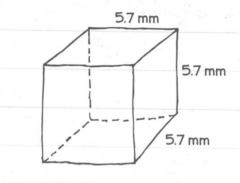

Then, I will imagine packing the crystal with grains of salt.

I know the edge lengths of the grains of table salt range from 0.2 mm to 0.4 mm. I can use 0.25 mm for the edge length of each grain of salt, since 0.25 mm is between 0.2 mm and 0.4 mm.

> **NOTICE THAT...**
> 0.25 is five hundredths greater than 0.2.

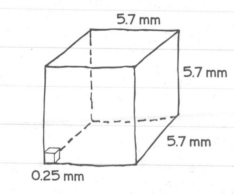

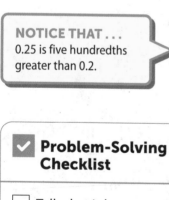

✓ Problem-Solving Checklist

- ☐ Tell what is known.
- ☐ Tell what the problem is asking.
- ☐ Show all your work.
- ☐ Show that the solution works.

Now, I can calculate the number of grains of salt that fit along the length, width, and height of the crystal.

I need to figure out how many 0.25s are in 5.7. So, I need to divide 5.7 mm by 0.25 mm.

$$0.25\overline{)5.7} \longrightarrow$$

```
        22.8
  25)570.0
   − 50
     70
   − 50
     20 0
   − 20 0
        0
```

NOTICE THAT...
The salt crystal and grain of table salt are both cubes. You only need to divide once to calculate the number of grains of salt that will fit along each edge of the crystal.

The number of grains will be a whole number, so I will round. About 23 grains of salt will fit along each edge of the salt crystal.

Finally, I will calculate the volume of a salt crystal in grains of salt.

I can use the formula for volume: $V = \ell wh$.

$$V = 23 \cdot 23 \cdot 23$$
$$= 12{,}167$$

Alberto's salt crystal is made from about 12,167 grains of salt.

NOTICE THAT...
You can also represent the volume using an exponent:
$23 \cdot 23 \cdot 23$ is the same as 23^3.

There are approximately 4.5 to 4.9 billion tons of salt in the Great Salt Lake.

Try Another Approach

➤ **There are many ways to solve problems. Think about how you might solve the Growing Salt Crystals problem in a different way.**

Growing Salt Crystals

In science club, Alberto looks at table salt under a microscope. Later, he mixes table salt with water to grow salt crystals. Read through Alberto's notes, and help him answer his question.

LAB NOTES

Table Salt Observations:

- The grains of salt are approximately cube-shaped.

- The edge lengths of the grains range from 0.2 mm to 0.4 mm.

Salt Crystal Observations:

salt crystal

- I grew 3 salt crystals. Each crystal is a cube.

- The edge length of the smallest cube is 4.5 mm.

- The edge length of the middle cube is 5.7 mm.

- The edge length of the largest cube is 6.3 mm.

(?) About how many grains of salt did it take to grow one of my salt crystals?

Plan It

➤ **Answer these questions to help you start thinking about a plan.**

a. Which of the three salt crystals will you use? What edge length of a grain of salt will you use?

b. Is there another way you could use the idea of volume to calculate how many grains of salt make up one crystal?

Solve It

➤ **Find a different solution for the Growing Salt Crystals problem. Show all your work on a separate sheet of paper. You may want to use the Problem-Solving Tips to get started.**

PROBLEM-SOLVING TIPS

Math Toolkit grid paper, isometric dot paper, unit cubes

Key Terms

| volume | dimensions | quotient |
| product | prism | formula |

Models You may want to use . . .

- a picture or diagram to organize your work.

- a formula to calculate volume: $V = Bh$ or $V = \ell wh$.

- an area model or the standard algorithm to multiply or divide decimals.

Reflect

Use Mathematical Practices As you work through the problem, discuss these questions with a partner.

- **Persevere** What is your first step? What will you do next?

- **Be Precise** Would it make sense to round the result of your calculations to get your final answer? Why or why not?

Discuss Models and Strategies

➤ **Read the problem. Write a solution on a separate sheet of paper. Remember, there can be lots of ways to solve a problem.**

Aquatic Ecosystem

Alberto wants to set up an aquarium as a demonstration of freshwater ecosystems for the science club. Read the information he finds about aquarium ecosystems. Then suggest a tank, a number of guppies, and an amount of gravel for Alberto to use to set up his ecosystem.

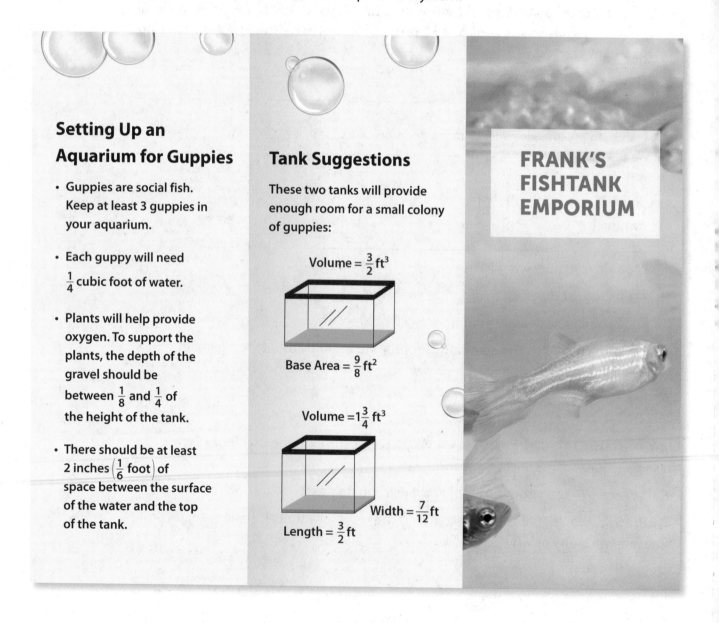

Setting Up an Aquarium for Guppies

- Guppies are social fish. Keep at least 3 guppies in your aquarium.

- Each guppy will need $\frac{1}{4}$ cubic foot of water.

- Plants will help provide oxygen. To support the plants, the depth of the gravel should be between $\frac{1}{8}$ and $\frac{1}{4}$ of the height of the tank.

- There should be at least 2 inches $\left(\frac{1}{6}\text{ foot}\right)$ of space between the surface of the water and the top of the tank.

Tank Suggestions

These two tanks will provide enough room for a small colony of guppies:

Volume = $\frac{3}{2}$ ft^3

Base Area = $\frac{9}{8}$ ft^2

Volume = $1\frac{3}{4}$ ft^3

Width = $\frac{7}{12}$ ft

Length = $\frac{3}{2}$ ft

FRANK'S FISHTANK EMPORIUM

Plan It and Solve It

➤ **Find a solution to the Aquatic Ecosystem problem.**

Write a detailed plan and support your answer. Be sure to include:

- the tank you suggest for Alberto.
- the amount of gravel (in cubic feet) needed for the tank.
- the amount of water (in cubic feet) to add to the tank.
- the number of guppies the tank can support.

PROBLEM-SOLVING TIPS

Math Toolkit grid paper, isometric dot paper, unit cubes

Key Terms

volume	dimension	height
base	area	formula

Questions

- Which tank do you suggest Alberto buy? How will you calculate the amount of gravel needed for the tank?
- What dimension(s) do you need to calculate for the tank before you can calculate the volume of water it will hold?

Reflect

Use Mathematical Practices As you work through the problem, discuss these questions with a partner.

- **Use Models** How can a sketch help you solve this problem?

- **Make an Argument** Does it make sense to suggest that Alberto put $4\frac{3}{4}$ guppies in the tank? Explain.

Guppies get their name from the British-born naturalist John Lechmere Guppy, who discovered them in Trinidad in 1866.

Persevere On Your Own

➤ **Read the problem. Write a solution on a separate sheet of paper.**

Making Slime

Alberto and Riley are choosing between two types of slime to make with the other members of the science club. Read an email from Riley about their plans, and help Alberto respond to Riley.

Delete   Archive   Reply   Reply All   Forward

To: Alberto
Subject: Planning our slime project!

Hi Alberto,

Here are my notes from when we tried making the two types of slime:

	Gooey Slime	Firm Slime
Mass of empty cup	0.007 kg	0.005 kg
Mass of water	0.36 kg	0.36 kg
Total mass after adding glue	0.492 kg	0.525 kg
Total mass after adding borax	0.5 kg	0.55 kg

Here is the glue and borax I saw at the store:

0.5 kg   1.84 kg

PLEASE LET ME KNOW:

• Which kind of slime do you want to make with the science club?
• How many boxes of borax and how many bottles of glue should we bring to the science club meeting? There are 24 members.
• How many batches of slime will the club be able to make?

Thanks!

Riley

Solve It

➤ **Find a solution to the Making Slime problem.**

- Choose one type of slime. Then calculate how much glue and borax is needed to make it.

- Determine how many bottles of glue and boxes of borax to bring to the science club meeting.

- Tell how many batches of slime the science club will be able to make with the materials.

Reflect

Use Mathematical Practices After you complete the problem, choose one of these questions to discuss with a partner.

- **Reason Mathematically** What operations did you use to find your solution? Explain why.

- **Critique Reasoning** Do you agree with the number of batches of slime your partner says the science club will be able to make? Explain.

In this unit you learned to . . .

Skill	Lesson
Add, subtract, and multiply multi-digit decimals using standard algorithms.	7
Divide multi-digit whole numbers and multi-digit decimals using standard algorithms.	8
Divide fractions.	9, 10
Solve real-world problems that involve dividing fractions.	9, 10
Find the volume of a right rectangular prism with fractional edge lengths.	11
Use math vocabulary and precise language to describe a strategy and how that strategy is used to solve a problem.	7–11

Think about what you have learned.

➤ **Use words, numbers, and drawings.**

1 One topic I could use in my everyday life is _____ because . . .

2 I worked hardest to learn how to . . .

3 One thing I could do better is . . .

Vocabulary Review

➤ **Review the unit vocabulary. Put a check mark by items you can use in speaking and writing. Look up the meaning of any terms you do not know.**

Math Vocabulary **Academic Vocabulary**

☐ dividend ☐ partial quotients ☐ additional

☐ divisor ☐ quotient ☐ combine

☐ estimate (verb) ☐ reciprocal ☐ maximum

☐ fraction ☐ remainder ☐ reasonable

➤ **Use the unit vocabulary to complete the problems.**

1 Use the four division problems shown below to answer questions 1a–1f.

$$84 \div 7 = 12 \qquad \frac{144}{8} = 18 \qquad 25\overline{)160.0}^{\,6.4} \qquad \frac{3}{4} \div \frac{1}{8} = \frac{3}{4} \times \frac{8}{1} = 6$$

a. What part of the problem is 144?

b. What part of the problem is 160.0?

c. What part of the problem is 6.4?

d. What part of the problem is 6?

e. What is the relationship between $\frac{8}{1}$ and $\frac{1}{8}$?

f. Name the divisors in each division problem.

2 160 divided by 25 equals 6.4. Why does the quotient contain a whole-number part and a decimal part? Use at least two math or academic vocabulary terms in your answer. Underline each term you use.

3 Is 20 a reasonable answer for 170 ÷ 15? Use at least two math or academic vocabulary terms in your answer. Underline each term you use.

➤ **Use what you have learned to complete these problems.**

1 What is the value of the expression $f - 2gh$ when $f = 4.5$, $g = 0.21$, and $h = 1.8$? Show your work.

SOLUTION _____

2 Lupe drives from Dallas to Anchorage, a total trip of 3,894 miles. She drives 348 miles to Wichita. For the rest of the trip, she will drive 394 miles each day. How many days does Lupe drive from Wichita to Anchorage? Complete the steps that can be used to solve the problem. Write your answers in the blanks.

Miles left to travel: 3,894 − _____ = _____

Number of days needed to travel: _____ ÷ 394 = _____ days

3 Ms. Guzman orders 6,370 marbles. Each package contains 182 marbles. How many packages does Ms. Guzman order? Record your answer on the grid. Then fill in the bubbles.

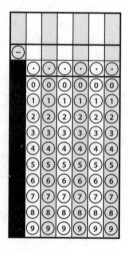

4 Carson fills each bird feeder with $\frac{3}{4}$ pound of birdseed. He has 12 pounds of birdseed. Carson says that to find how many bird feeders he can fill, he first finds how many $\frac{1}{4}$ pounds are in 12 pounds. What else does Carson need to do to find how many bird feeders he can fill?

SOLUTION _____

_____

5 It takes 126 cubes that have edge lengths of $\frac{1}{3}$ ft to completely fill this plastic bin.

What is the area of the base of the bin? Show your work.

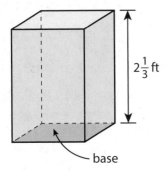

base

SOLUTION _____

6 What is $4\frac{2}{5} \div 1\frac{1}{10}$?

A $\frac{25}{121}$ **B** $\frac{1}{4}$

C 2   **D** 4

7 Bilal has 5 c of strawberries. He uses $2\frac{1}{6}$ c to make smoothies. He uses the rest of

the strawberries to make fruit cups. He needs $\frac{2}{3}$ c of strawberries for each fruit cup.

How many fruit cups can he make? Show your work.

SOLUTION _____

Performance Task

➤ **Answer the questions and show all your work on separate paper.**

Geraldine supplies number cubes to companies that make board games. Each number cube measures $\frac{3}{4}$ inch on each edge. For shipping, the number cubes can be packed into any of the boxes shown.

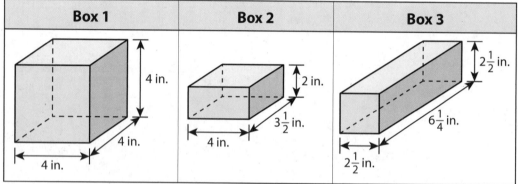

Box 1	Box 2	Box 3

Box 1: 4 in., 4 in., 4 in.
Box 2: 2 in., 4 in., $3\frac{1}{2}$ in.
Box 3: $2\frac{1}{2}$ in., $6\frac{1}{4}$ in., $2\frac{1}{2}$ in.

Geraldine receives an order for 780 number cubes. First, she needs to know the maximum number of cubes that can fit into each box. Then she needs a packing plan for the order. Remember: only whole cubes can be packed.

Design a packing plan for Geraldine. Your plan must meet the following requirements:

• The maximum number of cubes that can fit into each box is identified.

• The fewest number of boxes is used to pack the 780 number cubes.

• No box is packed with fewer than half the total number of cubes it can hold.

Reflect

Use Mathematical Practices After you complete the task, choose one of the following questions to answer.

• **Make Sense of the Problem** How are the dimensions of the number cubes related to the dimensions of the box?

• **Use Reasoning** How did you use the maximum capacity of each box to make your packing plan?

Unit 3

Ratio Reasoning

Ratio Concepts and
Equivalent Ratios

Self Check

Before starting this unit, check off the skills you know below.
As you complete each lesson, see how many more skills you can check off!

I can . . .	Before	After
Use ratio language to describe a ratio relationship between two quantities.	☐	☐
Use ratio reasoning to solve real-world problems.	☐	☐
Identify and write equivalent ratios.	☐	☐
Represent equivalent ratios as points in the coordinate plane.	☐	☐
Use tables to compare ratios.	☐	☐
Justify solutions to ratio problems by using ratio language and models, such as double number lines, tables, tape diagrams, and coordinate planes.	☐	☐

Prepare for Ratio Concepts and Equivalent Ratios

➤ **You have learned about patterns, ordered pairs, and graphing ordered pairs. Complete the table, and then graph the ordered pairs.**

x	y	(x, y)
0	0	(0, 0)
3	6	(3, 6)
6	12	(6, 12)
9		
12		
15		

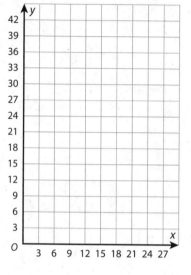

Use words and numbers to share as many ideas as you can about the graphed points. Then, meet with a partner and discuss your answers.

Dear Family,

This week your student is exploring ratio concepts. A **ratio** is a way of comparing quantities. Sometimes ratios compare a part and a part, and sometimes they compare a part and a whole.

For example, when making a total of 3 cups of lemonade, you might say:

• The ratio of cups of water to cups of lemon juice is 2 to 1.

• The ratio of cups of lemon juice to total cups of lemonade is 1 to 3.

Your student will be modeling ratios like the one below.

> To make a purple paint, you can use 3 cups of blue paint for every 2 cups of red paint.

➤ **ONE WAY** to model a ratio relationship is to use a diagram.

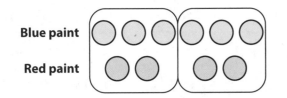

Blue paint
Red paint

➤ **ANOTHER WAY** is to use ratio language and symbols.

The ratio of cups of blue paint to cups of red paint is

   3 **to** 2   or   3 : 2

because there are 3 cups of blue paint **for every** 2 cups of red paint.

You can also change the order of the parts so that the amount of red paint is the first quantity in the ratio.

The ratio of cups of red paint to cups of blue paint is

   2 **to** 3   or   2 : 3

because there are 2 cups of red paint **for every** 3 cups of blue paint.

Both representations accurately compare the quantities of blue paint and red paint.

 Use the next page to start a conversation about ratios.

Activity Describing Ratios

➤ **Do this activity together to write sentences that describe ratios relationships.**

You can describe ratios using the language *for each* and *for every*.

- There are 2 red tulips *for each* yellow tulip.
- *For every* 1 yellow tulip, there are 2 red tulips.
- *For every* 4 red tulips, there are 2 yellow tulips.

Look at the models representing ratio relationships. Write two sentences using ratio language to describe each model.

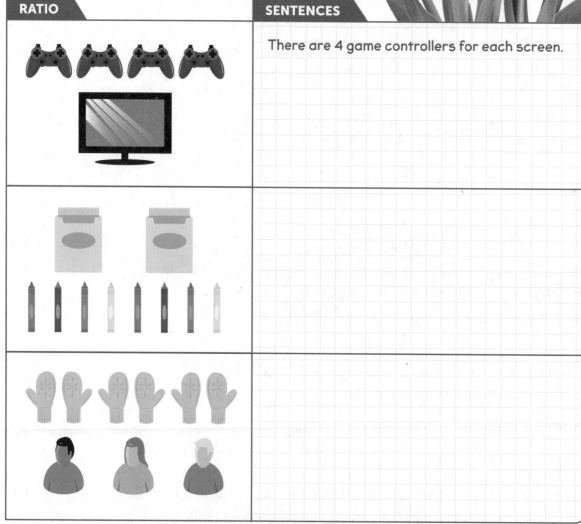

RATIO	SENTENCES
	There are 4 game controllers for each screen.

 ? Do you notice any similarities or differences between two sentences used to describe a ratio relationship?

Explore Ratio Concepts

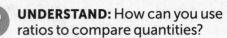

4 times as many test tubes as students

Model It

➤ **Complete the problems about comparing quantities.**

1 You can use multiplication as a way to compare two quantities.

a. In Charles's lab group, there are 4 times as many test tubes as students. Complete the model to show this comparison. A circle represents a student, and a rectangle represents a test tube.

Test Tubes ☐ ☐ ☐ ☐ ☐ ☐   ☐ ☐

Students   ○   ○   ○

b. One more student is added to Charles's group. How many more test tubes do you need to include in the model?

2 You can also use a **ratio** to compare two quantities. One way to describe a ratio relationship is to use the language *for every* or *for each*.

a. In Eldora's lab group, there are 3 test tubes for every 1 student. Complete the model to show this ratio relationship.

Test Tubes ☐

Students   ○   ○   ○

b. Use your model to complete these sentences that use ratio language.

For every 1 student, there are _____ test tubes.

There are _____ test tubes for each _____ .

There is _____ student for every _____ test tubes.

DISCUSS IT

Ask: How do your models in problems 1 and 2 help you to compare two quantities?

Share: I could use ratio language to describe my model in problem 1 by saying . . .

 Learning Target SMP 2, SMP 3, SMP 7
Understand the concept of a ratio and use ratio language to describe a ratio relationship between two quantities.

Model It

➤ **Complete the problems about ratio relationships.**

3 The Spanish Club is having a party. They plan to serve 6 tacos for every 3 guests.

  a. Complete the model to show this ratio relationship.

  Tacos [ ]

  Guests ◯

  b. Use ratio language to write two different sentences that compare numbers of tacos and guests.

  c. Ju-long says that there will be 2 tacos for every 1 guest. Use your model to help explain why Ju-long is correct.

4 **Reflect** Explain how the ratios *5 tacos for every 2 guests* and *2 tacos for every 5 guests* are different. Include a model in your explanation.

Prepare for Understanding of Ratio Concepts

1　Think about what you know about comparing numbers or quantities. Fill in each box. Use words, numbers, and pictures. Show as many ideas as you can.

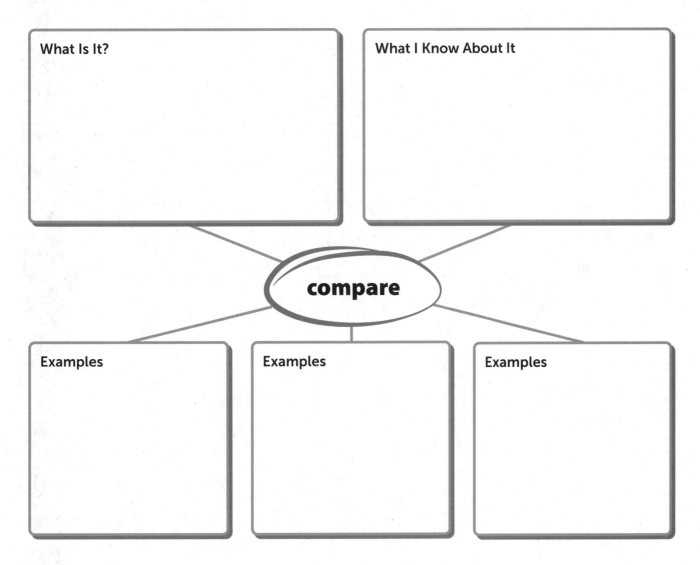

| What Is It? | What I Know About It |

compare

Examples　　Examples　　Examples

2　Write three sentences that compare the values 12 and 3 in different ways.

➤ **Complete problems 3–4.**

3 In a school band, there is 1 oboe player for every 6 clarinet players.

  a. Complete the model to show this ratio relationship.

  Oboe Players

  Clarinet Players

  b. Use your model to complete these sentences that use ratio language.

  There are _____ clarinet players for each _____ .

  For every _____ oboe player, there are _____ clarinet players.

  For every _____ clarinet players, there is _____ oboe player.

4 Emma sells flowers. She uses 9 ft of ribbon for every 3 wedding bouquets she sells.

  a. Complete the model to show this ratio relationship.

  Bouquets

  Feet of Ribbon

  b. Use ratio language to write two different sentences that compare the amount of ribbon and the number of bouquets.

  c. Adoncia says that Emma uses 3 ft of ribbon for every 1 bouquet. Use your model to help explain why Adoncia is correct.

Vocabulary

ratio

a way to compare two quantities when there are *a* units of one quantity for every *b* units of the other quantity.

---

272   **Lesson 12** Understand Ratio Concepts

Develop Understanding of Ratio Concepts

Model It: Compare with Ratios

➤ **Try these three problems involving ratios.**

1 Carlos is making baked pears. Complete the model to show the ratio relationships for the ingredients in the recipe.

Pears ◯ ◯ ◯ ◯

Cups of Yogurt ☐

Tablespoons of Granola △

2 You can compare two quantities in a ratio by using words or symbols. You can write a ratio using the word *to* or a colon.

There are **4 pears** **for every** **2 cups of yogurt**.

The ratio of **pears** **to** **cups of yogurt** is **4 to** 2 or **4 : 2**.

Write each ratio two different ways. Use the word *to* and a colon.

a. the ratio of cups of yogurt to pears

b. the ratio of cups of yogurt to tablespoons of granola

c. the ratio of tablespoons of granola to cups of yogurt

3 Use your model in problem 1 to complete the sentences.

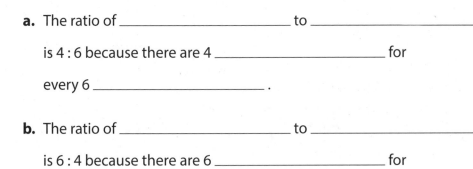

a. The ratio of _____ to _____

is 4 : 6 because there are 4 _____ for

every 6 _____ .

b. The ratio of _____ to _____

is 6 : 4 because there are 6 _____ for

every 4 _____ .

DISCUSS IT

Ask: How did you know which number to put first when writing the ratios?

Share: I noticed that the order of the numbers in a ratio matters because . . .

Model It: Parts and Wholes

➤ **Try these ratio problems involving parts of a whole.**

Type of Duck	Number Seen
Mallard	8
Ruddy Duck	5

4 Students record the types of ducks they see on a nature walk in Central Park in New York City. Draw a model to show the ratio of mallards to ruddy ducks.

Mallards

Ruddy Ducks

5 Some ratio relationships involve parts of a larger whole. For these relationships, ratios can compare two parts or a part and a whole.

Parts: mallards and ruddy ducks   **Whole:** total number of ducks

a. What does the ratio 8 to 13 represent?

b. Circle the type of ratio that 8 : 13 represents.

part to part   part to whole   whole to part

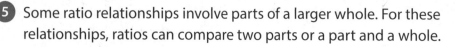

> **DISCUSS IT**
>
> **Ask:** How is the ratio 8 to 13 different from the ratio 8 to 5?
>
> **Share:** I noticed you can find a whole in a ratio relationship by . . .

CONNECT IT

➤ **Complete the problems below.**

6 Carlos uses 2 cups of yogurt and 6 tablespoons of granola for every 4 pears. Would it make sense to describe this situation with a part-to-whole ratio? Explain.

7 The puppies in a litter are either black or brown. The ratio of black puppies to the total number of puppies is 3 : 8. What is the ratio of brown puppies to black puppies? Draw a model to show how you found your answer.

Practice Ratio Concepts

➤ **Study how the Example shows ratio relationships. Then solve problems 1–5.**

Example

The students in the drama club are either actors or crew members. For every 6 actors in the club, there are 4 crew members. What is the ratio of actors to students in the drama club?

Draw a model to show **6 actors** for every **4 crew members**.

Actors ○○○○○○
Crew Members □□□□ } **10 students**

The model shows that there are **6 actors** for every **10 students** in the club.

The ratio of **actors** to **students** is 6 to 10, or 6 : 10.

---

1 a. What is the ratio of crew members to actors in the drama club in the Example? Write your answer in two different ways. Use the word *to* and a colon.

b. In your answer to problem 1a, why is the order of the numbers important?

2 Last season, the ratio of the number of soccer games won to the number of soccer games lost was 3 to 2.

a. Draw a model to represent this ratio relationship.

b. Tell what each ratio represents in this situation.

   2 to 3

   3 : 5

Vocabulary

ratio

a way to compare two quantities when there are *a* units of one quantity for every *b* units of the other quantity.

You can write the ratio in symbols as *a* : *b* and in words as *a* to *b*.

3 Paloma rides a scooter. She travels 10 ft for every 1 second.

a. Hannah says that Paloma's ratio of seconds traveled to feet traveled is 10 : 1. Is Hannah correct? Use a model to help explain your thinking.

5 ft   10 ft   15 ft   20 ft   25 ft

b. Gaspar also rides a scooter. He travels 2 ft farther for every 1 second than Paloma does. What is Gaspar's ratio of feet traveled to seconds traveled? Show your work.

SOLUTION _____

4 Describe a real-world ratio that the model could represent.

5 A hair stylist has three colors of hair dye. She has 4 bottles of chestnut, 7 bottles of blond, and 8 bottles of cherry. What does the ratio 8 : 19 represent in this situation? Explain your reasoning. Include a model in your explanation.

Refine Ideas About Ratio Concepts

Apply It

➤ **Complete problems 1–5.**

1 **Apply** When Akiko rides her bike to school, she travels 1 mi for every 6 min. Does this ratio mean that it takes Akiko 6 min to get to school? Explain.

2 **Analyze** A store sells variety packs of granola bars. The table shows the types of bars in each pack. Mason says that for every 7 bars in a pack, there is 1 cinnamon bar. Do you agree? Explain.

Type	Number of Bars
Cinnamon	1
Honey	4
Peanut Butter	3

3 **Evaluate** Bridget is filling welcome bags for several new students. Each bag gets 1 magnet. The ratio of magnets to pencils in each bag is 1 : 6, and the ratio of erasers to magnets is 2 : 1. Which statement below must be true? Use a model to help explain your thinking.

- Bridget needs 4 more pencils than erasers.

- Bridget needs 3 times as many pencils as erasers.

4 A national park has two types of bears: grizzly bears and black bears. A scientist reports that 9 out of the 12 bears she tagged are black bears.

PART A Draw a model that compares the number of black bears tagged to the number of grizzly bears tagged.

PART B Use your model to explain what the ratio 9 : 3 represents in this situation.

PART C Jelani says that for every 1 tagged grizzly bear, there are 3 tagged black bears. Use your model to explain why Jelani is correct.

5 **Math Journal** A store sells 1 smartwatch for every 8 smartphones. How can you use ratios to compare these quantities? Include a model in your explanation.

✓ **End of Lesson Checklist**

☐ **INTERACTIVE GLOSSARY** Find the entry for *ratio*. Add two important things you learned about ratios in this lesson.

Dear Family,

This week your student is learning how to find equivalent ratios.

Equivalent ratios are ratios that express the same comparison. For example, a rice recipe might require 2 cups of water for every 1 cup of rice.

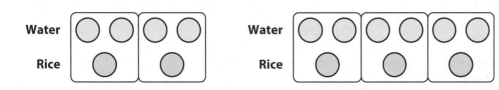

Water ○ ○

Rice ○

If you double the recipe, the ratio of cups of water to cups of rice is 4 to 2.
If you triple the recipe, the ratio of cups of water to cups of rice is 6 to 3.

Water / Rice diagrams

Your student will be learning how to solve problems like the one below.

> On a school field trip, there must be 1 teacher for every 10 students.
> If 40 students attend the field trip, how many teachers are needed?

➤ **ONE WAY** to find the number of teachers is to use addition.

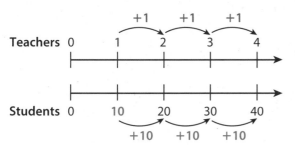

➤ **ANOTHER WAY** is to use multiplication.

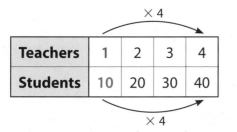

		$\times 4$		
Teachers	1	2	3	4
Students	10	20	30	40

Using either method, 4 teachers are needed for the field trip.

▶ Use the next page to start a conversation about ratios.

Activity Thinking About Ratios Around You

➤ **Do this activity together to investigate ratios in the real world.**

Have you ever watched a movie on TV and wondered why long black bars appear on the top and bottom of the screen? This happens because the ratios of width to length for TVs and movie screens are not equivalent!

Most TVs have 16 in. of width for every 9 in. of height. Most movie screens have 21.51 in. of width for every 9 in. of height. Without the long black bars, movies watched on TV might look stretched too tall.

 Where else do you see equivalent or non-equivalent ratios in the world around you?

Explore Equivalent Ratios

Henna

Henna Paste (1 batch)

- 2 tbsp henna powder
- 1 tsp oil
- 1 tsp sugar
- 2 tbsp water

Previously, you learned how to compare quantities by using ratios.
In this lesson, you will learn about equivalent ratios.

➤ **Use what you know to try to solve the problem below.**

Veda uses henna paste to paint designs on her friends' hands and
feet as they prepare to celebrate Diwali, a festival of lights. What is
the ratio of tablespoons of henna powder to teaspoons of oil if Veda
makes 3 batches of paste?

TRY IT

Math Toolkit connecting cubes, counters, grid paper

DISCUSS IT

Ask: How does your
model show 3 batches
of paste?

Share: My model
shows that . . .

◎ **Learning Targets** SMP 1, SMP 2, SMP 3, SMP 4, SMP 5, SMP 6
Use ratio and rate reasoning to solve real-world and mathematical problems.
- Make tables of equivalent ratios relating quantities with whole-number measurements, find missing values
  in the tables, and plot the pairs of values on the coordinate plane. Use tables to compare ratios.

CONNECT IT

1 **Look Back** What is the ratio of tablespoons of henna powder to teaspoons of oil for 3 batches of henna paste? Explain how you know.

2 **Look Ahead** **Equivalent ratios** are ratios that express the same comparison.

a. To find a ratio that is equivalent to the ratio *3 to 2*, you can combine equal groups of 3 circles and 2 squares. How does the model show that the ratios 3 : 2 and 6 : 4 are equivalent ratios?

3 circles to 2 squares   6 circles to 4 squares

b. Find another ratio that is equivalent to 3 : 2. Use a model to support your answer.

c. Explain why 3 : 2 and 9 : 8 are not equivalent ratios.

3 **Reflect** How can you tell whether two ratios are equivalent?

Prepare for Finding Equivalent Ratios

1 Think about what you know about ordered pairs. Fill in each box. Use words, numbers, and pictures. Show as many ideas as you can.

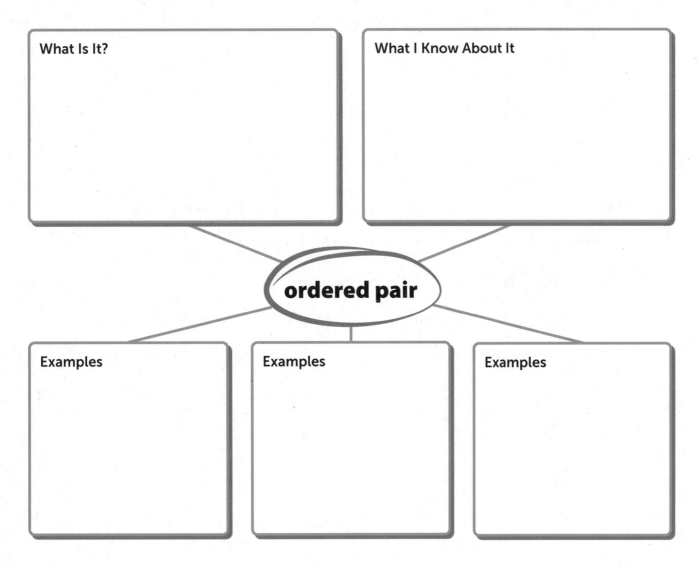

What Is It?

What I Know About It

ordered pair

Examples

Examples

Examples

2 Do the ordered pairs (1, 4) and (4, 1) represent the same point in the coordinate plane? Explain.

3 Felipe has a recipe for peanut butter dog treats.

a. What is the ratio of cups of flour to tablespoons of peanut butter if Felipe makes 3 batches of dog treats? Show your work.

Dog Treats (1 batch)	
Ingredient	**Amount**
Peanut Butter	4 tbsp
Flour	1 cup
Egg	1
Water	2 tbsp

SOLUTION _____

_____

b. Check your answer to problem 3a. Show your work.

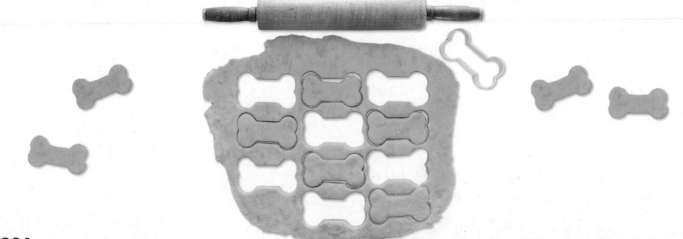

Develop Finding Equivalent Ratios

➤ **Read and try to solve the problem below.**

The ratio of picnic tables to garbage cans in a new national park should be 8 : 3. The park design shows plans for picnic tables in a small campground and a large campground. How many garbage cans should there be in each campground?

Number of Picnic Tables

40 in a small campground

120 in a large campground

TRY IT

Math Toolkit connecting cubes, counters, double number lines, grid paper

DISCUSS IT

Ask: How did you use the ratio 8 : 3 to find the number of garbage cans for 40 picnic tables?

Share: I used the ratio 8 : 3 when I . . .

➤ **Explore different ways to find equivalent ratios.**

The ratio of picnic tables to garbage cans in a new national park should be 8 : 3. The park design shows 40 picnic tables in a small campground and 120 picnic tables in a large campground. How many garbage cans should there be in each campground?

Model It

You can use addition to find equivalent ratios.

One way to show adding groups of **8 picnic tables** for every **3 garbage cans** is with a double number line.

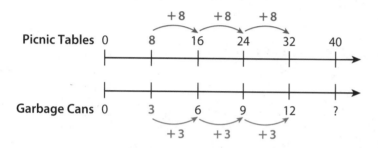

You can write ratios for number pairs that line up vertically. The double number line shows the equivalent ratios 8 : 3, 16 : 6, 24 : 9, and 32 : 12.

Model It

You can use multiplication to find equivalent ratios.

You can record equivalent ratios in a table.

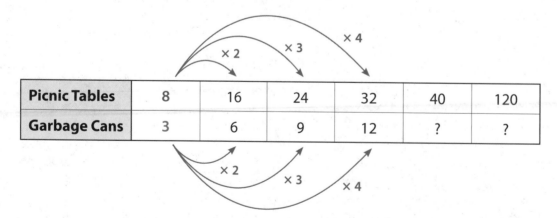

Picnic Tables	8	16	24	32	40	120
Garbage Cans	3	6	9	12	?	?

➤ **Use the problem from the previous page to help you understand how to find equivalent ratios.**

1 Look at the first **Model It**. How do you know that the ratios from the double number line are equivalent ratios?

2 Look at the second **Model It**. What number can you multiply 8 by to get 120? How can you use this number to solve part of the problem?

3 How many garbage cans should be placed in each campground? Explain how you can use addition or multiplication to find the answer.

4 Why can you multiply both quantities in a ratio by the same number to find an equivalent ratio?

5 Cai says you can divide both quantities in a ratio by the same nonzero number to find an equivalent ratio. Explain why Cai is correct.

6 **Reflect** Think about all the models and strategies you have discussed today. Describe how one of them helped you better understand how to find equivalent ratios.

Apply It

➤ **Use what you learned to solve these problems.**

7 Hailey makes a necklace with 24 blue beads and 32 purple beads. She wants to make a bracelet that uses the same ratio of blue beads to purple beads. She plans to use 6 blue beads for the bracelet. How many purple beads should Hailey use?

A 4 purple beads

B 8 purple beads

C 14 purple beads

D 18 purple beads

8 Kareem says that the ratio 4 : 1 is equivalent to the ratio 12 : 9 because $4 + 8 = 12$ and $1 + 8 = 9$. Is Kareem correct? Explain how you know.

9 The table shows that Marta's heart beats 18 times every 15 s. Use equivalent ratios to complete the table. Explain how you found the time in seconds for 180 heartbeats.

Marta's Heartbeats	
Time (s)	**Number of Beats**
15	18
30	
45	
	180

©Curriculum Associates, LLC   Copying is not permitted.

Name:

Practice Finding Equivalent Ratios

➤ **Study the Example showing how to find equivalent ratios. Then solve problems 1–5.**

Example

A soccer league has 60 returning players and 36 new players. Each team will have the same ratio of returning players to new players as the league has. How many new players will a team with 10 returning players have?

You can use a double number line to find ratios equivalent to **60 : 36**.
Number pairs that line up vertically represent equivalent ratios.

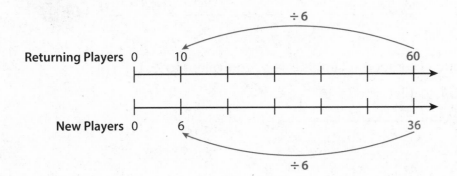

You can divide each quantity in 60 : 36 by 6 to find the equivalent ratio 10 : 6.

A team with 10 returning players will have 6 new players.

1 Sophia says that you can solve the problem in the Example by multiplying both quantities in the ratio 60 : 36 by $\frac{1}{6}$. Is Sophia correct? Explain.

2 Which ratios are equivalent to 8 : 12? Select all that apply.

A 4 : 6

B 12 : 8

C 16 : 20

D 24 : 36

E 56 : 84

Vocabulary

equivalent ratios
two ratios that express the same comparison.
Multiplying both numbers in the ratio $a : b$ by a nonzero number n results in the equivalent ratio $na : nb$.

3 A football field is 300 ft long. A sloth moving very quickly travels 60 ft every 5 min. Based on this ratio, how many minutes would it take a sloth to travel the length of a football field? Show your work.

SOLUTION _____

4 At a summer camp, the ratio of campers to adults is kept equivalent to 7 : 1.

   a. Use equivalent ratios to complete the table.

Campers	7		28	
Adults	1	2		30

   b. Next week, there will be 63 campers. How many adults should the camp have next week? Show your work.

SOLUTION _____

5 A manager of a clothing store always orders 2 small T-shirts and 3 large T-shirts for every 4 medium T-shirts. The manager plans to order 24 medium T-shirts. How many small T-shirts and large T-shirts should the manager order? Show your work.

SOLUTION _____

Develop Graphing a Table of Equivalent Ratios

➤ **Read and try to solve the problem below.**

A streaming music channel always plays the same ratio of pop songs to hip-hop songs. The point on the graph shows the number of hip-hop songs played for every 3 pop songs. Based on the relationship in the graph, how many hip-hop songs does the channel play for every 12 pop songs?

TRY IT

Math Toolkit connecting cubes, counters, double number lines, graph paper

DISCUSS IT

Ask: How does your model use the ordered pair from the graph?

Share: In my model, I used the ordered pair to . . .

➤ **Explore different ways to use a graph to show equivalent ratios.**

A streaming music channel always plays the same ratio of pop songs to hip-hop songs. The point on the graph shows the number of hip-hop songs played for every 3 pop songs. Based on the relationship in the graph, how many hip-hop songs does the channel play for every 12 pop songs?

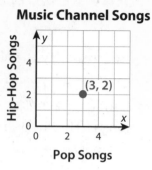

Music Channel Songs

Model It

You can make a table of equivalent ratios from the given ordered pair.

The ordered pair (3, 2) shows that the ratio of **pop songs** to **hip-hop songs** is 3 : 2.

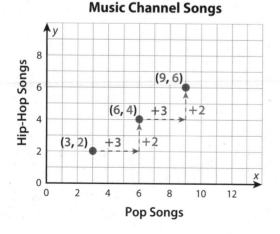

Pop Songs, x	Hip-Hop Songs, y
3	2
6	4
9	6
12	?

+3   +2
+3   +2
+3   +2

Model It

You can use the coordinates of the given ordered pair to find other ordered pairs that represent equivalent ratios.

Music Channel Songs

CONNECT IT

➤ **Use the problem from the previous page to help you understand how to use a graph to show equivalent ratios.**

1 How does the graph in the problem show that the ratio of pop songs to hip-hop songs is 3 : 2?

2 Look at the table in the first **Model It** and the graph in the second **Model It**. How is the addition pattern in the graph related to the addition pattern in the table?

3 How many hip-hop songs does the streaming music channel play for every 12 pop songs? Plot a point on the graph to model this relationship.

4 How can you use a point on a graph to find another point that represents an equivalent ratio? Explain why your method works.

5 How could you use ordered pairs and multiplication to find equivalent ratios?

6 **Reflect** Think about all the models and strategies you have discussed today. Describe how one of them helped you better understand using a graph to show equivalent ratios.

Apply It

➤ **Use what you learned to solve these problems.**

7 The ratio of the length of a fire hose in feet to the number of gallons of water the hose can hold is 100 : 4. Complete the table of equivalent ratios. Then write each ratio as an ordered pair.

Hose Length (ft)	Volume of Water (gal)	Ordered Pair
	1	
50		
100	4	
	12	

8 Enrique has a container of 32 fl oz of orange juice. He is filling glasses with 1 cup of juice. The point on the graph shows the ratio of fluid ounces to cups. Based on this ratio, how many glasses can Enrique fill from the container? Plot a point on the graph to show the number of cups in 32 fl oz. Show your work.

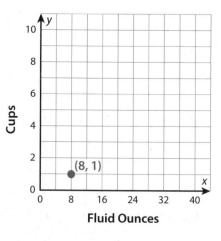

SOLUTION _____

9 Every 4-oz serving of Yum's Yogurt contains 8 g of protein. Complete the table of equivalent ratios. Then plot points on the graph to represent the ratios.

Yum's Yogurt

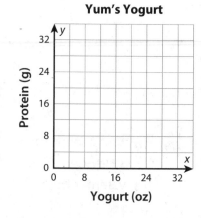

Yogurt (oz)	Protein (g)
4	
8	
12	
	32

Name:

Practice Graphing a Table of Equivalent Ratios

➤ **Study the Example showing how to graph a table of equivalent ratios. Then solve problems 1–5.**

Example

Jade reads 4 pages every 3 min. Make a table of equivalent ratios to show how many pages Jade can read in 3 min, 6 min, and 9 min. Then graph the equivalent ratios.

Record the ratio 3 to 4 in one row of a table. Find equivalent ratios for 6 min and 9 min by multiplying each number in the ratio 3 : 4 by 2 and by 3.

Time (min)	Pages Read
3	4
6	8
9	12

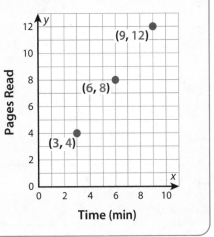

Think of each ratio in the table as an ordered pair (x, y). The x-coordinate is the **time in minutes** and the y-coordinate is the **number of pages read**.

---

1 How would the graph in the Example change if Jade reads 5 pages every 3 minutes instead of 4 pages every 3 minutes?

2 The point (7, 8) in the coordinate plane represents a ratio. Adela claims that you can find an equivalent ratio by adding the same number to both coordinates of the point. Is Adela correct? Explain.

Jordan and Mia are bringing napkins to a back-to-school picnic.
They decide to bring 35 napkins for every 10 people who plan to attend.
The point on the graph represents this ratio.

a. Plot another point that represents an equivalent ratio. Explain how
you found the coordinates of this point.

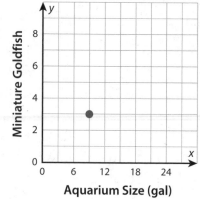

b. What do the coordinates of the point you plotted represent in this situation?

4 Allen is making a scarf for charity. He uses 4 yd of black yarn for
every 6 yd of yellow yarn.

a. Complete the table of equivalent ratios.

Black Yarn (yd)	2	4	12	
Yellow Yarn (yd)		6		30

b. Plot ordered pairs on the graph to represent the ratios.

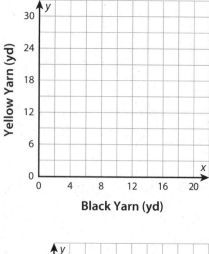

5 An aquarium that holds 9 gal is the correct size for 3 miniature
goldfish. The point on the graph represents this ratio relationship.
Which ordered pairs represent equivalent ratios that would also be
on the graph? Select all that apply.

A (1, 3)

B (3, 1)

C (12, 6)

D (15, 9)

E (18, 6)

Develop Using Equivalent Ratios

➤ **Read and try to solve the problem below.**

Ian travels 10 yd on his unicycle every 4 s. Based on this ratio, how many seconds does it take Ian to travel 25 yd on his unicycle?

TRY IT

Math Toolkit connecting cubes, counters, double number lines, graph paper

DISCUSS IT

Ask: How does your model show that Ian travels 10 yd every 4 s?

Share: I showed this ratio by . . .

➤ **Explore different ways to use equivalent ratios to solve problems.**

Ian travels 10 yd on his unicycle every 4 s. Based on this ratio, how many seconds does it take Ian to travel 25 yd on his unicycle?

Model It

You can use a double number line to solve the problem.

Choose scales to show that Ian travels 10 yd every 4 s.

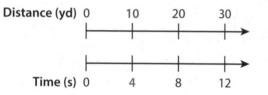

Add marks halfway between the existing marks to find additional equivalent ratios.

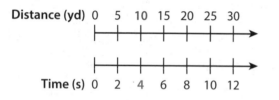

Model It

You can use a combination of multiplication and division to solve the problem.

Show the ratios in a table. Think of a way to get from 10 yd to 25 yd by using a combination of multiplication and division.

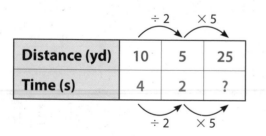

➤ **Use the problem from the previous page to help you understand how to use equivalent ratios to solve problems.**

1 Look at the first **Model It**. How do you know that 5 : 2, 15 : 6, and 25 : 10 are equivalent to the ratio 10 : 4?

2 Can you solve the **Try It** problem by multiplying both quantities in the ratio 10 to 4 by the same whole number? Why or why not?

3 Look at the second **Model It**. It shows that the ratio 10 to 4 can be written as the equivalent ratio 5 to 2. Why is this step helpful?

4 How many seconds does it take Ian to ride 25 yd on his unicycle? How do you know that your answer is reasonable?

5 Why is it sometimes helpful to use a combination of multiplication and division when finding equivalent ratios to solve problems?

6 **Reflect** Think about all the models and strategies you have discussed today. Describe how one of them helped you better understand how to solve the **Try It** problem.

Apply It

➤ **Use what you learned to solve these problems.**

7 A caterer typically uses 40 forks for every 25 knives. The caterer estimates that he will use 80 knives today. Use equivalent ratios to estimate the number of forks the caterer will use today. Show your work.

SOLUTION _____

8 Each day, a baker makes the same ratio of blueberry muffins to banana muffins. On Tuesday, she makes 96 blueberry muffins and 72 banana muffins. On Wednesday, she makes 36 blueberry muffins. How many banana muffins does the baker make on Wednesday?

A 12 banana muffins

B 27 banana muffins

C 48 banana muffins

D 132 banana muffins

9 An architect designs a skyscraper with 56 floors. The height of the skyscraper must increase by 45 m for every 10 floors. Based on this ratio, what is the planned height of the skyscraper? Show your work.

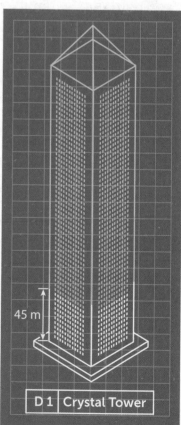

45 m

D 1 | Crystal Tower

SOLUTION _____

Name: _____

Practice Using Equivalent Ratios

➤ **Study the Example showing how to use ratios to solve problems. Then solve problems 1–5.**

Example

A company sells shampoo in two sizes of bottles. The ratio of the capacity of a bottle to its cost is the same for both sizes. A large bottle of shampoo contains 32 fl oz and costs $8. A small bottle contains 12 fl oz. What is the cost of a small bottle of shampoo?

You can use a table of equivalent ratios.

Think of a way to get from 32 to 12 by using a combination of multiplication and division. Then use this combination to find equivalent ratios.

÷ 8   × 3

Capacity (fl oz)	32	4	12
Cost ($)	8	1	3

÷ 8   × 3

A small bottle of shampoo costs $3.

1 The company in the Example decides to increase the capacity of its large bottles from 32 fl oz to 40 fl oz. It plans to keep the ratio of capacity to cost the same. How much should the company charge for a bottle that holds 40 fl oz? Show your work.

SOLUTION _____

2 Which ratio is equivalent to 3 : 18?

A 6 : 21

B 5 : 20

C 7 : 42

D 12 : 2

> **Vocabulary**
>
> **equivalent ratios**
> two ratios that express the same comparison.
> Multiplying both numbers in the ratio $a : b$ by a nonzero number n results in the equivalent ratio $na : nb$.

3 A community garden is surrounded by a fence. The total length of the fence is 3,000 ft. For every 48 ft of fence, there are 4 posts. What is the total number of posts in the fence? Show your work.

SOLUTION _____

4 A company makes first-aid kits in different sizes. The ratio of fabric bandages to plastic bandages in each kit is 3 to 9. A small kit has 16 fabric bandages. How many plastic bandages should a small kit have? Show your work.

SOLUTION _____

5 A bag contains 6 red tiles and 15 yellow tiles. Lilia removes 2 red tiles. How many yellow tiles should she remove so that the ratio of red tiles to yellow tiles in the bag stays equivalent to 6 : 15? Show your work.

SOLUTION _____

Refine Finding Equivalent Ratios

➤ **Complete the Example below. Then solve problems 1–9.**

Example

A picture-hanging kit contains 2 short nails for every 8 long nails. There are 28 short nails. How many long nails does the kit contain?

Look at how you could use a table of equivalent ratios.

Short Nails	2	4	6	28
Long Nails	8	16	24	?

In each ratio, the number of long nails is 4 times the number of short nails.

$? = 4 \times 28$

SOLUTION _____

Apply It

1 Nicanor keeps the tickets from all the sporting events he attends. The ratio of baseball tickets to basketball tickets in his collection is 3 : 5. Nicanor has 21 baseball tickets. How many more basketball tickets than baseball tickets does he have? Show your work.

SOLUTION _____

2 The graph shows the relationship between the number of steps Jamila takes and the distance she walks. Based on the equivalent ratios shown in the graph, how many steps does Jamila need to take to walk 120 ft? Show your work.

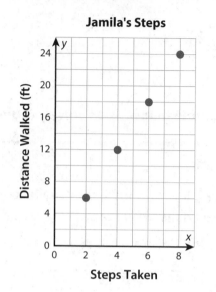

Jamila's Steps

CONSIDER THIS . . .
How can you show that the ordered pairs in the graph represent equivalent ratios?

SOLUTION _____

PAIR/SHARE
How does the graph indicate that the number of steps Jamila must take to walk 120 ft is less than 120?

3 Carson rides his bike for 30 min each day. He rides a total of 12 mi every 3 days. Based on this information, how many days will it take Carson to ride a total of 80 mi on his bike?

A 4 days

B 7 days

C 10 days

D 20 days

Galeno chose A as the correct answer. How might he have gotten that answer?

CONSIDER THIS . . .
How can you find the distance Carson rides in 1 day?

PAIR/SHARE
How can you check that your answer is reasonable?

4 Mr. Romano is ordering meat for a family reunion. He knows that 80 people plan to attend. He orders 1 lb of chicken for every 5 people and 3 lb of beef for every 10 people. Tell whether each statement is *True* or *False*.

	True	False
a. Mr. Romano orders 48 lb of beef.	○	○
b. Mr. Romano orders 16 lb of chicken.	○	○
c. The ratio of pounds of beef to pounds of chicken that Mr. Romano orders is 3 : 2.	○	○
d. The ratio of pounds of chicken to pounds of beef that Mr. Romano orders is 1 : 3.	○	○

5 Evelyn is making bows from blue and white ribbon. She uses 6 in. of blue ribbon for every 9 in. of white ribbon. Evelyn has 82 in. of blue ribbon and 114 in. of white ribbon. Which color of ribbon will she run out of first? Explain.

6 A dairy farm ships crates of milk to food stores. There are 48 quarts of milk for every 3 crates shipped. Plot points on the graph to show how many quarts of milk there are for shipments of 3, 4, 6, and 9 milk crates. Label each point with its ordered pair.

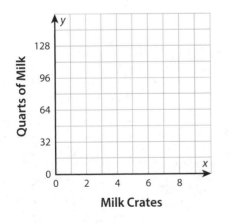

7 Last year, students planted 8 tomato plants and 16 pepper plants in a school garden. This year, the students planted 15 tomato plants. They want to have the same ratio of tomato plants to pepper plants as last year. Pepper plants cost $4.33 each. What is the cost, in dollars, of the pepper plants for this year's garden?

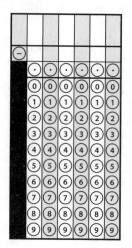

8 The graph shows four ordered pairs that represent ratios. Which ordered pair represents a ratio that is not equivalent to the others?

A (2, 12)

B (3, 18)

C (5, 24)

D (6, 36)

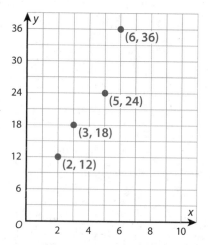

9 **Math Journal** Write a word problem that can be solved by finding an equivalent ratio. Show how to find the answer.

✓ **End of Lesson Checklist**

☐ **INTERACTIVE GLOSSARY** Find the entry for *equivalent ratios*. Add two important things you learned about equivalent ratios in this lesson.

☐ **SELF CHECK** Go back to the Unit 3 Opener and see what you can check off.

Dear Family,

This week your student is learning about ratios comparing parts and wholes.

Sometimes the two quantities in a ratio relationship can be combined to make a total amount, or a whole.

For example, a recipe might require 2 cups of pineapple juice for every 3 cups of cranberry juice. This would make a total of 5 cups of juice.

Pineapple

Cranberry

Total:
5 cups of juice

Your student will be learning to solve problems like the one below.

Leon needs 20 gal of fruit punch for a party. The recipe requires 2 parts pineapple juice and 3 parts cranberry juice. How much pineapple juice and how much cranberry juice does Leon need for the party?

➤ **ONE WAY** to find the parts that make up a whole is to use a tape diagram.

The 20 gal must be divided evenly between the 5 parts.

$$20 \div 5 = 4$$

Pineapple	4 gal	4 gal	
Cranberry	4 gal	4 gal	4 gal

Total:
20 gal of fruit punch
5 parts

➤ **ANOTHER WAY** is to use a table of equivalent ratios.

Pineapple (gal)	Cranberry (gal)	Total (gal)
2	3	5
8	12	20

$\times 4$

Both methods show that Leon needs 8 gal of pineapple juice and 12 gal of cranberry juice for the party.

 Use the next page to start a conversation about ratios with total amounts.

Activity Thinking About Ratios Around You

➤ **Do this activity together to investigate ratios in the real world.**

Plants need food to grow, just like humans and animals. Fertilizer is often used to help feed plants. A bag of fertilizer contains three major nutrients (nitrogen, phosphorus, and potassium), as well as some filler material.

To see how the amount of each nutrient compares to the total amount of fertilizer, look at the label on the bag. The label *10-30-10* on this bag shows that the fertilizer contains 10 parts nitrogen, 30 parts phosphorous, and 10 parts potassium.

? Where else do you see ratios that show parts of a whole in the world around you?

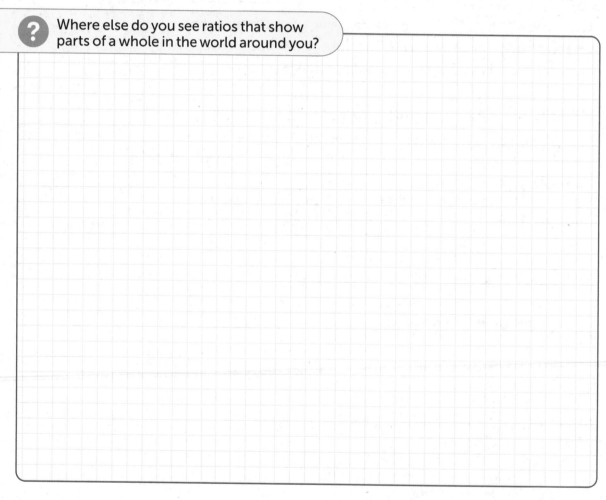

Explore Ratios That Describe Parts of a Whole

Green Tea Latte
4 : 3
Tea : Milk

Previously, you learned about equivalent ratios. In this lesson, you will learn about ratios that involve parts and a whole, or a total amount.

➤ **Use what you know to try to solve the problem below.**

Hasina is making green tea lattes. She steams milk to mix with hot tea. Hasina has 12 fl oz of hot tea. Based on the ratio in the recipe, how much milk does Hasina need to steam?

TRY IT

Math Toolkit connecting cubes, counters, double number lines, grid paper

DISCUSS IT

Ask: Would your model look different if Hasina used 12 cups of hot tea instead of 12 fl oz? Explain.

Share: In my model, . . .

Learning Targets SMP 1, SMP 2, SMP 3, SMP 4, SMP 5, SMP 6, SMP 7
Use ratio and rate reasoning to solve real-world and mathematical problems.
• Make tables of equivalent ratios relating quantities with whole-number measurements, find missing values in the tables, and plot the pairs of values on the coordinate plane. Use tables to compare ratios.

CONNECT IT

1 Look Back How much milk does Hasina need to steam to mix with 12 fl oz of hot tea? Explain how you know.

2 Look Ahead The ratio for Hasina's recipe could be given as 4 parts hot tea to 3 parts milk. Serafina's tea latte recipe calls for using **2 parts** hot tea to **4 parts** milk. A tape diagram is one way to model ratios that compare parts of a whole, or a total amount.

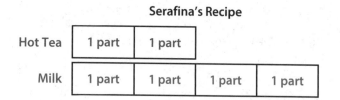

Serafina's Recipe

| Hot Tea | 1 part | 1 part | | |
| Milk | 1 part | 1 part | 1 part | 1 part |

This diagram is made up of six equal parts. Each part represents the same amount. This amount can be any measurement, such as 1 cup, 2 fl oz, or 3 gal.

a. What is the ratio of hot tea to the total amount of tea latte?

b. Suppose 1 part of the tape diagram represents 1 cup. What is the total amount of tea latte the recipe makes?

c. Suppose 1 part of the tape diagram represents 2 fl oz. What is the total amount of tea latte the recipe makes? What is the ratio of hot tea to the total amount of tea latte?

3 Reflect Suppose you change the amount that each equal part in a tape diagram represents. Does this change result in an equivalent ratio? Explain.

Prepare for Using Part-to-Part and Part-to-Whole Ratios

1 Think about what you know about using ratios to compare quantities. Fill in each box. Use words, numbers, and pictures. Show as many ideas as you can.

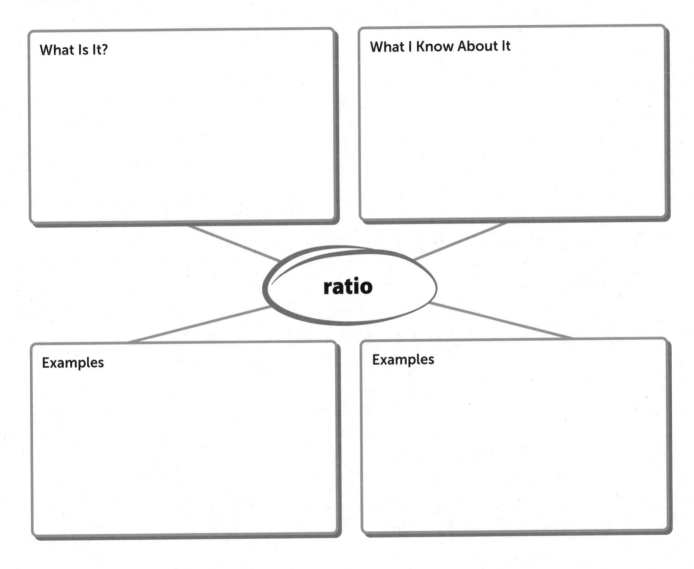

What Is It?	What I Know About It

ratio

Examples	Examples

2 Write three different ratios to describe this model. What do each of your ratios represent?

3 Dara is making salad dressing. The recipe calls for olive oil and vinegar to be mixed in the ratio 3 : 1.

    a. Dara has 4 tbsp of vinegar. Based on the ratio of olive oil to vinegar being 3 : 1, how much olive oil does Dara need? Show your work.

    SOLUTION _____

    b. Check your answer to problem 3a. Show your work.

    ©Curriculum Associates, LLC   Copying is not permitted.

Develop Solving Ratio Problems Involving Parts and Wholes

➤ **Read and try to solve the problem below.**

Tessa and her grandmother are decorating Tessa's quinceañera dress using two types of beads. They plan to use a total of 900 beads arranged in the pattern shown. How many of each type of bead do they need?

rhinestone

pearl

TRY IT

Math Toolkit connecting cubes, counters, double number lines, grid paper

DISCUSS IT

Ask: How did you use the total number of beads in your solution?

Share: In my solution, I . . .

➤ **Explore different ways to solve ratio problems involving parts and wholes.**

Tessa and her grandmother are decorating Tessa's quinceañera dress using two types of beads. They plan to use a total of 900 beads arranged in the pattern shown. How many of each type of bead do they need?

rhinestone

pearl

Model It

You can use a tape diagram to model the relationship between the parts and the total.

The ratio of rhinestones to pearls is 1 : 5.

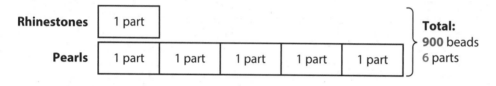

| Rhinestones | 1 part | | | | | | Total: |
| Pearls | 1 part | 1 part | 1 part | 1 part | 1 part | | 900 beads 6 parts |

The **total number** of beads is equal to the **number of equal parts** times the **value of each part**. Divide to determine the value of each part.

900 = 6 × ?

900 ÷ 6 = 150

There are **150** beads in each of the 6 parts.

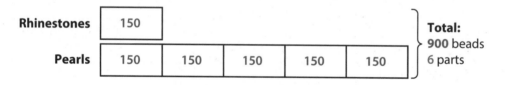

| Rhinestones | 150 | | | | | | Total: |
| Pearls | 150 | 150 | 150 | 150 | 150 | | 900 beads 6 parts |

Model It

You can make a table of equivalent ratios to represent the relationship between the parts and the total.

Multiply to find an equivalent ratio.

Rhinestones	Pearls	Total Beads
1	5	6
?	?	900

× 150

➤ **Use the problem from the previous page to help you understand how to solve ratio problems involving parts and wholes.**

1 Look at the first Model It. How are the values 1, 5, and 6 represented?

2 How do you determine the value of each part of the tape diagram? How does knowing this value help you solve the problem?

3 Look at the second Model It. How does the table show the same relationship between the parts and the total as the tape diagram?

4 When using a table of equivalent ratios to solve the problem, how do you determine what number to multiply by? How is this number related to the tape diagram?

5 How many rhinestones and how many pearls do Tessa and her grandmother need for the dress? How can you check your answer?

6 **Reflect** Think about all the models and strategies you have discussed today. Describe how one of them helped you better understand how to solve the Try It problem.

Apply It

> **Use what you learned to solve these problems.**

7 A store is handing out scratch-off cards to its customers. For each card, a customer wins either a coupon or a free T-shirt. The ratio of coupon cards to T-shirt cards is 9 : 2. The store orders a total of 8,250 cards. How many of the cards are T-shirt cards? Show your work.

SOLUTION _____

8 Raúl is mixing a cleaning spray. The instructions say to combine 2 parts vinegar and 1 part water. Raúl wants to make 24 fl oz of the spray. How many fluid ounces of vinegar and how many fluid ounces of water should Raúl use? Show your work.

SOLUTION _____

9 Emily makes 75 pins to sell at the school craft fair. She has two designs: a star and a bumblebee. She makes 2 star pins for every 3 bumblebee pins. How many pins of each type does Emily make? Show your work.

SOLUTION _____

Practice Solving Ratio Problems Involving Parts and Wholes

➤ **Study the Example showing how to solve ratio problems involving parts and wholes. Then solve problems 1–5.**

Example

Mr. Ramírez uses a ratio of 1 part pork to 3 parts beef when he makes meatloaf. He needs 32 oz of meat. How many ounces of beef and how many ounces of pork does Mr. Ramírez need for his meatloaf?

You can use a tape diagram to relate the parts to the total.

Divide the **total amount** by the **number of equal parts** to find the **value of each part.**

$32 \text{ oz} \div 4 = 8 \text{ oz}$

Pork: $1 \times 8 \text{ oz} = 8 \text{ oz}$

Beef: $3 \times 8 \text{ oz} = 24 \text{ oz}$

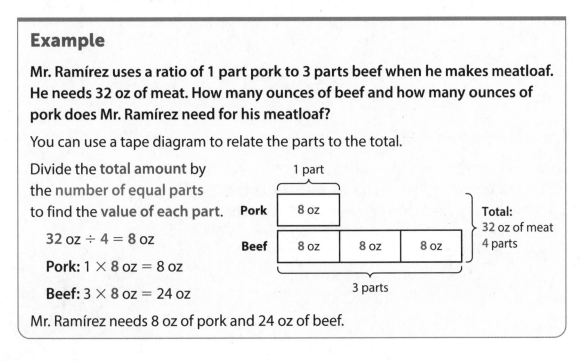

Mr. Ramírez needs 8 oz of pork and 24 oz of beef.

1 Suppose Mr. Ramírez from the Example needs 40 oz of meat.

a. What changes would you need to make to the tape diagram?

b. How many ounces of pork and how many ounces of beef would Mr. Ramírez need for a meatloaf with 40 oz of meat?

2 A movie theater sells only adult tickets and child tickets. For one movie, the theater sells 126 tickets in all. The tape diagram shows the ratio of adult tickets to child tickets the theater sells. What does each square of the diagram represent?

Adult tickets [ ][ ][ ][ ][ ][ ][ ]
Child tickets [ ][ ]

A 9 tickets

B 14 tickets

C 18 tickets

D 28 tickets

3 Indira finds that on a typical day, 4 out of every 5 students at her school eat a cafeteria lunch. The rest of the students bring their lunch from home. Indira's school has 495 students. On a typical day, how many students at her school bring their lunch from home? Show your work.

SOLUTION _____

4 Rhode Island Red chicks cost $3.20 each and Buckeye chicks cost $3.44 each. A farmer buys 4 Rhode Island Red chicks for every 3 Buckeye chicks. He buys 70 chicks in all. What is the total cost of the farmer's chicks? Show your work.

SOLUTION _____

5 A sixth-grade class collects 176 items for recycling. Three out of every eight items are cans, and the rest are bottles. How many bottles does the class collect? Show your work.

SOLUTION _____

Develop Comparing Ratios

➤ **Read and try to solve the problem below.**

Charlotte and Pablo are each making purple paint by mixing blue paint and red paint. Charlotte uses 1 cup of red paint for every 2 cups of blue paint. Pablo uses 2 cups of red paint for every 3 cups of blue paint. Whose paint is a bluer shade of purple?

TRY IT

Math Toolkit connecting cubes, counters, double number lines, grid paper

DISCUSS IT

Ask: How are your models similar to mine? How are they different?

Share: My models are similar to yours because . . . They are different because . . .

➤ **Explore different ways to compare ratios.**

Charlotte and Pablo are each making purple paint by mixing blue paint and red paint. Charlotte uses 1 cup of red paint for every 2 cups of blue paint. Pablo uses 2 cups of red paint for every 3 cups of blue paint. Whose paint is a bluer shade of purple?

Model It

You can use part-to-part ratios to compare two ratios.

Charlotte	
Red (cups)	**Blue (cups)**
1	2
2	4
3	6
4	8
5	10
6	12

Pablo	
Red (cups)	**Blue (cups)**
2	3
4	6
6	9
8	12
10	15
12	18

Model It

You can use part-to-whole ratios to compare ratios.

Charlotte		
Red (cups)	**Blue (cups)**	**Total (cups)**
1	2	3
2	4	6
3	6	9
4	8	12
5	10	15
6	12	18

Pablo		
Red (cups)	**Blue (cups)**	**Total (cups)**
2	3	5
4	6	10
6	9	15
8	12	20
10	15	25
12	18	30

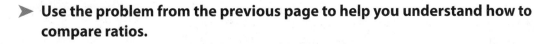
➤ **Use the problem from the previous page to help you understand how to compare ratios.**

1 Look at the ratios 2 : 4 and 2 : 3 in the first **Model It**. What quantity is the same in the ratios? How can the ratios help you compare the two shades of purple paint?

2 Look at the second **Model It**. Instead of listing all the batches shown, how could you use multiplication to find equivalent ratios with the same total amount?

3 Is Charlotte's paint or Pablo's paint a bluer shade of purple? Use either pair of tables to explain how you know.

4 To compare ratios, why is it helpful to find equivalent ratios in which one quantity in each ratio is the same?

5 **Reflect** Think about all the models and strategies you have discussed today. Describe how one of them helped you better understand how to compare ratios.

Apply It

➤ **Use what you learned to solve these problems.**

6 Darius and Khadija are learning to play chess. Darius's ratio of wins to losses is 2 to 13. Khadija's ratio of wins to losses is 3 to 17. Who has the better winning record? Explain how you know.

7 Arturo's food coloring uses the ratio 30 drops yellow to 27 drops blue. Ravi's food coloring uses the ratio 30 drops yellow to 24 drops blue. Linda says that Arturo's food coloring is yellower because 27 > 24. Do you agree? Explain.

8 Efia and Mora are mixing oils to make scented candles. Whose oil mixture has a stronger vanilla smell? Explain.

Scented Candle Ratios

Efia's oil	Mora's oil
12 parts vanilla to 8 parts lavender	10 parts vanilla to 6 parts lavender

Practice Comparing Ratios

➤ **Study the Example showing how to compare ratios. Then solve problems 1–5.**

Example

A science teacher makes two mixtures of red dye and water. Mixture A has 3 mL of red dye for every 20 mL of water. Mixture B has 4 mL of red dye for every 30 mL of water. Which mixture is redder?

You can use tables to find equivalent ratios with the same amount of water.

Mixture A		Mixture B	
Red Dye (mL)	Water (mL)	Red Dye (mL)	Water (mL)
3	20	4	30
6	40	8	60
9	60	12	90

When both mixtures have 60 mL of water, Mixture A has more red dye than Mixture B. So, Mixture A is redder.

1 In the Example problem, how could you use multiplication to find equivalent ratios with the same amount of water?

2 Adsila's recipe for peach frozen yogurt says to mix 3 cups blended peaches for every 2 cups vanilla yogurt. Which of these frozen yogurt recipes has a stronger peach taste than Adsila's? Select all that apply.

A 5 cups blended peaches for every 3 cups vanilla yogurt

B 8 cups blended peaches for every 5 cups vanilla yogurt

C 9 cups blended peaches for every 6 cups vanilla yogurt

D 10 cups blended peaches for every 8 cups vanilla yogurt

E 14 cups blended peaches for every 10 cups vanilla yogurt

3 Ramón makes nectar for a hummingbird feeder by mixing 8 cups of water with 2 cups of sugar. Tiffany makes nectar by mixing 9 cups of water with 3 cups of sugar. Whose nectar is more sugary? Explain.

4 To make cherry trail mix, Sebastián needs 4 oz of nuts for every 3 oz of dried cherries. To make sunflower trail mix, he needs 5 oz of nuts for every 2 oz of sunflower seeds. Can Sebastián make more cherry trail mix or sunflower trail mix with 20 oz of nuts? Show your work.

SOLUTION _____

5 An artist combines copper and other metals to make bronze. A bronze sculpture of a dolphin contains 43 g of copper for every 7 g of other metals. A bronze sculpture of a bird contains 83 g of copper for every 17 g of other metals. Which sculpture is more coppery? Explain.

Refine Using Part-to-Part and Part-to-Whole Ratios

➤ **Complete the Example below. Then solve problems 1–9.**

Example

A pet store sells brown mice and white mice. The ratio of brown mice to white mice is 5 : 3. The store has 6 more brown mice than white mice. What is the total number of mice at the store?

Look at how you could show your work with tape diagrams.

2 parts represent 6 mice, so 1 part represents 3 mice.

6 mice

| Brown mice | 3 mice | 3 mice | 3 mice | 3 mice | 3 mice | } 15 mice |

| White mice | 3 mice | 3 mice | 3 mice | } 9 mice |

SOLUTION _____

CONSIDER THIS . . .
How do you decide how many equal parts to use for the tape diagram?

PAIR/SHARE
How can you check that your answer is correct?

Apply It

1 Dawn is ordering 1 veggie sandwich for every 3 ham sandwiches. She needs 12 sandwiches in all. Veggie sandwiches cost $4.00 each, and ham sandwiches cost $4.50 each. How much will Dawn spend on sandwiches? Show your work.

CONSIDER THIS . . .
How could a table help you find the number of each type of sandwich Dawn orders?

PAIR/SHARE
Explain how you know that the amount Dawn spends must be greater than the cost of 12 veggie sandwiches and less than the cost of 12 ham sandwiches.

SOLUTION _____

2 In science class, students are mixing water and a citric acid solution. The table shows how much water and acid solution two students use. Whose mixture is more acidic? Show your work.

Student	Water (mL)	Acid Solution (mL)
Bao	26	4
Moses	17	3

CONSIDER THIS...
You can use the information in the table to find the total volume of each mixture.

SOLUTION _____

PAIR/SHARE
How did equivalent ratios help you solve this problem?

3 Amata mixes 2 parts black paint with 3 parts white paint to make 90 mL of gray paint. How much white paint does Amata use to make the gray paint?

A 18 mL

B 30 mL

C 45 mL

D 54 mL

José chose A as the correct answer. How might he have gotten that answer?

CONSIDER THIS...
How many equal parts does Amata mix in all?

PAIR/SHARE
How can you use the answer to the problem to find how much white paint Amata would use to make 30mL of gray paint?

4 The graph shows the ratio of goals attempted to goals made for two soccer players, Andres and Deyvi. Which player has a better record of making goals? Explain how you know.

Soccer Goals

5 Kwame and Olivia each combine orange juice and mango juice. Kwame makes a total of 12 cups, and Olivia makes a total of 20 cups. Kwame uses less orange juice than Olivia, but his orange-mango juice tastes more like oranges than hers does. Give an example of the number of cups of each ingredient each person could have used. Explain your thinking.

6 There are 39 people on a city bus. The ratio of adults to children is 10 : 3. At the next stop, 3 adults get off the bus. What is the new ratio of adults to children on the bus?

A 3 : 1

B 9 : 2

C 7 : 3

D 12 : 1

39 people
10 : 3
adults : children

7 A box holds red pens and blue pens. The ratio of red pens to blue pens is 1 to 4. The box holds 12 more blue pens than red pens. What is the total number of pens in the box? Show your work.

SOLUTION _____

8 Lulu and Cece collect a total of 35 shells from the beach. At first, the ratio of Lulu's shells to Cece's shells is 5 : 2. Then Lulu gives 5 of her shells to Cece. Tell whether each statement is *True* or *False*.

	True	False
a. At first, Lulu has 25 shells.	○	○
b. After Lulu gives Cece 5 shells, Cece has 15 shells.	○	○
c. After Lulu gives Cece 5 shells, the ratio of Lulu's shells to Cece's shells is 5 : 3.	○	○

9 **Math Journal** In cooking class, Lupita and Jacob each make a mixture of basil and oregano. Lupita uses 2 tsp basil for every 3 tsp oregano. Jacob uses 4 tsp basil for every 5 tsp oregano. Lupita says the two mixtures will taste the same. Jacob says his will have a stronger basil taste than Lupita's. Who is correct? Explain.

✓ **End of Lesson Checklist**

☐ **INTERACTIVE GLOSSARY** Write a new entry for *determine*. Write at least one synonym for *determine*.

☐ **SELF CHECK** Go back to the Unit 3 Opener and see what you can check off.

Math IN Action

SMP 1 Make sense of problems and persevere in solving them.

Study an Example Problem and Solution

➤ **Read this problem involving equivalent ratios. Then look at one student's solution to this problem on the following pages.**

Counting Heartbeats

Josephine is planning an exercise program for some of her family members, based on their ages. Josephine is 10 years old, and her brother, Dylan, is 20 years old. Their mother, Zahara, is 40 years old, and their grandfather, Reth, is 70 years old.

Read about how to calculate the target number of heartbeats for different types of exercise. Choose one member of Josephine's family. Then for each type of exercise, use ratio language to describe the number of heartbeats that family member should count over a period of time between 10 and 20 seconds.

HOME   NEWS   TIPS   ABOUT US

What Is a Target Number of Heartbeats?

It is the approximate number of times your heart should beat during 60 seconds of exercise. It is not an exact goal, but it can be used to track if you are getting the most benefit from your exercise.

A target number of heartbeats:

- is a healthy number of heartbeats in 60 seconds.
- depends on the person's age, a.
- varies depending on the type of exercise.

Type of Exercise	Target Number of Heartbeats in 60 Seconds
Low Intensity (walking or stretching)	$0.5 \times (220 - a)$
Moderate Intensity (jogging or weight training)	$0.6 \times (220 - a)$
High Intensity (sprinting or jumping rope)	$0.8 \times (220 - a)$

While exercising, people usually count their heartbeats for a shorter period of time, often between 10 and 20 seconds. Then they use that number to calculate the target number for 60 seconds.

An adult heart beats about 100,000 times a day. It pumps about 2,000 gallons of blood through the body each day.

One Student's Solution

> **NOTICE THAT...**
> All three expressions use the same variable, *a*, to represent the family member's age. The expressions also use multiple operations and grouping symbols. After substituting, be sure to follow the order of operations.

First, I have to choose a family member.

I will calculate the target numbers for Zahara.

So, I will find the number of times Zahara's heart should beat for every 60 seconds.

I will substitute Zahara's age, 40, into each expression to calculate the target number of heartbeats for each type of exercise.

Low Intensity:	Moderate Intensity:	High Intensity:
$0.5 \times (220 - a)$	$0.6 \times (220 - a)$	$0.8 \times (220 - a)$
$0.5 \times (220 - 40)$	$0.6 \times (220 - 40)$	$0.8 \times (220 - 40)$
$0.5 \times (180)$	$0.6 \times (180)$	$0.8 \times (180)$
90 heartbeats	108 heartbeats	144 heartbeats

> **NOTICE THAT...**
> Each sentence tells how many times Zahara's heart should beat for every 60 seconds of exercise.

Next, I will use ratio language to describe the target number of heartbeats for each type of exercise.

While doing **low** intensity exercise, Zahara's heart should beat about 90 times for every 60 seconds.

While doing **moderate** intensity exercise, Zahara's heart should beat about 108 times for every 60 seconds.

While doing **high** intensity exercise, Zahara's heart should beat about 144 times for every 60 seconds.

> **✓ Problem-Solving Checklist**
>
> ☐ Tell what is known.
> ☐ Tell what the problem is asking.
> ☐ Show all your work.
> ☐ Show that the solution works.

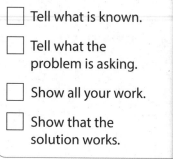

high intensity exercise

144 heartbeats for every 60 seconds

Now, I need to find the number of heartbeats Zahara should count in a shorter period of time.

I will use double number lines to find equivalent ratios when the number of seconds is 20.

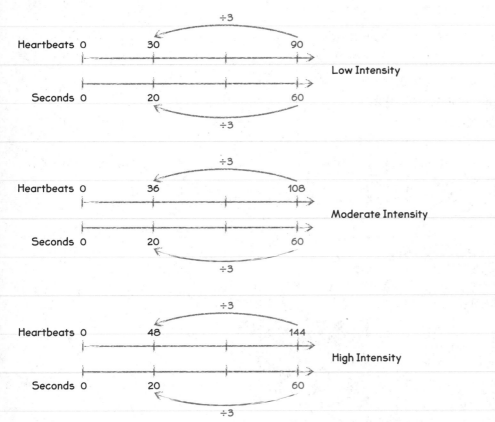

NOTICE THAT...
60 ÷ 3 = 20.
90, 108, and 144 are also divisible by 3, so equivalent ratios using 20 seconds will give a whole number of heartbeats.

Finally, I will use ratio language to describe the target number of heartbeats for 20 seconds of each type of exercise.

While doing **low** intensity exercise, Zahara should count about 30 heartbeats for every 20 seconds.

While doing **moderate** intensity exercise, Zahara should count about 36 heartbeats for every 20 seconds.

While doing **high** intensity exercise, Zahara should count about 48 heartbeats for every 20 seconds.

NOTICE THAT...
These ratios are equivalent to the ratios that tell how many times Zahara's heart should beat for every 60 seconds of exercise.

Try Another Approach

➤ **There are many ways to solve problems. Think about how you might solve the Counting Heartbeats problem in a different way.**

Counting Heartbeats

Josephine is planning an exercise program for some of her family members, based on their ages. Josephine is 10 years old, and her brother, Dylan, is 20 years old. Their mother, Zahara, is 40 years old, and their grandfather, Reth, is 70 years old.

Read about how to calculate the target number of heartbeats for different types of exercise. Choose one member of Josephine's family. Then for each type of exercise, use ratio language to describe the number of heartbeats that family member should count over a period of time between 10 and 20 seconds.

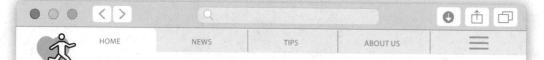

HOME   NEWS   TIPS   ABOUT US

What Is a Target Number of Heartbeats?

It is the approximate number of times your heart should beat during 60 seconds of exercise. It is not an exact goal, but it can be used to track if you are getting the most benefit from your exercise.

A target number of heartbeats:

- is a healthy number of heartbeats in 60 seconds.
- depends on the person's age, a.
- varies depending on the type of exercise.

Type of Exercise	Target Number of Heartbeats in 60 Seconds
Low Intensity (walking or stretching)	$0.5 \times (220 - a)$
Moderate Intensity (jogging or weight training)	$0.6 \times (220 - a)$
High Intensity (sprinting or jumping rope)	$0.8 \times (220 - a)$

While exercising, people usually count their heartbeats for a shorter period of time, often between 10 and 20 seconds. Then they use that number to calculate the target number for 60 seconds.

Plan It

➤ **Answer these questions to help you start thinking about a plan.**

a. How are the expressions for each target number of heartbeats alike? How are they different?

b. What number of seconds will you use to write the equivalent ratios? Why did you choose this number?

Solve It

➤ **Find a different solution for the Counting Heartbeats problem. Show all your work on a separate sheet of paper. You may want to use the Problem-Solving Tips to get started.**

PROBLEM-SOLVING TIPS

Math Toolkit double number lines, grid paper

Key Terms

ratio	equivalent	substitute
evaluate	variable	expression

Models You may want to use . . .

• pictures or ratio language to represent a ratio relationship.

• tables or double number lines to find equivalent ratios.

• multiplication or division to find equivalent ratios or to check your work.

Reflect

Use Mathematical Practices As you work through the problem, discuss these questions with a partner.

• **Persevere** How can your answers to the Plan It questions help you plan how to solve the problem?

• **Make an Argument** During which type of exercise should the family member you chose count the greatest number of heartbeats? Why?

Discuss Models and Strategies

➤ **Read the problem. Write a solution on a separate sheet of paper. Remember, there can be lots of ways to solve a problem.**

Staying Hydrated

Josephine and her family set goals for how much water to drink compared to other beverages.

Choose two family members. Use ratio tables to determine who will drink more water compared to other beverages. Make a graph comparing the two goals that Josephine can share with her family.

Daily Goals:

Josephine:
10 ounces of water for every 5 ounces of other beverages

Zahara:
12 ounces of water for every 8 ounces of other beverages

Reth:
15 ounces of water for every 9 ounces of other beverages

Dylan:
8 ounces of water for every 6 ounces of other beverages

Family Member: _____

Amount of Water (ounces)	Amount of Other Beverages (ounces)

Family Member: _____

Amount of Water (ounces)	Amount of Other Beverages (ounces)

Plan It and Solve It

➤ **Find a solution to the Staying Hydrated problem.**

Write a detailed plan and support your answer. Be sure to include:

- the names of the family members you chose.
- ratio tables that show your analysis for the two family members.
- a graph that uses a different color for each family member.
- the family member who drinks more water compared to other beverages.

PROBLEM-SOLVING TIPS

Math Toolkit connecting cubes, counters, coordinate planes, double number lines, grid paper

Key Terms

ratio	equivalent	part
whole	compare	table
graph		

Questions

- How will you write ratios that can be compared for the family members you chose?
- How will you label the axes of your graph?

Reflect

Use Mathematical Practices As you work through the problem, discuss these questions with a partner.

- **Reason Mathematically** How did you determine which person drinks more water compared to other beverages?

- **Use Models** How can you use your graph to find an equivalent ratio that is not shown in your table?

Many people choose stainless steel bottles for drinking water on the go. The bottles do not rust, are durable, and keep water cooler longer than plastic or glass bottles.

Persevere On Your Own

➤ **Read the problem. Write a solution on a separate sheet of paper.**

Making a Sandwich

Dylan reads that meals with a total carbohydrate to fiber ratio of less than 10 to 1 tend to be healthier. Look at the nutrition information for the ingredients he might use in a sandwich.

Using at least three ingredients, help Dylan make a sandwich with a carbohydrate to fiber ratio that is less than 10 to 1.

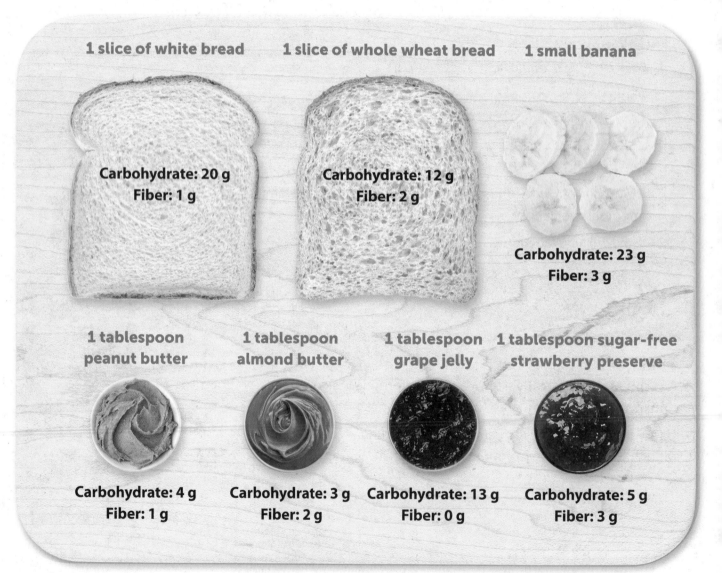

1 slice of white bread
Carbohydrate: 20 g
Fiber: 1 g

1 slice of whole wheat bread
Carbohydrate: 12 g
Fiber: 2 g

1 small banana
Carbohydrate: 23 g
Fiber: 3 g

1 tablespoon peanut butter
Carbohydrate: 4 g
Fiber: 1 g

1 tablespoon almond butter
Carbohydrate: 3 g
Fiber: 2 g

1 tablespoon grape jelly
Carbohydrate: 13 g
Fiber: 0 g

1 tablespoon sugar-free strawberry preserve
Carbohydrate: 5 g
Fiber: 3 g

Solve It

➤ **Find a solution to the Making a Sandwich problem.**

- Name at least three ingredients Dylan can use to make his sandwich. Tell how much of each ingredient to use.

- Calculate the total amount of carbohydrates and fiber in the sandwich.

- Use ratio language and symbols to compare the total amount of carbohydrates in the sandwich to the total amount of fiber two different ways.

- Show that the ratio of carbohydrates to fiber in the sandwich is less than 10 to 1.

Reflect

Use Mathematical Practices   After you complete the problem, choose one of these questions to discuss with a partner.

- **Persevere** Did you try different combinations of ingredients before deciding which ones to use? Explain.

- **Use Models** What models did you use, and how did they help you find a solution?

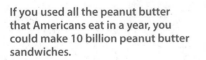

If you used all the peanut butter that Americans eat in a year, you could make 10 billion peanut butter sandwiches.

In this unit you learned to . . .

Skill	Lesson
Use ratio language to describe a ratio relationship between two quantities.	**12, 13, 14**
Use ratio reasoning to solve real-world problems.	**12, 13, 14**
Identify and write equivalent ratios.	**13, 14**
Represent equivalent ratios as points in the coordinate plane.	**13**
Use tables to compare ratios.	**14**
Justify solutions to ratio problems by using ratio language and models, such as double number lines, tables, tape diagrams, and coordinate planes.	**12–14**

Think about what you have learned.

➤ **Use words, numbers, and drawings.**

1 Two important things I learned are . . .

 2 A mistake I made that helped me learn was . . .

 3 One thing I am still confused about is . . .

Vocabulary Review

➤ Review the unit vocabulary. Put a check mark by items you can use in speaking and writing. Look up the meaning of any terms you do not know.

Math Vocabulary   **Academic Vocabulary**

☐ compare   ☐ ratio   ☐ determine

☐ coordinate plane   ☐ scale   ☐ graph (verb)
                         (on a graph)
☐ equivalent ratios   ☐ relationship
                       ☐ x-coordinate
☐ ordered pair
                       ☐ y-coordinate

➤ Use the unit vocabulary to complete the problems.

 1 One student describes a ratio by saying *There are 5 teachers for every 2 students.* Another student describes a ratio by saying *There are 2 students for every 5 teachers.* What is the same and different about these two ratios?

2 Use at least two math or academic vocabulary terms to describe the table. Underline each term you use.

Distance (ft)	3	6	9	
Time (min)	1	2	3	4

3 The graph represents a ratio relationship. Use at least three math or academic vocabulary terms to describe the graph. Underline each term you use.

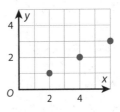

➤ **Use what you have learned to complete these problems.**

1 An art supply store sells two colors of ink. The store has 6 cases of black ink and 8 cases of blue ink. What does the ratio 6 : 14 represent in this situation? Explain your reasoning.

SOLUTION _____

_____

_____

2 There are 114 cans of soup in a grocery store. The ratio of large cans of soup to small cans of soup is 12 : 7. A customer buys 2 large cans of soup. What is the new ratio of large cans of soup to small cans of soup in the grocery store? Choose all the correct answers.

A 3 : 5   **B** 5 : 3

C 8 : 5   **D** 10 : 7

E 35 : 21   **F** 37 : 21

3 Jetia mixes 5 parts cranberry juice with 8 parts apple juice to make 117 cups of cran-apple juice. How much apple juice does Jetia use to make the cran-apple juice? Show your work.

SOLUTION _____

4 A pet store has two types of betta fish: red betta fish and blue betta fish. A customer notices that 7 out of the 12 betta fish in the store are red. What is the ratio of blue betta fish to red betta fish? Write your answer in the blanks.

_____ : _____

5 A weaver creates a cloth. He can weave 1 yd for every 3 hours worked. Plot points on the graph to show how many yards he can create in 3, 6, 9, and 12 hours. Label each point with its ordered pair.

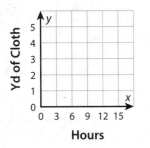

6 Haruto stretches the same number of minutes before each workout. He stretches a total of 105 minutes every 7 workouts. Based on this information, how many minutes does Haruto stretch for 4 workouts?

A 15 minutes

B 30 minutes

C 60 minutes

D 90 minutes

7 Devon and Kylie each make a cheese sauce. Devon uses 8 oz of cheese for every 9 oz of cream. Kylie uses 11 oz of cheese for every 12 oz of cream. Whose cheese sauce will have a stronger cheese flavor? Show your work.

SOLUTION _____

_____

Performance Task

➤ **Answer the questions and show all your work on separate paper.**

Candace runs an art studio. She has primary colors of paint: red, blue, and yellow. There are a total of 60 cups of red paint, 20 cups of blue paint, and 30 cups of yellow paint. Candace needs to make orange and purple paint. She mixes her orange and purple paints using the following specifications.

- To make orange paint, Candace combines 5 parts yellow paint for every 3 parts red paint.

- To make purple paint, Candace combines 7 parts red paint for every 2 parts blue paint.

- She only uses whole cups when measuring.

- She needs at least 40 cups of orange and 40 cups of purple paint.

Create a plan for Candace to mix the paint she needs. Include the amount of each primary color of paint she will use and the amount of orange and purple paint she will make.

Reflect

Use Mathematical Practices After you complete the task, choose one of the following questions to answer.

- **Make Sense of the Problem** How do the ratios of each primary color relate to the total amount of each new color?

- **Use Reasoning** How did you make sure that your plan doesn't use more primary color paint than Candace has?

✔ **Self Check**

Before starting this unit, check off the skills you know below.
As you complete each lesson, see how many more skills you can check off!

I can . . .	Before	After
Compare rates to solve real-world problems.	☐	☐
Use unit rates to find equivalent ratios.	☐	☐
Convert measurement units using rates.	☐	☐
Express a percent as a decimal or a fraction.	☐	☐
Find a given percent of a number.	☐	☐
Find what percent one number is of another number.	☐	☐
Find the whole when given a part and a percent.	☐	☐
Use math vocabulary and precise language to explain ratios, rates, and percents.	☐	☐

➤ **Write what you know about comparing ratios in each box.**
  Share your ideas with a partner and write in any new information you learn.

I Can Compare Ratios Using:

diagrams

Words and Phrases I Use When Discussing
How to Compare Ratios:

**comparing
ratios**

My Examples or Drawings:

Types of Ratios That Can Be Compared:

Dear Family,

This week your student is exploring rates. You may be familiar with rates such as *miles per hour, words per minute,* or *price per pound.*

A **rate** is a ratio that compares the number of units of one quantity to 1 unit of another quantity. You can write two rates to represent a given ratio relationship.

Ratio of cost to pounds of apples
$4 for every 2 pounds

Rate per pound
$2 for every 1 pound
$2 per pound

Rate per dollar
0.5 pound for every $1
0.5 pound per dollar

Your student will be modeling rates for ratio relationships like the one below.

A computer uploads 15 photos every 5 minutes.

➤ **ONE WAY** to model the two rates for a ratio relationship is to use a double number line.

The double number line shows the number of photos uploaded in **1 minute** and the number of minutes needed to upload **1 photo**.

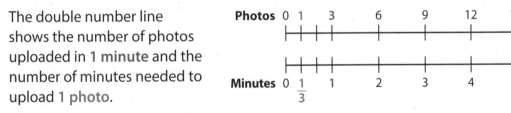

➤ **ANOTHER WAY** is to use a table of equivalent ratios.

Divide both quantities in the ratio 15 : 5 by 5 to make the second quantity 1.

Then divide both quantities in the ratio 3 : 1 by 3 to make the first quantity 1.

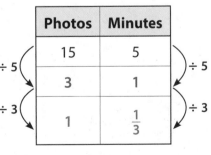

Photos	Minutes
15	5
3	1
1	$\frac{1}{3}$

Both models show that you can think of the uploading rate as 3 photos per minute or as $\frac{1}{3}$ minute per photo.

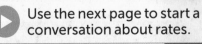

Use the next page to start a conversation about rates.

Activity Thinking About Rates in the World Around You

➤ **Do this activity together to investigate rates in the real world.**

When making a movie, directors must consider how many frames per second they want audiences to see. The rate *frames per second* represents how many images flash across the screen in one second.

Many movie directors use 24 frames per second because this makes the movie scenes look smooth. Have you ever noticed some movie scenes look very choppy? It may seem like the camera is shaking, but this choppiness is actually caused by the movie director choosing 12 frames per second instead of 24!

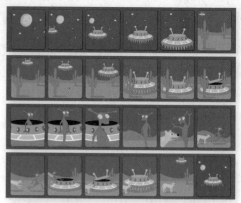

24 frames per second

12 frames per second

? Where else do you see rates in the world around you?

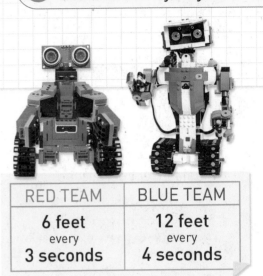

Explore Rate Concepts

Model It

➤ **Complete the problems about equivalent ratios.**

1 Teams of students in Ms. Seda's class make robots. The Red Team's robot travels 6 feet every 3 seconds. The model shows the ratio 6 : 3. Complete the model to show the equivalent ratio that tells how far the Red Team's robot travels in 1 second.

RED TEAM	BLUE TEAM
6 feet	12 feet
every	every
3 seconds	4 seconds

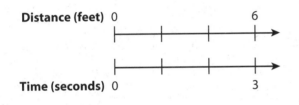

Distance (feet) 0   6

Time (seconds) 0   3

2 A ratio that compares the number of units of one quantity to 1 unit of another quantity is a **rate**. You can use the word **per,** which means *for each* or *for every,* to write a rate. A speed in feet per second is a rate that compares distance to time.

a. The Red Team's robot travels at a rate of _____ feet per second.

b. The Blue Team's robot travels 12 feet every 4 seconds. Complete the model to show this robot's rate in feet per second.

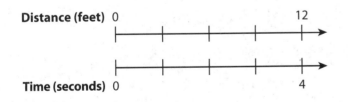

Distance (feet) 0   12

Time (seconds) 0   4

The Blue Team's robot travels at a rate of _____ feet per second.

◎ Learning Target SMP 2, SMP 3, SMP 7
Understand the concept of a unit rate $\frac{a}{b}$ associated with a ratio $a : b$ with $b \neq 0$, and use rate language in the context of a ratio relationship.

Model It

➤ **Complete the problems about rates.**

3 The Yellow Team's robot is not working properly. It travels only 4 feet every 12 seconds.

a. Complete the model to show the robot's rate in feet per second.

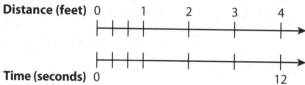

Distance (feet) 0   1   2   3   4

Time (seconds) 0   12

b. Does your model show that the Yellow Team's robot travels *more than 1 foot* or *less than 1 foot* in 1 second? Explain.

c. Use your model to complete the sentences.

In 1 second, the Yellow Team's robot travels _____ foot.

The robot travels at a rate of _____ foot per second.

d. The Red Team, the Blue Team, and the Yellow Team race their robots. Which robot will win? Justify your answer.

DISCUSS IT

Ask: How can division help you write a rate?

Share: A rate will include a fraction when . . .

4 **Reflect** How is writing a rate related to what you know about writing equivalent ratios?

Prepare for Understanding Rate Concepts

1 Think about what you know about ratios. Fill in each box. Use words, numbers, and pictures. Show as many ideas as you can.

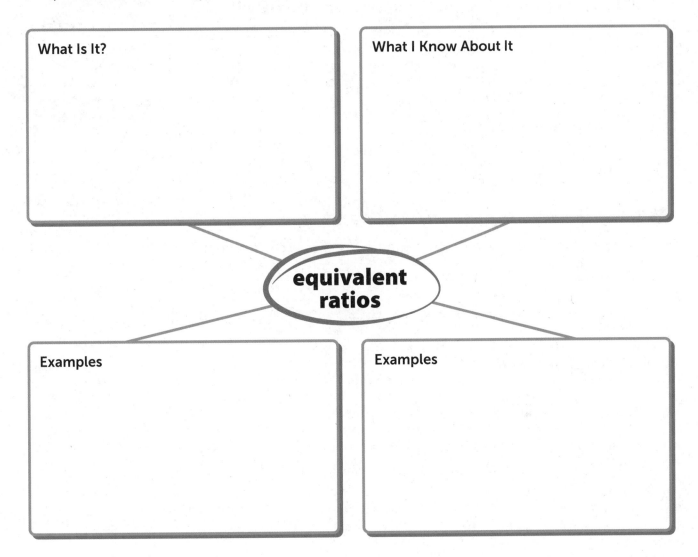

What Is It?

What I Know About It

equivalent ratios

Examples

Examples

2 The ratio of minutes to gallons of water flowing through a garden hose is 2 to 12. Carlota says that an equivalent ratio of minutes to gallons is 6 to 1. Is Carlota correct? Explain how you know.

➤ **Complete problems 3–5.**

3 Three friends are buying food for an end-of-school party. Adrian spends $16 for 2 pounds of sliced turkey.

   a. Complete the model to show the cost for 1 pound of turkey.

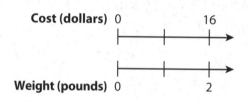

              Cost (dollars) 0   16

            Weight (pounds) 0   2

   b. The turkey costs $ _____ per pound.

4 Gabriel spends $18 for 3 pounds of sliced cheese.

   a. Complete the model to show how much the cheese costs per pound.

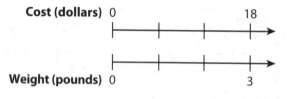

              Cost (dollars) 0   18

            Weight (pounds) 0   3

   b. The cheese sells at a rate of $ _____ per pound.

   c. How can you use the rates you found in problems 3b and 4b to tell whether turkey or cheese is less expensive per pound?

5 Jia spends $4 for 8 pounds of bananas.

   a. Complete the model to show the cost of the bananas per pound.

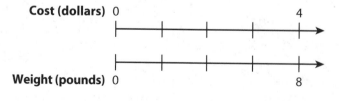

              Cost (dollars) 0   4

            Weight (pounds) 0   8

   b. The bananas sell at a rate of $ _____ per pound.

> **Vocabulary**
>
> **rate**
> a ratio that tells the number of units of one quantity for 1 unit of another quantity.
>
> **per**
> *for each* or *for every*. The word *per* can be used to express a rate, such as $2 per pound.

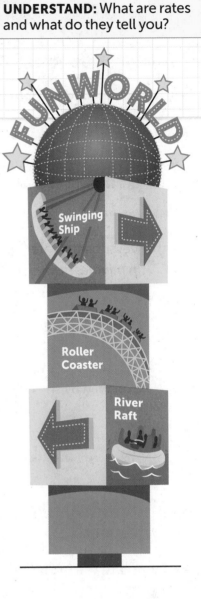

? **UNDERSTAND:** What are rates and what do they tell you?

Develop Understanding of Rate Concepts

Model It: Compare Rates

➤ **Try these two problems involving rates.**

1 At a theme park, passengers are waiting in line for three rides.

a. The Roller Coaster can load 60 passengers every 5 minutes. Complete the model to show the rate at which passengers are loaded per minute.

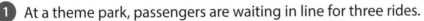

Passengers 0

Minutes 0

b. The loading rate is _____ passengers per minute.

c. The Swinging Ship can load more passengers than the Roller Coaster in the same amount of time. Is the loading rate for the Swinging Ship faster or slower than the rate for the Roller Coaster?

2 **a.** Every 8 minutes, the River Raft can load 88 passengers. Complete the model to show the rate at which passengers are loaded per minute.

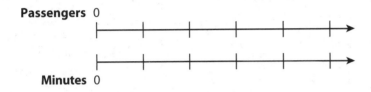

Passengers 0

Minutes 0

b. The loading rate is _____ passengers per minute.

c. Suppose the same number of passengers are in line for the Roller Coaster, the Swinging Ship, and the River Raft. If you want to get on a ride as quickly as possible, which line should you get in? Explain how you know.

DISCUSS IT

Ask: How can you determine whether the Swinging Ship or the River Raft has a faster loading rate?

Share: I think that a faster rate means . . .

Model It: Two Rates for a Ratio Relationship

➤ **Try this problem about rates.**

3 You can write two rates for any ratio relationship.

 a. It takes Adriana 20 minutes to walk 5 blocks to the library. Complete the table of equivalent ratios to show Adriana's two rates.

Minutes	Blocks
20	5
1	
	1

 b. Describe the rate that Adriana walks in *blocks per minute* and in *minutes per block*.

 c. Adriana wants to know how many blocks she can walk in 45 minutes. Explain why she can use her rate in *blocks per minute* to find the answer.

DISCUSS IT

Ask: How does the table of equivalent ratios show two rates?

Share: I can write two rates for any ratio relationship by . . .

CONNECT IT

➤ **Complete the problems below.**

4 Suppose Adriana walks faster on her way home from the library. How will this change affect her rate in *blocks per minute*? Explain.

5 Use a model to show the snail's rate in *centimeters per minute* and its rate in *minutes per centimeter*. Describe each rate in words.

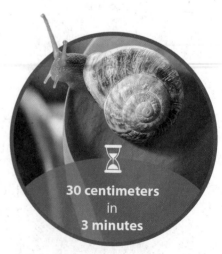

30 centimeters in 3 minutes

Practice Rate Concepts

➤ **Study how the Example shows writing two rates for a ratio relationship. Then solve problems 1–5.**

Example

A train uses 48 gallons of fuel for every 8 miles it travels. Write the train's rate of fuel use in *gallons per mile* and in *miles per gallon*.

Write equivalent ratios that make comparisons to **1 unit**.

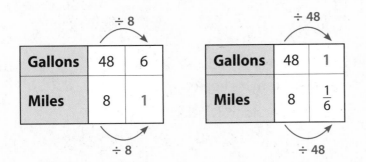

The ratio 6 to 1 shows that the train uses 6 gallons per mile.

The ratio $\frac{1}{6}$ to 1 shows that the train travels $\frac{1}{6}$ mile per gallon.

1 The Example shows how to use division to write equivalent ratios that make comparisons to 1 unit. How do you know what numbers to divide by?

2 Edward buys 6 yards of fabric for $15. He says that the fabric costs $0.40 per yard. Complete the model to show cost of fabric per yard. Do you agree with Edward? Explain.

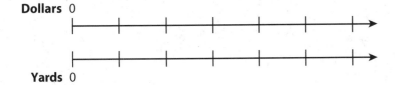

©Curriculum Associates, LLC   Copying is not permitted.

Vocabulary

rate
a ratio that tells the number of units of one quantity for 1 unit of another quantity. Rates are often expressed using the word *per*, such as 5 miles per hour or 2 cups per serving.

per
for each or *for every*.

3 An elevator in the Seattle Space Needle can rise 100 meters in 50 seconds. Use a model to show the elevator's rate of travel in *meters per second* and in *seconds per meter*. Describe each rate in words.

The Space Needle is an observation tower in Seattle, Washington.

4 Zahara rides with her dad to her grandmother's house. They travel 159 miles in 3 hours. Her uncle, Jorge, drives there separately from his home.

a. At what speed does Zahara's dad drive, in miles per hour? Draw a model to show your work.

SOLUTION _____

b. Jorge's trip takes the same amount of time as Zahara's, but he travels a shorter distance. Does Jorge drive faster or slower than Zahara's dad?

5 A store changes the cost of a package of batteries. Now customers pay more money for the same number of batteries. Did the cost per battery increase, decrease, or stay the same? Explain how you know.

Refine Ideas About Rate Concepts

Apply It

➤ **Complete problems 1–5.**

1 **Apply** Malcolm is making chicken rice soup. The recipe calls for 5 cups of chicken broth per cup of brown rice. How many cups of brown rice are needed for 20 cups of chicken broth? Explain how you know.

2 **Analyze** At a tea shop, a package of vanilla tea weighs 1 ounce and costs $2. Cinnamon tea is priced at 2 ounces per dollar. Use rates to show which tea is more expensive per ounce. Include a model in your response.

3 **Critique** A school laser printer prints 72 pages in 6 minutes. Alanna's home printer prints twice as many pages in twice as many minutes. Alanna says her printer's rate in pages per minute is two times the rate of the school printer. Do you agree or disagree? Explain.

4 A box holds 12 cups of cereal. This amount is equivalent to 16 servings.

PART A Use a model to show the number of cups of cereal per serving and the number of servings per cup of cereal.

PART B Explain how your model shows each rate.

PART C If you wanted to know how many cups of the cereal are in a box that holds 24 servings, which rate would you use? Explain.

5 **Math Journal** A farm stand sells 3 quarts of peaches for $15. Use a model to write a rate for this situation. What does this rate tell you?

✓ End of Lesson Checklist

☐ **INTERACTIVE GLOSSARY** Find the entry for *rate*. Rewrite the definition in your own words.

Dear Family,

This week your student is learning how to solve problems that involve rates. Using **unit rates** can help you find equivalent ratios or compare ratios.

For example, a pastry recipe uses 3 cups of flour for every 6 servings. Suppose you have 4 cups of flour. Dividing 6 by 3 finds the number of servings you can make per cup, or the **unit rate**. Then, multiply the unit rate by 4 to find that you can make **8** servings.

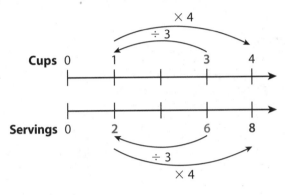

Your student will be learning how to solve problems like the one below.

> City A receives 21 inches of snow in 12 hours. City B receives 27 inches of snow in 15 hours. Which city has a heavier snowfall rate?

➤ **ONE WAY** to find and compare rates is to use tables of equivalent ratios.

Divide to find the **unit rate** for inches of snow in 1 hour for each city.

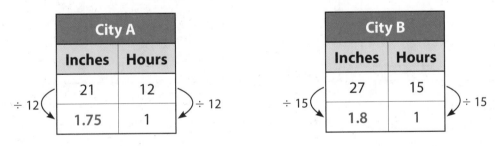

City A	
Inches	**Hours**
21	12
1.75	1

$\div 12$ $\div 12$

City B	
Inches	**Hours**
27	15
1.8	1

$\div 15$ $\div 15$

➤ **ANOTHER WAY** is to use equations to find the unit rates.

Inches per hour for City A

inches → $\frac{21}{12}$ = 21 ÷ 12 = **1.75**
hours →

Inches per hour for City B

inches → $\frac{27}{15}$ = 27 ÷ 15 = **1.8**
hours →

Since 1.8 > 1.75, City B receives more snow per hour than City A.

Using either method, City B has the heavier snowfall rate.

 Use the next page to start a conversation about unit rates.

Activity Exploring Unit Rates

➤ **Do this activity together to explore patterns in unit rates.**

Each table below represents a ratio and two unit rates.

What patterns do you notice in each table?

The peregrine falcon, one of the world's fastest birds, has been known to fly at a speed of 4 miles per minute.

TABLE 1

Miles	Minutes
8	2
4	1
1	$\frac{1}{4}$

TABLE 2

Pounds	Dollars
4	2
2	1
1	$\frac{1}{2}$

TABLE 3

Inches	Hours
5	2
$\frac{5}{2}$	1
1	$\frac{2}{5}$

 What patterns do you notice between all three tables?

Explore Unit Rates

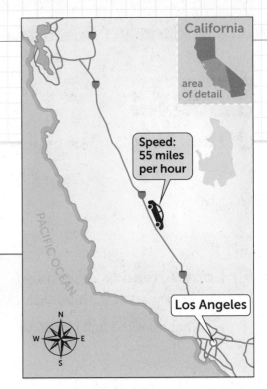

California

area of detail

Speed: 55 miles per hour

PACIFIC OCEAN

Los Angeles

N W E S

Previously, you learned about rates. In this lesson, you will learn how to use rates and unit rates to solve problems.

➤ **Use what you know to try to solve the problem below.**

Chloe is driving on the freeway. She is 200 miles from Los Angeles. She drives at a constant speed of 55 miles per hour. Can Chloe get to Los Angeles in less than $3\frac{1}{2}$ hours?

TRY IT

Math Toolkit double number lines, grid paper

◎ **Learning Targets** SMP 1, SMP 2, SMP 3, SMP 4, SMP 5, SMP 6, SMP 8
• Solve unit rate problems including those involving unit pricing and constant speed.
• Use ratio reasoning to convert measurement units; manipulate and transform units appropriately when multiplying or dividing quantities.

CONNECT IT

1 Look Back Can Chloe get to Los Angeles in less than $3\frac{1}{2}$ hours? Explain.

2 Look Ahead Chloe's constant speed of **55 miles per hour** is a **rate**. The numerical part of the rate, **55**, is called the **unit rate**.

a. What does the unit rate 55 tell you in this situation?

b. On another trip, Chloe drives at a constant speed of 60 miles per hour. What is Chloe's unit rate? What does the unit rate tell you?

c. The table shows that Chloe travels 240 miles in 4 hours. Complete the equivalent ratios in the first two columns. Where do you see Chloe's unit rate?

d. The third column of the table shows the quotient of the numbers in each equivalent ratio. Complete the third column. What do you notice?

Miles, a	Hours, b	$\frac{a}{b} = a \div b$
	1	
	2	
180		
240	4	$\frac{240}{4} = 240 \div 4 = 60$

3 Reflect How could you use unit rates to help you identify equivalent ratios?

Prepare for Using Unit Rates to Solve Problems

1 Think about what you know about rates. Fill in each box. Use words, numbers, and pictures. Show as many ideas as you can.

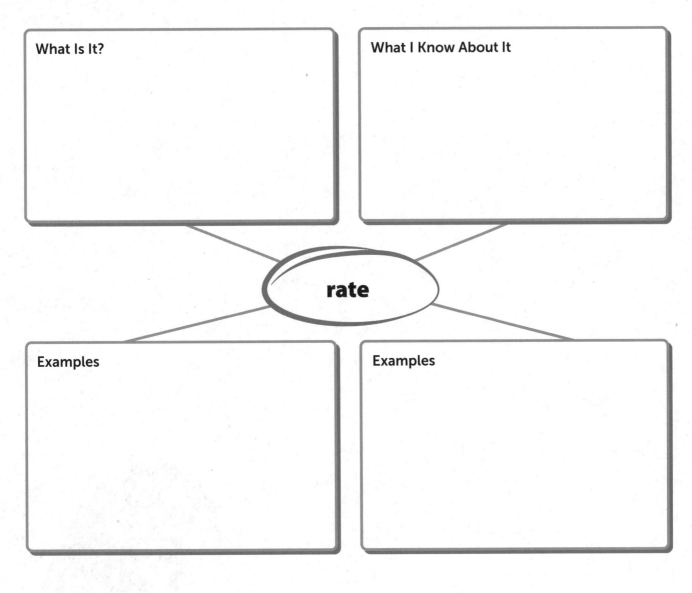

What Is It?	What I Know About It

rate

Examples	Examples

2 What two rates can you write for the ratios shown by the double number line? What do they tell you?

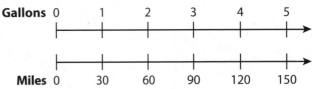

| **Gallons** | 0 | 1 | 2 | 3 | 4 | 5 |

| **Miles** | 0 | 30 | 60 | 90 | 120 | 150 |

3 Deon feeds his Great Dane 62 cups of dog food per week. He has a new bag with 160 cups of dog food.

a. Deon will pick up more dog food at the pet store in $2\frac{1}{2}$ weeks. Will the new bag of food last until then? Show your work.

SOLUTION _____

b. Check your answer to problem 3a. Show your work.

Develop Using Unit Rates to Find Equivalent Ratios

➤ **Read and try to solve the problem below.**

Ashwini jogs on the track at her school. She uses a watch to track her progress. At this rate, how long will it take her to jog 16 laps?

15 minutes
6 laps

TRY IT

 Math Toolkit double number lines, grid paper

DISCUSS IT

Ask: How does your model show Ashwini's rate?

Share: My model shows Ashwini's rate . . .

➤ **Explore different ways to understand how to use a unit rate to find equivalent ratios.**

Ashwini jogs on the track at her school. She uses a watch to track her progress. It takes her 15 minutes to jog 6 laps. At this rate, how long will it take her to jog 16 laps?

Model It

You can use a table of equivalent ratios to solve the problem.

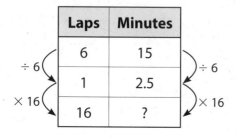

Laps	Minutes
6	15
1	2.5
16	?

÷ 6   ÷ 6
× 16   × 16

Model It

You can find the unit rate and then use it to find equivalent ratios.

Divide the numbers in the ratio 15 : 6 to find the unit rate for minutes per lap.

$$\text{minutes} \rightarrow \frac{15}{6} = \frac{5}{2} = 2.5 \leftarrow \text{laps}$$

Multiply the **number of laps** by the **unit rate** for minutes per lap.

Laps	Minutes
6	15
16	?

× 2.5

➤ **Use the problem from the previous page to help you understand how to use a unit rate to find equivalent ratios.**

1 Look at the table in the first **Model It**. Where do you see the unit rate for the ratio of minutes to laps? Describe how the unit rate is found.

2 Look at the second **Model It**. Why can you use a fraction to show the unit rate for the ratio of minutes to laps?

3 Write a multiplication expression that uses the unit rate to find the missing value of the equivalent ratio. How long will it take Ashwini to jog 16 laps?

4 How long will it take Ashwini to jog 22 laps? Explain how you can use the unit rate to find the total number of minutes it takes Ashwini to run any number of laps.

5 How does a unit rate relate the two quantities in a ratio? How can a unit rate help you solve problems involving equivalent ratios?

6 **Reflect** Think about all the models and strategies you have discussed today. Describe how one of them helped you better understand how to use a unit rate to find equivalent ratios.

Apply It

➤ **Use what you learned to solve these problems.**

WEEKLY SPECIAL
BBQ Chicken **4 lb for $5.00**

7 Alejandro is buying chicken for a barbecue. At the rate shown in the Weekly Special, what does 7 lb of chicken cost? Show your work.

SOLUTION _____

8 Look at problem 7. How much chicken can Alejandro buy for $8? Show your work.

SOLUTION _____

9 Anica volunteers to fold T-shirts for the runners at a marathon. She folds 8 T-shirts every 6 minutes. At this rate, how many T-shirts does Anica fold in 45 minutes? Show your work.

SOLUTION _____

Practice Using Unit Rates to Find Equivalent Ratios

➤ **Study the Example showing how to use a unit rate to find an equivalent ratio. Then solve problems 1–5.**

Example

Winona and Reth are adding money to their subway fare cards. Winona pays $26 for 8 rides. Each ride costs the same amount. How much does Reth pay for 7 rides?

The ratio of dollars to rides is 26 : 8. Divide to find the **unit rate**.

$$\text{dollars} \rightarrow \frac{26}{8} = \frac{13}{4} = 3.25 \leftarrow \text{rides}$$

The rate is $3.25 per ride.

Multiply the **number of rides** by the **unit rate** to find the missing value of the equivalent ratio.

$7 \times 3.25 = 22.75$

Reth pays $22.75 for 7 rides.

Dollars	Rides
26	8
?	7

× 3.25

---

1 Look at the problem in the Example. Rolando also adds money to his subway fare card. How much does Rolando pay for 20 rides? Show your work.

SOLUTION _____

2 Look at the problem in the Example. Vinh adds $39 to his subway fare card. How many rides does Vinh buy? Explain how you can use the unit rate for rides per dollar to find the answer.

3 Angela starts a blog about wheelchair basketball. In the first 4 days, the blog gets 22 new subscribers. At this rate, how many new subscribers can Angela expect in 30 days? Show your work.

SOLUTION _____

4 Ximena is typing a 2,500-word essay. In 9 minutes she types 396 words. At this rate, can Ximena type the essay in an hour? Explain.

5 Andrew saves the same amount of money each week. The table shows the amount he saves in different numbers of weeks. How much money does Andrew save in 40 weeks? Show your work.

Weeks	Dollars
7	224
9	288
11	352

SOLUTION _____

Develop Using Unit Rates to Compare Ratios

Comparing Dish Soap Brands

Brand **A**	Brand **B**
32 fl oz $2.56	48 fl oz $4.80

➤ **Read and try to solve the problem below.**

Antonio uses dish soap in his recipe for giant bubbles. He compares the prices of two brands of dish soap. Which brand is the better buy?

TRY IT

Math Toolkit double number lines, grid paper

DISCUSS IT

Ask: What was the first thing you did to compare the prices of the brands?

Share: First I . . .

➤ **Explore different ways to use unit rates to compare ratios.**

Antonio uses dish soap in his recipe for giant bubbles. He compares the prices of two brands of dish soap. Which brand is the better buy?

Dish Soap	Fluid Ounces	Price
Brand A	32	$2.56
Brand B	48	$4.80

Model It

You can find the better buy by comparing the unit rates for dollars per fluid ounce.

Use a table to find the price per fluid ounce for each brand.

Brand A ÷ 32

Price ($)	2.56	0.08
Fluid Ounces	32	1

÷ 32

Brand B ÷ 48

Price ($)	4.80	0.10
Fluid Ounces	48	1

÷ 48

A price for 1 unit, such as 1 fl oz, is called a unit price.

The unit price for Brand A is $**0.08** per fluid ounce.

The unit price for Brand B is $**0.10** per fluid ounce.

Model It

You can find the better buy by comparing the unit rates for fluid ounces per dollar.

Brand A ÷ 2.56

Fluid Ounces	32	12.5
Price ($)	2.56	1

÷ 2.56

Brand B ÷ 4.80

Fluid Ounces	48	10
Price ($)	4.80	1

÷ 4.80

For Brand A, you get **12.5** fluid ounces per dollar.

For Brand B, you get **10** fluid ounces per dollar.

➤ **Use the problem from the previous page to help you understand how to use rates and unit rates to compare ratios.**

1 Look at the first **Model It**. Why do you divide by 32 to find the unit price for Brand A and divide by 48 to find the unit price for Brand B?

2 How can you use the unit prices to find which brand is the better buy?

3 Look at the second **Model It**. How can you use the unit rates for fluid ounces per dollar to find which brand is the better buy?

4 How are the strategies in the two **Model Its** similar? How are they different?

5 Why can you compare two ratios by comparing their unit rates?

6 **Reflect** Think about all the models and strategies you have discussed today. Describe how one of them helped you better understand how to solve the **Try It** problem.

Apply It

➤ **Use what you learned to solve these problems.**

7 The table shows the top running speeds for a giraffe and a zebra. Which animal can run faster? Show your work.

Animal	Meters	Seconds
Giraffe	280	20
Zebra	204	12

SOLUTION _____

8 Four friends make chili for a chili cook-off. Each of them uses a different amount of hot sauce to make the chili spicy. Which ratio of hot sauce to chili makes the spiciest chili?

A 15 tsp hot sauce for 6 pt of chili

B 18 tsp hot sauce for 15 pt of chili

C 12 tsp hot sauce for 8 pt chili

D 24 tsp hot sauce for 10 pt chili

9 DeAndre's laptop downloads a 9 GB (gigabyte) file in 15 seconds. It takes Cheryl's laptop 80 seconds to download a 32 GB file. Whose laptop downloads files at a faster rate? Show your work.

DeAndre's laptop	Cheryl's laptop
9 GB 15 seconds	32 GB 80 seconds

SOLUTION _____

Practice Using Unit Rates to Compare Ratios

➤ **Study the Example showing how to use unit rates to compare ratios. Then solve problems 1–5.**

Example

Two teams of students are painting fences at Lakeside Middle School. The Blue Team paints 15 square meters in 6 hours. The Red Team paints 8 square meters in 4 hours. Which team paints faster?

You can compare the unit rates for square meters painted per hour.

Blue Team

square meters ⟶ $\dfrac{15}{6} = 2.5$
hours ⟶

Red Team

square meters ⟶ $\dfrac{8}{4} = 2$
hours ⟶

The team with the greater unit rate paints more square meters per hour.

$2.5 > 2$

The Blue Team paints faster.

---

1 Show how to solve the problem in the Example by comparing the unit rates for hours per square meter.

2 A news site offers a subscription that costs $28.50 for 6 months. What is the unit price per month? Show your work.

SOLUTION _____

3 Khalid wants to buy a long sandwich for a party. Store A sells a 5-foot sandwich for $42.50. Store B sells a 6-foot sandwich for $49.50. Which store has the better buy? Show your work.

Store A

Store B

SOLUTION _____

4 A store sells two brands of hand lotion. Brand X costs $3.25 for 5 fluid ounces. Brand Y costs $6 for 8 fluid ounces. How much less per fluid ounce does Brand X cost than Brand Y? Show your work.

SOLUTION _____

5 Three friends make lemonade with different recipes. The table shows the ratio of lemon juice to the total amount of lemonade. Which friend makes lemonade with the strongest lemon flavor? Explain how to use unit rates to decide.

Name	Lemon Juice (cups)	Lemonade (cups)
Erin	2	12
Damita	4	16
Jayden	3	15

Develop Using Unit Rates to Convert Measurements

800 meters every 15 minutes

➤ **Read and try to solve the problem below.**

A band marches in the African American Day Parade in New York City. The band marches 800 meters every 15 minutes. At this rate, how many kilometers does the band march in 1 hour?

TRY IT

Math Toolkit double number lines, grid paper, rulers

DISCUSS IT

Ask: How do you know your answer is reasonable?

Share: My answer makes sense because . . .

➤ **Explore different ways to convert between units of measure.**

A band marches in the African American Day Parade in New York City. The band marches 800 meters every 15 minutes. At this rate, how many kilometers does the band march in 1 hour?

Model It

You can use a table of equivalent ratios to convert between units of measure.

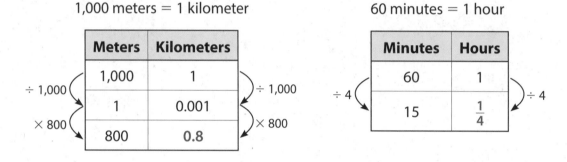

1,000 meters = 1 kilometer

Meters	Kilometers
1,000	1
1	0.001
800	0.8

÷ 1,000   ÷ 1,000
× 800   × 800

60 minutes = 1 hour

Minutes	Hours
60	1
15	$\frac{1}{4}$

÷ 4   ÷ 4

The band marches **0.8** kilometers in $\frac{1}{4}$ hour. Multiply by 4 to find the number of kilometers the band marches in 1 hour.

    4 × 0.8

Model It

You can multiply by a unit rate to convert between units of measure.

Write the rate for kilometers per meter.

    1 kilometer = 1,000 meters

    $\frac{1}{1,000}$ kilometer per meter

Find the number of meters the band marches in 1 hour.

    4 × 800 = 3,200

To convert 3,200 meters to kilometers, multiply by the unit rate.

    meters   kilometers per meter
      ↓   ↓
    3,200 × $\frac{1}{1,000}$

➤ **Use the problem from the previous page to help you understand how to convert between units of measure.**

1 Look at the first **Model It**. How are the relationships 1,000 meters = 1 kilometer and 60 minutes = 1 hour similar to rates?

2 Look at the second **Model It**. The relationship 1 kilometer = 1,000 meters is used to write the rate $\frac{1}{1,000}$ kilometer per meter. How is this rate shown by a row of the table of meters and kilometers in the first **Model It**?

3 There are two rates that relate meters and kilometers. In the second **Model It**, why is $\frac{1}{1,000}$ the unit rate that is used to convert 3,200 meters to kilometers?

4 How many kilometers does the band march in 1 hour?

5 How is converting between measurements similar to finding equivalent ratios?

6 **Reflect** Think about all the models and strategies you have discussed today. Describe how one of them helped you better understand how to convert between units of measure.

LESSON 16 Use Unit Rates to Solve Problems   **377**

Apply It

➤ **Use what you learned to solve these problems.**

7 The unit of money in England is the pound (£). When Anne visits England, £10 equals $13. She sees a bike rental that costs £3 per hour. Anne wants to spend less than $20. Can Anne rent the bike for 5 hours? Explain.

8 A can contains 4 cups of pineapple juice. The can of juice costs $2.56. What is the unit price in dollars per fluid ounce?

   A $12.50 per fluid ounce

   B $1.56 per fluid ounce

   C $0.64 per fluid ounce

   D $0.08 per fluid ounce

9 A model train takes 10 seconds to travel along a section of track that is 5 yards long. At this rate, how many feet does the model train travel every minute? Show your work.

SOLUTION _____

Practice Using Unit Rates to Convert Measurements

➤ **Study the Example showing how to solve a measurement conversion problem. Then solve problems 1–4.**

Example

The table shows the prices of two brands of flour. Which brand is the better buy?

Convert the weight of Brand A to ounces.

  1 pound = 16 ounces

The rate is 16 ounces per pound.

pounds   ounces per pound

  ↓   ↓

  $5 \times 16 = 80$

Brand A weighs **80** ounces.

Find the unit prices in dollars per ounce, as shown in the tables.

Brand A costs **$0.03** per ounce.

Brand B costs **$0.04** per ounce.

Brand A is the better buy.

Flour	Weight	Price
Brand A	5 pounds	$2.40
Brand B	48 ounces	$1.92

Brand A   ÷ 80

Dollars	2.40	0.03
Ounces	80	1

Brand B   ÷ 48

Dollars	1.92	0.04
Ounces	48	1

1 Show how you can solve the problem in the Example by comparing the unit prices in dollars per pound.

Vocabulary

convert
to write an equivalent measurement using a different unit.

2 Vivian is getting a pet snake. She is choosing between the ball python and the corn snake. Vivian wants the shorter snake. Which snake should she get? Show your work. (12 in. = 1 ft)

Ball python	Corn snake
$4\frac{1}{2}$ ft long	45 in. long

SOLUTION _____

3 Kenji walks 44 feet in 10 seconds. At this rate, how many miles does Kenji walk in an hour? Show your work. (1 mile = 5,280 feet)

SOLUTION _____

4 A 2-liter bottle is full of water. The bottle leaks 80 milliliters of water every 3 minutes. Will the bottle be empty in 1 hour? Explain why or why not. (1 liter = 1,000 milliliters)

Refine Using Unit Rates to Solve Problems

➤ **Complete the Example below. Then solve problems 1–9.**

Example

An elm tree is 20 feet tall. A poplar tree is 6.4 meters tall. Which tree is taller?

Look at how you could use a rate to convert measurement units.

Convert 6.4 meters to feet.

For every 100 meters there are about 328 feet.

The rate is 3.28 feet per meter. The unit rate is 3.28.

meters   feet per meter

$6.4 \times 3.28 = 20.992$

The height of the poplar tree is about 21 feet.

SOLUTION _____

CONSIDER THIS . . .
The relationship you use to convert between the customary unit *feet* and the metric unit *meters* is an approximation: 100 meters is about 328 feet.

PAIR/SHARE
How would the steps of the solution be different if you compared the heights in meters?

Apply It

1 Lucía and Quinn train for a bike race. Lucía bikes 46 miles in 240 minutes. Quinn bikes 51 miles in 5 hours. Who bikes at a faster rate? Show your work.

CONSIDER THIS . . .
You can compare the rates in miles per hour, hours per mile, miles per minute, or minutes per mile.

PAIR/SHARE
Does knowing which person bikes farther give you enough information to decide who bikes faster? Why or why not?

SOLUTION _____

2 Elisa packs her suitcase before a trip. The suitcase weighs 49 pounds. The airline only allows suitcases that weigh up to 23 kilograms. Can Elisa take the suitcase on the plane? Show your work. (For every 10 kilograms there are about 22 pounds.)

CONSIDER THIS...
What comparison do you need to make to solve this problem?

SOLUTION _____

PAIR/SHARE
How could you solve the problem a different way?

3 Issay works at a restaurant. Today, it takes him 16 minutes to fold 40 napkins. He plans to fold napkins for 30 minutes tomorrow. If he works at the same rate, how many napkins will he fold tomorrow?

CONSIDER THIS...
Do you expect the answer to be less than 40 or greater than 40?

A 12

B 54

C 75

D 100

Destiny chose C as the correct answer. How might she have gotten that answer?

PAIR/SHARE
How did you decide which strategy or model to use to solve this problem?

4 A desktop aquarium can hold 5 gallons of water. Desiderio fills it at a rate of 40 fluid ounces per minute. How long does it take him to fill the aquarium? Show your work. (1 gallon = 128 fluid ounces)

SOLUTION _____

5 Glen is asked to convert 21 feet to yards. He knows that 3 feet = 1 yard. His work is shown. Explain Glen's error and show how to use a rate to find the correct solution.

The rate is 3 feet per yard.

21 • 3 = 63

So, the length in yards is 63 yards.

6 A mouse runs 24 meters in 8 seconds. Tell whether each statement is *True* or *False*.

	True	False
a. At this rate, the mouse runs 30 meters in 14 seconds.	○	○
b. The mouse runs faster than a mouse who runs 26 meters in 13 seconds.	○	○
c. At this rate, it takes the mouse 5 seconds to run 15 meters.	○	○
d. The mouse runs at a rate of $\frac{1}{3}$ second per meter.	○	○

7 Soledad buys 5 ounces of frozen yogurt for $2.25. What is the unit price of the frozen yogurt in dollars per ounce?

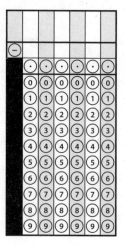

8 Which rate is faster, 2 feet per second or 2 seconds per foot, or are both rates the same? Explain.

9 **Math Journal** At a county fair, a strip of 20 ride tickets costs $13. The manager thinks they should also sell a strip of 8 ride tickets. Describe how the manager can use a unit rate to decide on a fair price for the strip of 8 tickets.

✓ End of Lesson Checklist

☐ **INTERACTIVE GLOSSARY** Find the entry for *unit rate*. Give an example of a unit rate and tell how the unit rate is related to a ratio.

☐ **SELF CHECK** Go back to the Unit 4 Opener and see what you can check off.

Dear Family,

This week your student is exploring percents. A **percent** is a rate that shows an amount per 100. You can represent a percent as a fraction or a decimal.

Percents are often written with the percent symbol, %. This model shows 10% because 10 out of 100 equal parts are shaded. This is the same as saying $\frac{10}{100}$, or $\frac{1}{10}$, of the grid is shaded. The decimal 0.1 also represents 10%.

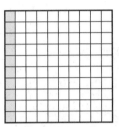

This model shows 25% because 25 out of 100 equal parts are shaded. This is the same as saying $\frac{25}{100}$, or $\frac{1}{4}$, of the grid is shaded. The decimal 0.25 also represents 25%.

Your student will be modeling percents like the one below.

> During a field trip to the science museum, 50% of 200 students decide to see the butterfly exhibit.

➤ **ONE WAY** to model a percent is to use a bar model.

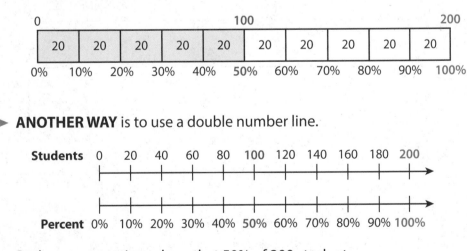

➤ **ANOTHER WAY** is to use a double number line.

Both representations show that 50% of 200 students, or 100 students, decide to see the butterfly exhibit.

Use the next page to start a conversation about percents.

Activity Exploring Percents

➤ **Do this activity together to look for patterns in percents.**

Each set shows three statements about percents. What patterns do you notice in each set?

SET 1

10% of 100 is 10.

20% of 100 is 20.

30% of 100 is 30.

SET 2

50% of 100 is 50.

50% of 200 is 100.

50% of 300 is 150.

SET 3

10% of 200 is 20.

20% of 200 is 40.

30% of 200 is 60.

 Do you notice any patterns between two of the sets?

Explore Percents

Keith has mowed $\frac{1}{2}$ of the lawn.

Model It

➤ **Complete the problems about fractions and percents.**

1 Keith and his friends mow lawns to earn money.

    a. The model represents a lawn that Keith is mowing. So far, he has mowed $\frac{1}{2}$ of the lawn. Shade the model to show how much of the lawn Keith has mowed.

    b. You can write $\frac{1}{2}$ as an equivalent fraction with different denominators. Write numerators to show three fractions that are equivalent to $\frac{1}{2}$.

$$\frac{\Box}{8} \qquad\qquad \frac{\Box}{40} \qquad\qquad \frac{\Box}{100}$$

2 In problem 1b, you wrote the fraction of the lawn Keith has mowed as a number of equal parts out of 100. You can use a **percent** to represent an amount *per 100*. You can think of a percent as a rate, with the whole divided into 100 equal parts.

    a. The fraction $\frac{50}{100}$ means 50 parts out of 100 equal parts, or 50 parts per 100 parts.

    The fraction $\frac{50}{100}$ represents _____ percent.

    b. When you write a percent, you can use the percent symbol (%) in place of the word *percent*. Look back at problem 1. Complete this sentence that uses a percent to describe how much of the lawn Keith has mowed so far.

    Keith has mowed _____ % of the lawn.

> ## DISCUSS IT
>
> *Ask:* How would you change your model in problem 1 to show that Keith has mowed $\frac{50}{100}$ of the lawn?
>
> *Share:* I think $\frac{50}{100}$ and $\frac{1}{2}$ both represent 50% because . . .

 Learning Targets   SMP 2, SMP 3, SMP 7

Use ratio and rate reasoning to solve real-world mathematical problems.
• Find a percent of a quantity as a rate per 100; solve problems involving finding the whole, given a part and the percent.

Model It

➤ **Complete the problems about percents.**

3 You can use a hundredths grid to show a percent.

a. Esteban mows 50% of a lawn.
Shade the model to show 50%.

b. Emma mows 10% of a lawn.
Shade the model to show 10%.

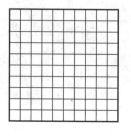

DISCUSS IT

Ask: What is a different way you can shade the model in problem 3b to show 10%?

Share: I think I can represent 10% with the decimal 0.1 because . . .

c. Does this model also represent the percent of the lawn Emma has mowed? Explain how you know.

4 **Reflect** How is using a model to show a percent similar to using a model to show a fraction? Use either 50% or 10% as an example in your explanation.

©Curriculum Associates, LLC Copying is not permitted.

Name:

Prepare for Understanding Percents

1 Think about what you know about ratios, rates, and the word *per*. Fill in each box.
Use words, numbers, and pictures. Show as many ideas as you can.

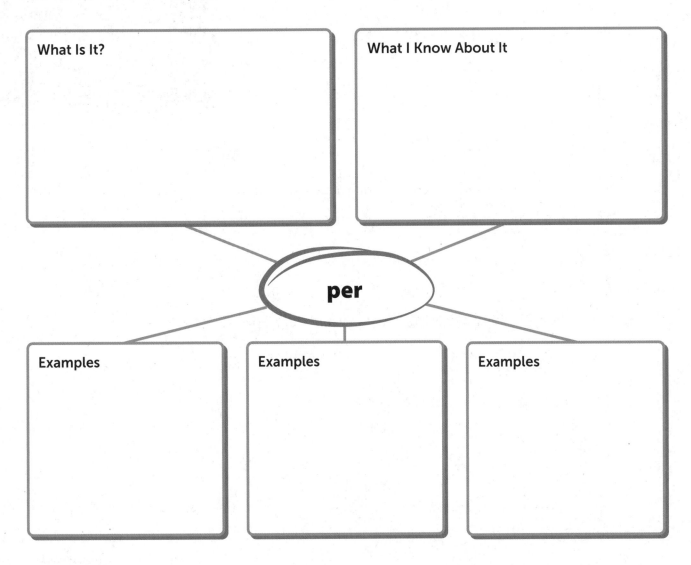

What Is It?

What I Know About It

per

Examples

Examples

Examples

2 Tara makes two batches of purple food coloring.
The table shows the number of drops of red and blue
food coloring she uses for each batch. Do the two
batches use the same number of drops of red per
drop of blue? Explain.

Batch	Drops of Red	Drops of Blue
Batch 1	100	20
Batch 2	75	15

➤ **Complete problems 3 and 4.**

3 Kadeem made a rectangular pan of enchiladas for his family. So far, they have eaten $\frac{1}{5}$ of the enchiladas.

a. Shade the model to show $\frac{1}{5}$ of the pan.

b. You can write $\frac{1}{5}$ as an equivalent fraction with different denominators.

Write numerators to show three fractions that are equivalent to $\frac{1}{5}$.

$\dfrac{\square}{10}$ $\qquad$ $\dfrac{\square}{40}$ $\qquad$ $\dfrac{\square}{100}$

4 **a.** The fraction $\frac{20}{100}$ means 20 out of 100 equal parts, or 20 parts per 100 parts.

The fraction $\frac{20}{100}$ represents _____ percent.

b. Shade the hundredths grid to show 20%.

c. Why does your model in problem 3a represent the same percent as your model in problem 4b?

Vocabulary

percent

per 100. A percent is a rate per 100. A percent can be written using the percent symbol (%) and represented as a fraction or a decimal. For example, 15% can be represented as $\frac{15}{100}$ or as 0.15.

d. Kadeem's family has eaten _____ % of the enchiladas.

> **?** **UNDERSTAND:** What do percents mean and how are they related to fractions?

Develop Understanding of Percents

Model It: Bar Models

 Try these two problems involving percents.

1 A group of students is raising money for a trip to Washington, D.C. They use a model that looks like a thermometer to track their progress toward their goal.

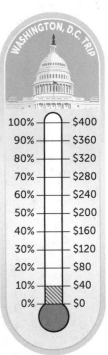

a. The line at 100% represents the students' goal. What amount of money are the students trying to raise?

b. The shading between 0% and 10% shows that the students have reached 10% of their goal. How much money have the students raised so far?

c. After 1 week, the students reach 50% of their goal. Shade the model to show how much money the students have raised.

d. Use your model to complete this sentence.

50% of $_____ is $_____ .

2 Another group of students is also raising $400 for the trip.

a. On Monday, the students reach 25% of their goal. Label and shade the bar model to show their progress.

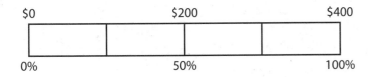

b. How much money have the students raised so far? Justify your answer.

> **DISCUSS IT**
>
> *Ask:* How are the two models on this page alike? How are they different?
>
> *Share:* The bar model is divided into four parts because . . .

c. What fraction of their goal have the students reached?

Model It: Double Number Lines

➤ **Try this problem using a double number line to show percents.**

U.S. Capitol

Lincoln Memorial

3 A total of 300 students go to Washington, D.C.

   a. Label the tick marks on the double number line.

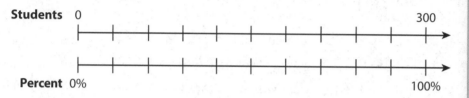

Students 0   300

Percent 0%   100%

   b. Ayana finds that 50% of the students visit the Capitol.

   What number of students lines up with 50%?

   This means _____ % of 300 students is _____ students.

   c. Ayana finds that 0.1 of the students visit the Lincoln Memorial. Do more students visit the Capitol or the Lincoln Memorial? How do you know?

> **DISCUSS IT**
>
> **Ask:** How could you use a double number line to find 25% of 300?
>
> **Share:** In this situation, 100% represents . . .

CONNECT IT

➤ **Complete the problems below.**

4 How do bar models and double number lines show percents in a similar way?

5 Heidi is driving 200 miles. She has finished 80% of the drive. Draw a model to show 80% of Heidi's drive.

Practice Modeling Percents

➤ **Study how the Example shows modeling a percent. Then solve problems 1–5.**

Example

The drama club hopes to sell 600 tickets for a school play. So far, they have sold 20% of the tickets. Use a model to show 20% of 600.

You can use a bar model.

The whole is **600**. It lines up with **100%**.

Divide the whole into 10 equal parts of 60. Each part is 10%. Shade two parts to show **20%**.

0		120								600
60	60	60	60	60	60	60	60	60	60	

0%   10%   20%   30%   40%   50%   60%   70%   80%   90%   100%

1 **a.** What amount lines up with 20% in the Example? What does this mean?

b. What fraction of the tickets have students sold so far? Explain how you know.

2 Tomás is reading a 100-page book. He has read 40% of the book so far.

    a. Label and shade the model to show 40% of 100.

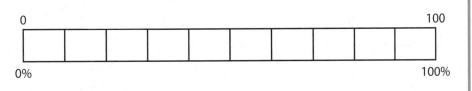

0   100

0%   100%

b. How many pages has Tomás read? What fraction of the pages has he read?

> ### Vocabulary
>
> **percent (%)**
>
> *per 100*. A percent is a rate per 100. A percent can be written using the percent symbol (%) and represented as a fraction or decimal. For example, 15% can be represented as $\frac{15}{100}$ or 0.15.

3 Mr. Aba's class is making 200 origami cranes for an art project. So far, they have made $\frac{3}{4}$ of the cranes.

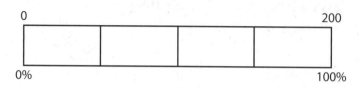

a. Label and shade the bar model to show their progress.

```
0                                    200
┌──────┬──────┬──────┬──────┐
│      │      │      │      │
└──────┴──────┴──────┴──────┘
0%                                  100%
```

b. What percent of the cranes have they made? How many have they made? Explain.

4 On Monday, 30% of the 900 students at Maple Middle School walk to school.

a. Label the tick marks on the double number line.

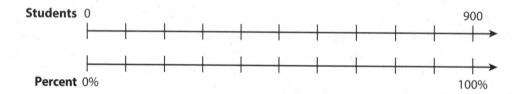

Students 0   900

Percent 0%   100%

b. How many students walk to school on Monday? What fraction of the 900 students walk to school?

5 Eduardo's juice box contains 500 mL of juice. The juice box label says *Contains 10% real fruit juice*. How many mL of real fruit juice are in Eduardo's juice box? Draw a model to show your work.

SOLUTION _____

Refine Ideas About Percents

Apply It

➤ **Complete problems 1–5.**

1 **Interpret** Some students have a goal of collecting 200 leaves for a science project. What does 0% of the goal mean in this situation? What does 100% mean?

2 **Analyze** Maya is helping a gardener plant 300 bulbs. They plant 20% of the bulbs on Monday and 30% of the bulbs on Tuesday. Maya says this means they have planted 50 bulbs so far. Label and shade the model. Then use your model to explain why Maya's statement is not reasonable.

0   300
```
┌─────────────────────────────────────────────────────────────┐
│                                                               │
└─────────────────────────────────────────────────────────────┘
```
0%   100%

3 **Apply** Elizabeth buys a jar of 100 dog treats. In one month, she gives her dog 80 of the treats. What percent is this? What fraction is this? Draw a model to support your answers.

4 Ms. Duda's class is hanging 500 red lanterns around the school for Lunar New Year. Before lunch, the class hangs 100 of the lanterns.

PART A Draw a model to show what percent of 500 lanterns the class hangs before lunch.

PART B How many lanterns are left to hang? What percent of the lanterns are left to hang? Use your model in Part A to explain your answer.

5 **Math Journal** Choose one of the following percents: 25%, 40%, or 60%. Use a model and words to explain what that percent means. Write at least two fractions that represent your percent.

✓ **End of Lesson Checklist**

☐ **INTERACTIVE GLOSSARY** Write a new entry for *symbol*. Give an example of using the percent symbol and show what the percent symbol means.

Dear Family,

This week your student is learning how to use percents to solve problems.

Similar strategies can be used to solve two types of problems:

• A shirt costs $20 and is marked 40% off. How much money will you save?

• A shirt is on sale for 40% off. You will save $8. What was the original price?

Your student will be learning to solve problems like the one below.

> At an aquarium, 30% of the fish are freshwater fish. There are
> 120 freshwater fish. How many fish are at the aquarium?

➤ **ONE WAY** to find a whole amount when you know a part and the percent is to use a double number line.

You know that 120 is 30% of the whole. First, **divide by 3** to find 10%. Then, **multiply by 10** to find 100%.

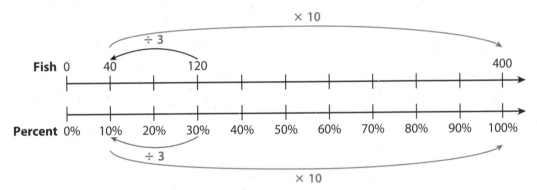

➤ **ANOTHER WAY** is to make a table of equivalent ratios.

$$\div 3 \quad \times 10$$

Fish	120	40	400
Percent (%)	30	10	100

$$\div 3 \quad \times 10$$

Using either method, there are 400 fish at the aquarium.

Use the next page to start a conversation about percents.

Activity Thinking About Percents Around You

➤ **Do this activity together to investigate percents in the real world.**

Do you ever read the sports page or listen to the news and wonder how they figure out the standings for the teams? They use percents!

Percents can help you compare the teams, especially if they have not played the same number of games.

SPORTS NEWS
BASEBALL STANDINGS

	W	L	PCT
Clippers	11	9	.550
Generals	13	12	.520
Sox	10	10	.500

Number of games won

Number of games lost

Percent of games won

? Where else do you see percents in the world around you?

Explore Percent Problems

Wins

Carolina	Aniyah
19 out of 25 games	**17** out of 20 games

Previously, you learned about representing percents. In this lesson, you will learn about solving problems with percents.

➤ **Use what you know to try to solve the problem below.**

Carolina and Aniyah are playing in an Oware tournament. Who has the better winning record so far?

TRY IT

Math Toolkit double number lines, grid paper, hundredths grids

DISCUSS IT

Ask: How did you decide which player has the better winning record?

Share: At first, I thought . . .

◎ **Learning Targets**   SMP 1, SMP 2, SMP 3, SMP 4, SMP 5, SMP 6
Use ratio and rate reasoning to solve real-world and mathematical problems.
• Find a percent of a quantity as a rate per 100; solve problems involving finding the whole, given a part and the percent.

CONNECT IT

 Look Back Does Carolina or Aniyah have the better winning record? Explain how you know.

 Look Ahead Carolina, Aniyah, and their friend Keith keep track of how many Oware games they play and how many games they win during one month. They can use percents to compare their winning records.

a. Carolina wins 77 out of 100 games. What percent of her games does she win? Explain how you know.

b. Kyle wins 14 out of 20 games.

$\frac{14}{20} = \frac{\square}{100}$, so Kyle wins _____ % of his games.

c. Aniyah wins 32 out of 40 games. Complete the table of equivalent ratios.

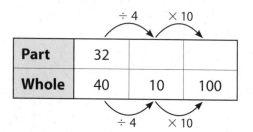

What is 32 out of 40 games expressed as a percent?

d. Who has the best winning record? Explain how you know.

③ Reflect How can writing ratios as percents help you compare the ratios?

Prepare for Using Percents to Solve Problems

1 Think about what you know about percents. Fill in each box. Use words, numbers, and pictures. Show as many ideas as you can.

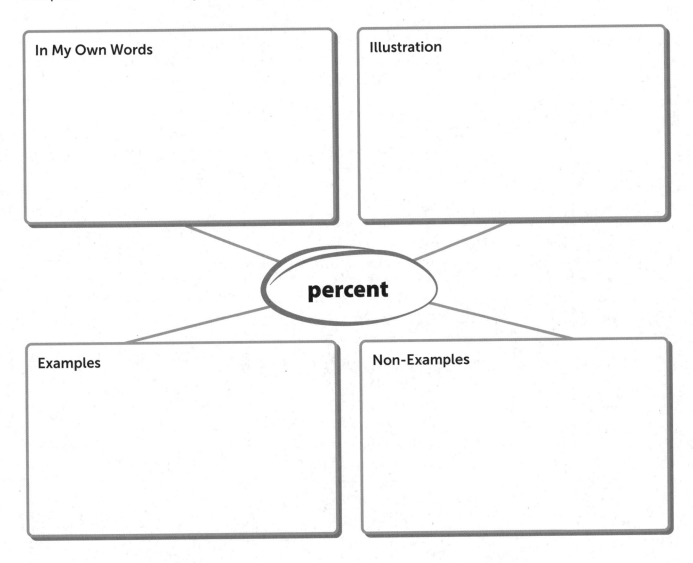

In My Own Words

Illustration

percent

Examples

Non-Examples

2 Explain how the model shows 80%.

3 In a survey, 13 out of 20 teachers respond *yes* to a proposal for a new after-school club. In the same survey, 37 out of 50 students respond *yes*.

   a. Which group is more in favor of the new after-school club, *teachers* or *students*? Show your work.

SOLUTION _____

   b. Check your answer to problem 3a. Show your work.

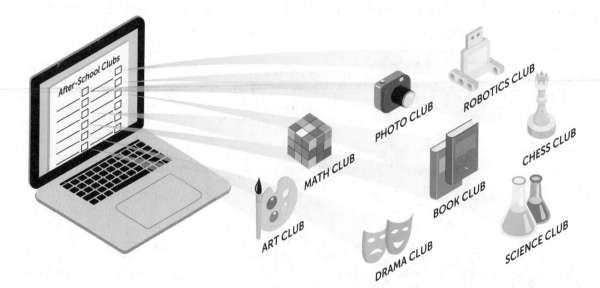

Develop Finding a Percent of a Quantity

75% of 800 students

➤ **Read and try to solve the problem below.**

At Gordon Middle School, 75% of the 800 students participate in the music program. How many students participate in the music program?

TRY IT

Math Toolkit base-ten grid paper, double number lines, fraction bars, hundredths grids

DISCUSS IT

Ask: How does your model show 75%?

Share: My model shows 75% by . . .

➤ **Explore different ways to understand finding a percent of a quantity.**

At Gordon Middle School, 75% of the 800 students participate in the music program. How many students participate in the music program?

Picture It

You can use hundredths grids to show a percent of a number.

75% means 75 out of every 100, and there are 8 hundreds in 800.

Model It

You can write a multiplication expression to find a percent of a number.

Write the percent as a fraction.

75%	of	800 students
↓	↓	↓
$\frac{75}{100}$	×	800

➤ **Use the problem from the previous page to help you understand how to find a percent of a quantity.**

1 Look at **Picture It**. Why can you use 8 hundredths grids to show the school's 800 students? How many students does each grid square represent?

2 You can also use a single hundredths grid to represent the school's 800 students. How many students does each grid square represent now? What percent of 800 students does each grid square represent? Explain.

3 How many students participate in the music program? Explain why you can use the expression 75 × 8 to find 75% of 800.

4 Look at **Model It**. How does the hundredths grid in problem 2 represent the expression $\frac{75}{100}$ × 800? Show that the expression is equivalent to 75 × 8.

5 One way to find p% of a number is to multiply the number by the percent written as the fraction $\frac{p}{100}$. Why does this give the same result as first finding 1% of the number and then multiplying by p?

6 **Reflect** Think about all the models and strategies you have discussed today. Describe how one of them helped you better understand how to solve the **Try It** problem.

Apply It

➤ **Use what you learned to solve these problems.**

7 Bruno is setting up a school garden. His budget is $400. He spends 5% of the budget on gardening tools. He spends 95% of the budget on plants. How much money does Bruno spend on each? Show your work.

SOLUTION _____

8 To pass a test in a water safety course, a student must get 80% of the questions correct. There are 90 questions on the test. How many questions must a student answer correctly to pass the test?

A 64 questions

B 72 questions

C 80 questions

D 81 questions

9 A school will have a fall festival if at least 40% of the 450 students plan to attend. How many students must plan to attend in order for the school to have the festival? Show your work.

SOLUTION _____

Practice Finding a Percent of a Quantity

➤ **Study the Example showing how to find a percent of a quantity. Then solve problems 1–5.**

Example

There are 500 students who participate in an after-school sports program. Of these students, 25% play field hockey. How many students play field hockey?

You can use a model to find 25% of 500.

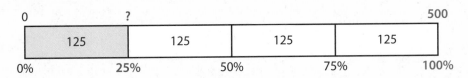

The model shows **500** divided into 4 groups of 125. Each group of 125 represents 25% of 500. This means that 25% of 500 is 125.

There are 125 students who play field hockey.

---

1 **a.** What is 25% written as a fraction?

   b. What is 25% written as a decimal?

   c. Write and evaluate a multiplication expression that represents 25% of 500.

   d. Compare your answer to problem 1c to the answer in the Example.

2 How could you use the bar model in the Example to find 75% of 500?

3 Suppose 30% of 500 students play an instrument. Describe one way to find 30% of 500.

> **Vocabulary**
>
> **percent**
>
> *per 100.* A percent is a rate per 100. A percent can be written using the percent symbol (%) and represented as a fraction or decimal.
>
> For example, 15% can be represented as $\frac{15}{100}$ or as 0.15.

4 The results of a survey show that 40% of 300 students choose recycling as the top priority for their generation.

a. How many students choose recycling? Show your work.

SOLUTION _____

b. Suppose 20% of 300 students choose recycling. How many students choose recycling? Explain how you found your answer.

5 There are 20 puzzles in Magdalena's puzzle book. Magdalena completes 55% of the puzzles. How many puzzles does Magdalena have left to complete? Show your work.

SOLUTION _____

Develop Finding the Whole

40%
of race completed

24
miles completed

➤ **Read and try to solve the problem below.**

Akira is checking his progress in a bike race. How many miles is the race?

TRY IT

Math Toolkit base-ten grid paper, double number lines, fraction bars, hundredths grids

DISCUSS IT

Ask: How is your strategy similar to mine? How is it different?

Share: My model shows . . .

➤ **Explore different ways to understand finding the whole when a part and the percent are given.**

Akira is checking his progress in a bike race. He has biked 24 mi so far, and that is 40% of the race. How many miles is the race?

Model It

You can use a double number line to find the whole when a part and the percent are given.

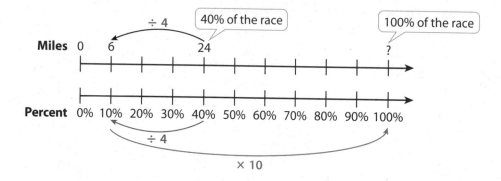

Model It

You can make a table of equivalent ratios to find the whole when a part and the percent are given.

Start with the ratio 24 : 40.

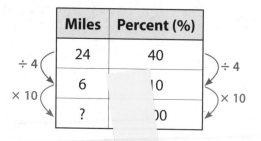

Miles	Percent (%)
24	40
6	10
?	00

÷ 4 ×10 (left), ÷ 4 ×10 (right)

➤ **Use the problem from the previous page to help you understand how to find the whole when a part and the percent are given.**

1 Look at the double number line and the table in the **Model Its**. How do both models use the relationship between 40% and 10%?

2 How many miles make up 10% of the race? Explain how you know.

3 Suppose Akira completes 100% of the race. How many miles does he bike? Explain how you know.

4 Mavis used another method. First, she divided 24 mi by 8 to get 3 mi. Then, she multiplied 3 mi by 20 to get 60 mi. What percent of the whole race is 3 mi? Why did Mavis multiply 3 mi by 20?

5 How can you find the whole when you know a part and the percent?

6 **Reflect** Think about all the models and strategies you have discussed today. Describe how one of them helped you understand finding the whole when you know the part and the percent.

Apply It

➤ **Use what you learned to solve these problems.**

7 At Shaw Middle School, 150 students take part in cleaning up the school. This is 30% of the students that attend the school. How many students attend Shaw Middle School? Show your work.

SOLUTION _____

8 At a basketball game, the home team scores 60% of the points. The home team scores 45 points. How many points are scored in all?

A 27 points

B 70 points

C 75 points

D 225 points

9 Lamont spends $120 on groceries. This is 25% of the money he earns this week. How much money does Lamont earn? Show your work.

SOLUTION _____

Practice Finding the Whole

➤ **Study the Example showing how to find the whole when a part and the percent are given. Then solve problems 1–5.**

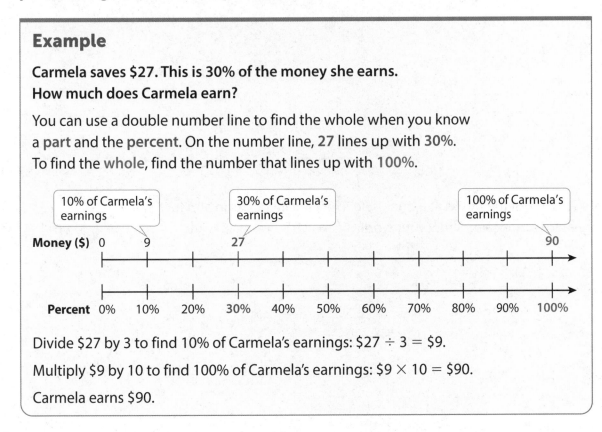

Example

Carmela saves $27. This is 30% of the money she earns. How much does Carmela earn?

You can use a double number line to find the whole when you know a **part** and the **percent**. On the number line, **27** lines up with **30%**. To find the **whole**, find the number that lines up with **100%**.

| 10% of Carmela's earnings | 30% of Carmela's earnings | 100% of Carmela's earnings |

Money ($) 0   9   27   90

Percent 0%   10% 20% 30% 40% 50% 60% 70% 80% 90% 100%

Divide $27 by 3 to find 10% of Carmela's earnings: $27 ÷ 3 = $9.

Multiply $9 by 10 to find 100% of Carmela's earnings: $9 × 10 = $90.

Carmela earns $90.

1 In the Example, why is it helpful to find 10% of Carmela's earnings before finding 100% of her earnings?

2 Aiden spends $18 on souvenirs during a school trip to New York City. This is 45% of the money he brings on the trip. How much money does Aiden bring on the trip? Show your work.

SOLUTION _____

3 Angel is running for school council president. He receives 300 votes, which is 60% of all the votes. How many students vote in the election? Explain how you found your answer.

4 Students sell 80% of the books at a book sale. They sell 48 books in all. How many books are at the book sale? Show your work.

SOLUTION _____

5 Aiyana reads 147 pages of a book. She completes 70% of the book. How many pages does Aiyana still have left to read? Show your work.

SOLUTION _____

Refine Using Percents to Solve Problems

➤ **Complete the Example below. Then solve problems 1–9.**

Example

Alison is driving from Houston to Dallas. She drives 180 mi. This is 75% of the trip. What is the distance from Houston to Dallas?

Look at how you could show your work using a table of equivalent part-to-whole ratios.

75% is 75 parts out of a whole made up of 100 equal parts.

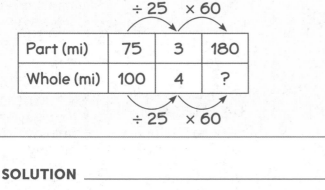

SOLUTION _____

Apply It

1 Tarik turns in his third research report. His teacher says that 20% of his reports for the year are done. How many research reports will Tarik complete during the school year? Show your work.

SOLUTION _____

2 Rani takes a 40-question test. She answers 5% of the questions incorrectly. How many questions does she answer incorrectly? Show your work.

CONSIDER THIS...
What operation do you use to find a fraction of a number?

PAIR/SHARE
What strategy did you use to solve this problem? Why?

SOLUTION _____

3 Two sixth grade classes are raising money. Mrs. Shen's class raises $120. Mr. McClary's class raises 50% of the amount Mrs. Shen's class raises. How much money do the two classes raise in all?

CONSIDER THIS...
You could use a fraction to help you solve this problem.

A $60

B $170

C $180

D $240

Jake chose A as the correct answer. How might he have gotten that answer?

PAIR/SHARE
How would you solve the problem if Mr. McClary's class raises 60% of the amount Mrs. Shen's class raises?

4 What percent of 20 is 5?

A 1%

B 4%

C 25%

D 85%

5 Three basketball players take different numbers of shots during practice. They each record the number of baskets made out of the number of shots taken. The players in order from greatest percent of baskets made to least percent of baskets made are

_____ , _____ , and _____ .

Number of Baskets Made

Diego **21** out of **60** shots
Amare **16** out of **40** shots
Paula **17** out of **50** shots

6 Rosa has a limit to the time she may play video games each day. She plays for 9 min on Monday, which is 30% of the time she can play. How many more minutes can Rosa play on Monday? Show your work.

SOLUTION _____

7 Tell whether each statement is *True* or *False*.

	True	False
a. 80% of 90 is the same as $\frac{8}{9}$ of 90.	○	○
b. 45% of 60 is 27.	○	○
c. 20% of 90 is the same as $\frac{1}{5}$ of 90.	○	○
d. 25 is 35% of 80.	○	○

8 In the seahorse tank at an aquarium, 70% of the male seahorses have eggs in their pouches. There are 20 male seahorses in the tank. Kennedy uses the expression 0.07 × 20 to find the number of male seahorses with eggs. Explain why Kennedy's expression is incorrect. How many male seahorses have eggs in their pouches?

9 **Math Journal** Choose one of the following percents: 15%, 35%, or 85%. Write and solve a word problem that uses your percent and involves finding the whole.

✔ **End of Lesson Checklist**

☐ **INTERACTIVE GLOSSARY** Find the entry for *percent*. Add two important things you learned about percents in this lesson.

☐ **SELF CHECK** Go back to the Unit 4 Opener and see what you can check off.

Study an Example Problem and Solution

➤ **Read this problem involving rates and unit rates. Then look at one student's solution to this problem on the following pages.**

Sending Fresh Food to Space

As part of a science experiment, students are sending a package of fresh fruits and vegetables to the International Space Station (ISS) to find out how long each food remains edible in space. The package can include between 0.5 kilogram and 1.2 kilograms of fresh food. Read the information about the available types of food and the shipping costs for sending cargo to the ISS.

Choose at least three types of food for the science experiment. Determine about how much it will cost each company to ship the food to the ISS, and then compare these costs.

In order to escape the gravity of Earth, a rocket needs to travel at a speed of 7 miles per second.

Space Station Grocery Delivery

Type of Fresh Food	Average Mass (grams)
apple	202
avocado	211
carrot sticks (1 package)	122
grapefruit	255
jalapeño	35
onion	226
pear	142
tomato	120

Shipping Cargo to the ISS

Company A:
About $1,275,000 for every 25 kg of cargo

Company B:
About $3,500,000 for every 50 kg of cargo

One Student's Solution

✓ Problem-Solving Checklist

- ☐ Tell what is known.
- ☐ Tell what the problem is asking.
- ☐ Show all your work.
- ☐ Show that the solution works.

First, I have to choose at least three types of fresh food for the science experiment.

I will choose four types of food: apple, grapefruit, onion, and pear.

Next, I need to check that the items I chose have a total mass of at least 0.5 kilogram and no more than 1.2 kilograms.

I will add to find the total mass in grams.

$$202 + 255 + 226 + 142 = 825$$

The items have a mass of 825 grams.

I know that 1 kilogram = **1,000** grams, so I can use the rate $\frac{1}{1,000}$ kilogram per gram to find the mass of the items in kilograms.

grams   kilograms per gram
↓   ↓
$$825 \times \frac{1}{1,000} = 0.825$$

NOTICE THAT . . .
To convert from grams to kilograms, multiply by the unit rate.

The total mass of the items is 0.825 kilogram, which is more than 0.5 kilogram and less than 1.2 kilograms.

Then, I will find the cost of sending 0.825 kilogram of fresh food to the ISS with Company A.

I can use a table of equivalent ratios.

NOTICE THAT . . .
The first row shows the cost for 25 kg, which is given in the problem. Dividing both values in this row by 25 gives the cost for each kilogram.

Company A	
Mass	**Approximate Cost**
25 kg	$1,275,000
1 kg	$51,000
0.825 kg	$42,075

÷ 25
× 0.825

÷ 25
× 0.825

It will cost about $42,075 to send 0.825 kilogram of fresh food with Company A.

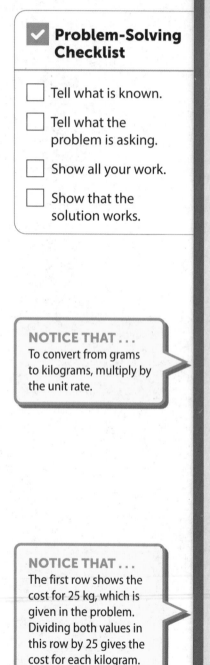

Now, I will find the cost of sending 0.825 kilogram of fresh food to the ISS with Company B.

Company B	
Mass	**Estimated Cost**
50 kg	$3,500,000
1 kg	$70,000
0.825 kg	$57,750

÷ 50
× 0.825

÷ 50
× 0.825

> **NOTICE THAT ...**
> The table shows that the rate of shipping cargo to the ISS with Company B is about $70,000 per kilogram.

It will cost about $57,750 to send 0.825 kilogram of fresh food with Company B.

So, I now have the information I need to compare the costs.

I will subtract the cost of Company A from the cost of Company B.

$57,750 - 42,075 = 15,675$

It will cost about $15,675 less to send the fresh food to the ISS with Company A than with Company B.

Finally, I can check that my answer is reasonable.

My earlier work shows that shipping 1 kilogram of cargo to the ISS costs about $51,000 with Company A and about $70,000 with Company B.

$70,000 - 51,000 = 19,000$

> **NOTICE THAT ...**
> You can subtract the unit rates to find how much less it costs to ship 1 kilogram of cargo with Company A than with Company B.

So, it costs about $19,000 less per kilogram to ship cargo with Company A than with Company B. I will multiply the mass of the fresh food by $19,000 less per kilogram.

kilograms   dollars less per kilogram
↓   ↓
$0.825 \times 19,000 = 15,675$

$0.825 \times 19,000 = 15,675$

The check shows that my answer is reasonable.

Try Another Approach

➤ **There are many ways to solve problems. Think about how you might solve the Sending Fresh Food to Space problem in a different way.**

Sending Fresh Food to Space

As part of a science experiment, students are sending a package of fresh fruits and vegetables to the International Space Station (ISS) to find out how long each food remains edible in space. The package can include between 0.5 kilogram and 1.2 kilograms of fresh food. Read the information about the available types of food and the shipping costs for sending cargo to the ISS.

Choose at least three types of food for the science experiment. Determine about how much it will cost each company to ship the food to the ISS, and then compare these costs.

Space Station Grocery Delivery

Type of Fresh Food	Average Mass (grams)
apple	202
avocado	211
carrot sticks (1 package)	122
grapefruit	255
jalapeño	35
onion	226
pear	142
tomato	120

Shipping Cargo to the ISS

Company A: About $1,275,000 for every 25 kg of cargo

Company B: About $3,500,000 for every 50 kg of cargo

Plan It

➤ **Answer these questions to help you start thinking about a plan.**

   a. Which fresh foods will you select for the science experiment?

   b. How can you determine whether the total mass of the fresh foods you select is between 0.5 kilogram and 1.2 kilograms?

Solve It

➤ **Find a different solution for the Sending Fresh Food to Space problem. Show all your work on a separate sheet of paper. You may want to use the Problem-Solving Tips to get started.**

PROBLEM-SOLVING TIPS

Math Toolkit double number lines, graph paper

Key Terms

convert	equivalent ratios	rate
ratio	unit rate	

Models You may want to use . . .

* double number lines to find equivalent ratios.
* tables of equivalent ratios to find rates or unit rates.
* division to find unit rates.

Reflect

Use Mathematical Practices As you work through the problem, discuss these questions with a partner.

* **Repeated Reasoning** How can you find the cost of shipping a package of any mass to the ISS using Company A or Company B?

* **Reason Mathematically** You can write two rates for any ratio relationship. How do you know which of the two rates to use when solving the problem?

Because there is no refrigerator on the ISS, fresh food does not last very long. New supplies of fresh food are brought to the shuttle by unmanned supply ships.

Discuss Models and Strategies

➤ **Read the problem. Write a solution on a separate sheet of paper. Remember, there can be lots of ways to solve a problem.**

Going on a Spacewalk

Astronauts Francisco and Mei are going on a spacewalk. Their main task is to install two new cameras on the outside of the International Space Station (ISS). After they complete their main task, they will perform get-ahead tasks. Read the information about the get-ahead tasks, and then look at the data about the astronauts' oxygen levels.

Assume that Francisco and Mei continue to use oxygen at the same rate. Assign each of them a get-ahead task. Then show that each astronaut has enough oxygen to complete his or her assigned task and return to the airlock at the ISS.

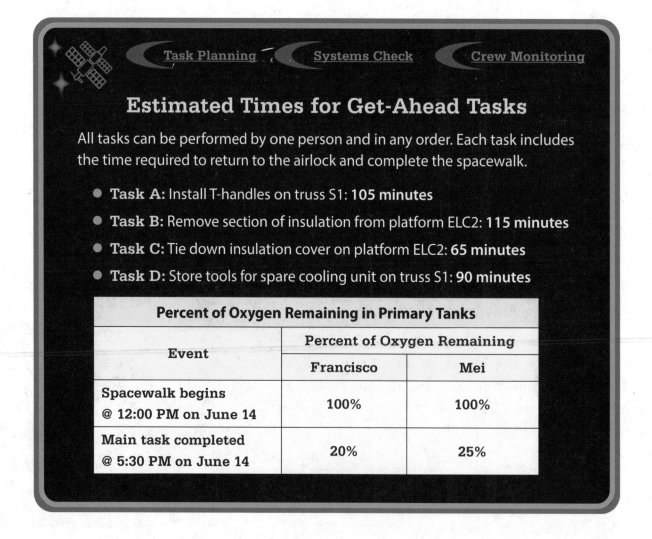

Task Planning | Systems Check | Crew Monitoring

Estimated Times for Get-Ahead Tasks

All tasks can be performed by one person and in any order. Each task includes the time required to return to the airlock and complete the spacewalk.

- **Task A:** Install T-handles on truss S1: **105 minutes**
- **Task B:** Remove section of insulation from platform ELC2: **115 minutes**
- **Task C:** Tie down insulation cover on platform ELC2: **65 minutes**
- **Task D:** Store tools for spare cooling unit on truss S1: **90 minutes**

Percent of Oxygen Remaining in Primary Tanks

Event	Percent of Oxygen Remaining	
	Francisco	Mei
Spacewalk begins @ 12:00 PM on June 14	100%	100%
Main task completed @ 5:30 PM on June 14	20%	25%

Plan It and Solve It

➤ **Find a solution to the Going on a Spacewalk problem.**

Write a detailed plan and support your answer. Be sure to include:

• an assignment of one get-ahead task to Francisco and a different get-ahead task to Mei.

• work showing that Francisco and Mei each have enough oxygen to do the assigned get-ahead task and return to the airlock at the ISS.

PROBLEM-SOLVING TIPS

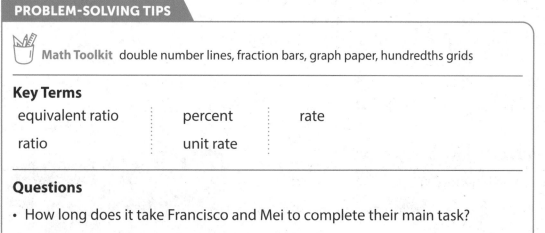 **Math Toolkit** double number lines, fraction bars, graph paper, hundredths grids

---

Key Terms

equivalent ratio	percent	rate
ratio	unit rate	

Questions

• How long does it take Francisco and Mei to complete their main task?

• What percent of the oxygen in Francisco's primary tank does he use while completing the main task? How do you know?

Reflect

Use Mathematical Practices As you work through the problem, discuss these questions with a partner.

• **Use Models** What models can you use to help you determine how much time Francisco and Mei can each spend on a get-ahead task without running out of oxygen?

• **Make an Argument** Can either Francisco or Mei complete more than one get-ahead task? How do you know?

Spacewalking astronauts can face temperatures ranging from −250°F to 250°F. A spacesuit protects astronauts from extreme temperatures.

Persevere On Your Own

➤ **Read the problem. Write a solution on a separate sheet of paper.**

Writing an Article

Troy is a journalist writing an article about Francisco's mission on the International Space Station (ISS). Troy wants to help his readers understand just how fast the ISS travels.

Read Troy's notes from a portion of his interview with Francisco, as well as his research about the ISS. Help Troy answer the questions he still has about the sunrises. Then write a paragraph for Troy's article that includes the answers to his questions.

Interview and Research Notes

- Francisco will spend 198 Earth days on board the ISS.

- He likes to photograph sunrises and sunsets from the ISS.

- A sunrise occurs on the ISS each time it orbits Earth.

- The time it takes the ISS to orbit Earth varies from 90 minutes to 93 minutes, depending on its altitude.

Idea for Article

Start by discussing Francisco's photography. Compare the number of sunrises that will happen on the ISS to the number that will happen on Earth during Francisco's mission.

WHAT I STILL NEED TO DO

- Answer these questions:

  - About how many sunrises occur each Earth day on the ISS?

  - About how many more sunrises will occur on the ISS during Francisco's mission than on Earth?

- Write a paragraph for the article that includes the answers to the questions.

Solve It

➤ **Find a solution to the Writing an Article problem.**

- Determine the approximate number of sunrises that occur each Earth day on the ISS.

- Estimate how many more sunrises will occur on the ISS during Francisco's mission than will occur on Earth during the same time period.

- Write a paragraph for Francisco's article that includes the information you determined.

Reflect

Use Mathematical Practices After you complete the problem, choose one of these questions to discuss with a partner.

- **Make Sense of Problems** What equivalent ratios can you use to convert among minutes, hours, and days? How can you use these ratios to help solve the problem?

- **Critique Reasoning** Does your partner's estimate of the number of sunrises that will occur on the ISS during Francisco's mission agree with yours? If not, explain why the estimates are different and whether they are both reasonable.

The ISS orbits Earth at an average altitude of 248 miles, traveling at a speed of about 17,500 miles per hour. It appears as a bright light in the night sky and can be seen from Earth without a telescope.

In this unit you learned to . . .

Skill	Lesson
Compare rates to solve real-world problems.	**15, 16**
Use unit rates to find equivalent ratios.	**16**
Convert measurement units using rates.	**16**
Express a percent as a decimal or a fraction.	**17, 18**
Find a given percent of a number.	**17, 18**
Find what percent one number is of another number.	**17, 18**
Find the whole when given a part and a percent.	**18**
Use math vocabulary and precise language to explain ratios, rates, and percents.	**15–18**

Think about what you have learned.

➤ **Use words, numbers, and drawings.**

1 The most important math I learned was _____ because . . .

2 The hardest thing I learned to do was _____ because . . .

3 I could use more practice with . . .

➤ **Review the unit vocabulary. Put a check mark by items you can use in speaking and writing. Look up the meaning of any terms you do not know.**

Math Vocabulary

☐ equivalent ratios ☐ rate

☐ per ☐ ratio

☐ percent ☐ unit rate

Academic Vocabulary

☐ justify

☐ relationship

☐ survey

➤ **Use the unit vocabulary to complete the problems.**

1 Use the table of equivalent ratios to answer questions 1a–1c.

Miles	10	5	15	1
Hours	2	1	3	$\frac{1}{5}$

a. How can you describe the relationship between 10 : 2 and 5 : 1?

b. How are the ratios 5 : 1 and 1 : $\frac{1}{5}$ different from the other ratios in the table?

c. What do the numbers 5 and $\frac{1}{5}$ represent in the ratio relationship between miles and hours?

2 The town of Newburg has 1,200 students. The blue squares on the hundredths grid represent students who walk to school. The white squares represent students who take the bus. Use at least two math or academic vocabulary terms to describe the grid. Underline each term you use.

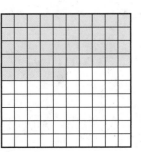

➤ **Use what you have learned to complete these problems.**

1 Brenda completes her sixth hiking trail in a state park. A park ranger tells her that she has hiked 25% of the trails. How many trails are there to hike in the state park? Show your work.

SOLUTION _____

2 A website sells two brands of face paint. Brand A costs $3 for 4 fl oz. Brand B costs $7 for 10 fl oz. How much more per fluid ounce does Brand A cost than Brand B? Show your work.

SOLUTION _____

3 There are 175 glasses Ellen needs to wash. She washes 68% of the glasses. How many glasses does Ellen have left to wash? Show your work.

SOLUTION _____

4 Kurtis is watching a movie. The movie lasts 280 min. Kurtis has watched 30% of the movie so far. How many minutes of the movie has Kurtis watched?
Show your work.

SOLUTION _____

5 On Saturday, 960 people visit the zoo. Of the visitors, 40% are children. How many of the visitors on Saturday were children? Record your answer on the grid. Then fill in the bubbles.

6 A package contains 20 golf balls. The total weight of the golf balls is 32 ounces. Use the model to show the number of ounces per golf ball and the number of golf balls per ounce. Write your answers in the blanks.

Golf Balls	20		1
Ounces	32	1	

7 A snail takes 24 min to travel 5 ft. At this rate, how many inches does the snail travel every hour?

A 4.8

B 12.5

C 150

D 288

Performance Task

➤ **Answer the questions and show all your work on separate paper.**

Alexandria, Bettina, and Crystal are planning a road trip together. The road trip is 1,100 miles. They plan to drive 50 miles per hour for the entire trip and have agreed on the following conditions.

- Alexandria will drive 60% of the road trip.

- Bettina will drive 1 mile for every 10 minutes of the road trip.

- Crystal will drive the remainder of the road trip.

Find the total driving time for the trip. Then determine the amount of time and how many miles each person will drive.

Reflect

Use Mathematical Practices After you complete the task, choose one of the following questions to answer.

- **Model** How would drawing diagrams or using tables help organize your work?

- **Be Precise** How would you test your solution to prove it answers the task?

Set 1 Volume

➤ **Find the volume of each rectangular prism. Show your work.**

1 Find the volume of the rectangular prism shown below.

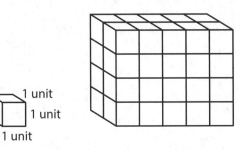

1 unit
1 unit
1 unit

2 A rectangular prism with length 6 in., width 5 in., and height 4 in.

3 A rectangular prism with height 7 in. and base with area 12 in.^{2}

Set 2 Multiply and Divide Multi-Digit Numbers

➤ **Multiply or divide. Show your work.**

1 $4,307 \times 16$ **2** $434 \div 14$ **3** $1,472 \div 16$

     UNIT 1 • Cumulative Practice   **CP1**

Set 3 Decimal Place Value and Rounding Decimals

➤ **Fill in the blanks.**

1 _____ is 10 times 0.07.

2 _____ is 10^2 times 0.0003.

3 _____ is $\frac{1}{10}$ of 0.002.

4 _____ is 10^4 times 0.00025.

➤ **Round to the nearest hundredth.**

5 4.157 _____

6 349.332 _____

7 21.034 _____

8 6.976 _____

➤ **Round to the nearest tenth.**

9 27.371 _____

10 792.42 _____

11 5.948 _____

12 0.168 _____

Set 4 Add and Subtract Decimals

➤ **Add or subtract. Show your work.**

1 2.34 + 3.1 + 0.09

2 11.52 − 5.74

3 8.5 + 3.08

4 14 − 6.73

5 12.45 − 3.2

6 10.09 + 6.33

Set 5 Add and Subtract Fractions in Word Problems

➤ **Write an equation to represent and solve each problem. Show your work.**

1 Aniyah has $2\frac{2}{3}$ cups of oats in one container. She has $4\frac{3}{4}$ cups of oats another container. How many cups of oats does she have in total?

2 Jason has $4\frac{3}{10}$ feet of string. He uses $2\frac{2}{5}$ feet of string. How much string does he have left?

Set 6 Multiply and Divide Decimals

➤ **Multiply or divide. Show your work.**

1 4.15×6 **2** 0.2×0.3 **3** $9 \div 0.03$

Set 7 Multiply Fractions

➤ **Solve the problems. Multiply.**

1 $\frac{2}{3} \times \frac{1}{4} =$ **2** $\frac{1}{3} \times \frac{4}{3} =$ **3** $\frac{5}{3} \div \frac{1}{5} =$

4 A rectangle with length $\frac{7}{4}$ inches and width $\frac{1}{3}$ inch. What is the area of the rectangle? Show your work.

Set 8 Multiply Fractions in Word Problems

➤ **Write a multiplication equation to represent and solve each problem. Show your work.**

1 Manuel has $4\frac{1}{2}$ cups of flour. He plans to use $\frac{2}{3}$ of the flour to bake bread. How many cups of flour will Manuel use to bake bread?

2 Mary plays soccer for $\frac{2}{5}$ hour on Monday. She plays for $2\frac{1}{3}$ times as long on Tuesday. How long does Mary play on Tuesday?

3 Niesha's brother is $3\frac{1}{2}$ feet tall. Niesha is $1\frac{1}{3}$ times as tall as her brother. How tall is Niesha?

Set 9 Divide with Unit Fractions in Word Problems

➤ **Write a division equation to represent and solve each problem. Show your work.**

1 Amelia makes 5 cups of muffin batter. Each muffin requires $\frac{1}{3}$ cup of batter. How many muffins can Amelia make?

2 Drew has $\frac{1}{2}$ of a package of raisins. He shares it equally among himself and 4 friends. What fraction of the original package does each person receive?

3 Pablo cuts 8 apples into quarters. How many apple pieces does he have?

Cumulative Practice

Set 1 Write Algebraic Expressions

➤ **Write an algebraic expression for each word phrase.**

1 2.5 more than 6 times a number x

2 The product of 8 and the sum of s and 3

3 6 more than half of a number m

4 5 less than the quotient of 16 and a number y

Set 2 Write Algebraic Expressions in Real-World Problems

➤ **Write an algebraic expression for each situation.**

1 A movie ticket for an adult costs $10 and a movie ticket for a child costs $7. Write an expression that represents the total cost in dollars of tickets for a adults and c children.

2 Ji has 40 stickers. She gives 4 stickers each to some friends. Write an expression that represents the number of stickers she has after giving stickers to f friends.

3 Lucas makes 24 muffins. He eats 2 muffins, and then divides the rest equally among f friends. Write an expression that represents the number of muffins each friend receives.

Set 3 Interpret Algebraic Expressions

➤ **Use the expression $2x + 4$ for problems 1–4. Fill in the blanks.**

1 _____ is a coefficient.

2 _____ is a variable.

3 _____ and _____ are factors.

4 _____ is a sum.

➤ **Use the expression $5(m - 4)$ for problems 5–8. Fill in the blanks.**

5 _____ is a product.

6 _____ is a variable.

7 _____ is a difference.

8 _____ and _____ are factors.

Set 4 Interpret Algebraic Expressions in Real-World Problems

➤ **Identify and interpret the parts of each expression.**

1 A pen costs $2.50. The expression $4n + 2.50$ represents the cost of buying 4 notebooks and a pen. What is the product in the expression? What does the product represent?

2 Henry has 50 apples. He gives 4 apples each to f friends. What is the difference in the expression $50 - 4f$? What does the difference represent?

3 The number of roses and daisies in 5 bouquets is $5(r + d)$. What is the sum in the expression? What does the sum represent?

Set 5 Evaluate Algebraic Expressions

➤ **Evaluate the expressions. Show your work.**

1 Evaluate $3n + 4$ when $n = 3$.

2 Evaluate $4 - \dfrac{2}{x}$ when $x = 6$.

3 Evaluate $3(x - 2y)$ when $x = 4$ and $y = 2$.

4 Evaluate $(4a + 2) \div 3$ when $a = 10$.

5 Evaluate $4q + p$ when $q = 3$ and $p = 2$.

6 Evaluate $60 \div c + 2$ when $c = 3$.

7 Evaluate $3 + \dfrac{h}{3}$ when $h = 8$.

8 Evaluate $5(x + y)$ when $x = 2$ and $y = \dfrac{1}{3}$.

Set 6 Evaluate Algebraic Expressions in Real-World Problems

➤ **Solve the problems. Show your work.**

1 Lin uses c to represent the regular cost of her meal at a restaurant. She has a coupon to get her meal at half price. The expression $\frac{c}{2} + 3$ represents how much she will pay, including the tip. The regular cost of Lin's meal is $16. How much does she pay in total?

2 The expression $8b + 15t$ represents how much money, in dollars, Kanesha earns babysitting and tutoring, where b is the number of hours she babysits and t is the number of hours she tutors. Kanesha babysits for 5 hours and tutors for 2 hours. How much money does she earn?

Set 7 Write and Evaluate Expressions with Exponents

➤ **Write each expression as a power for problems 1 and 2.**

1 $6 \cdot 6 \cdot 6 \cdot 6 =$ _____

2 $2 \cdot 2 \cdot 2 \cdot 2 \cdot 2 \cdot 2 =$ _____

➤ **Evaluate the expressions for problems 3–6. Show your work.**

3 $4(15 - 2^3)$

4 $2 + 3n^2$ when $n = 3$

5 $2x^3$ when $x = \frac{1}{4}$

6 $a^2 - \frac{1}{9}$ when $a = \frac{4}{3}$

Set 8 Write and Evaluate Expressions in Real-World Problems

➤ **Solve the problems. Show your work.**

1 The volume of a cube with edge length s units is s^3 cubic units. A rectangular box is a cube with edge length 30 cm. What is the volume of the box?

2 Jordan has two pieces of fabric. One piece has area 14 in.^{2}. The other piece has area $2x^2$ in.^{2}. Write an algebraic expression Jordan can use to find the total area of the fabric. Then find the total area when x is 8 in.

3 The volume of an inflatable pool is $3 \cdot 4^2$ cubic feet. The number of trips it takes to fill the pool with a bucket that holds m cubic feet of water is $3 \cdot 4^2 \div m$. How many trips does it take to fill the pool with a bucket that holds $\frac{1}{2}$ cubic foot of water?

4 A biologist puts n cells in a Petri dish. The number of cells in the Petri dish triples every hour. After 5 hours, the number of cells is $n \cdot 3^5$. How many cells are in the Petri dish after 5 hours when the biologist puts 5 cells in the Petri dish?

Cumulative Practice

Name: _____

Set 1 Models of Division with Fractions

➤ **Complete the model to show the division equation for problem 1. Find the quotient.**

1 $\frac{4}{3} \div \frac{1}{9} =$ _____

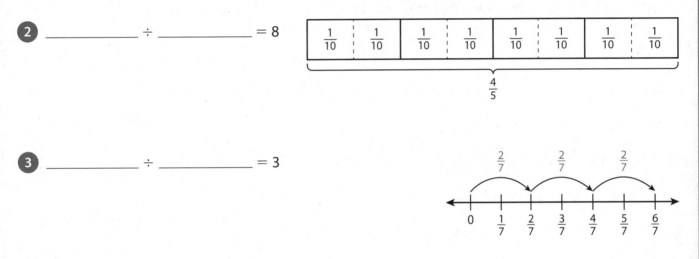

➤ **Write the division equation that each model represents for problems 2 and 3.**

2 _____ ÷ _____ = 8

3 _____ ÷ _____ = 3

Set 2 Solve Fraction Division Problems

➤ **Write and solve an equation to solve the problems. Show your work.**

1 A pumpkin weighs $7\frac{1}{2}$ pounds. An apple weighs $\frac{1}{3}$ pound. How many times the apple's weight is the pumpkin's weight?

2 A rectangle has an area of $\frac{9}{10}$ in.² and a width of $\frac{3}{4}$ in. What is its length?

Set 3 Divide Fractions by Whole Numbers

➤ **Divide. Fill in the blanks for problems 1–6.**

1 $\frac{2}{3} \div 4$

2 $\frac{8}{10} \div 10$

3 $\frac{9}{2} \div 3$

4 $\frac{3}{5} \div 2$

5 $\frac{5}{6} \div 6$

6 $\frac{4}{2} \div 2$

➤ **Write and evaluate a division expression to solve problem 7. Show your work.**

7 A ribbon that is $\frac{3}{4}$ ft long is cut into 5 pieces of equal length. How long is each piece?

Set 4 Divide Whole Numbers by Fractions

➤ **Divide. Show your work for problems 1–6.**

1 $9 \div \frac{4}{5}$

2 $6 \div \frac{2}{5}$

3 $7 \div \frac{3}{7}$

4 $1 \div \frac{2}{3}$

5 $2 \div \frac{4}{9}$

6 $8 \div \frac{4}{7}$

➤ **Write and evaluate a division expression to solve problem 7. Show your work.**

7 A recipe for 1 batch of muffins calls for $\frac{3}{4}$ cup of almond milk. Rose has 6 cups of almond milk. How many batches of muffins could she make?

Set 5 Divide Mixed Numbers by Fractions

➤ **Divide. Show your work for problems 1–9.**

1 $2\frac{2}{3} \div \frac{2}{3}$

2 $4\frac{1}{2} \div \frac{3}{4}$

3 $2\frac{1}{2} \div \frac{2}{5}$

4 $2\frac{4}{5} \div \frac{4}{5}$

5 $2\frac{1}{4} \div \frac{1}{3}$

6 $5\frac{3}{4} \div \frac{2}{3}$

7 $3\frac{2}{5} \div \frac{2}{5}$

8 $2\frac{1}{2} \div \frac{3}{4}$

9 $2\frac{2}{9} \div \frac{5}{6}$

➤ **Write and evaluate a division expression to solve problem 10. Show your work.**

10 Mateo has a piece of fabric that is $2\frac{1}{4}$ yards long. He cuts it into pieces that are each $\frac{3}{8}$ yard long. How many pieces of fabric does Mateo cut?

Set 6 Write Algebraic Expressions

➤ **Write an algebraic expression for each word phrase.**

1 2 more than the product of 6 and a number x _____

2 The product of 4 and the sum of n and 9 _____

3 $\frac{1}{2}$ more than twice a number y _____

4 5 more than the quotient of 6 and a number a _____

5 Half the sum of 8 and a number m _____

6 The difference between 15 and $4x$ _____

Set 7 Describe Algebraic Expressions

➤ **Fill in the blanks to describe the algebraic expressions.**

1 In the expression $2x + 7$, _____ is a coefficient.

2 In the expression $4(y - 2)$, _____ is a difference and _____ is a product.

3 In the expression $6y + (9 + x)$, the factors of the first term are _____ and _____.

4 In the expression $2p + \frac{6}{r} - 3$, _____ is the quotient.

5 In the expression $5(2 + n)$, the factors are _____ and _____.

6 In the expression $4x + \frac{y}{2}$, _____ is a sum and _____ is a product.

7 In the expression $2 + 4y + 2x$, the first term is _____ and the second term is _____.

Set 8 Evaluate Algebraic Expressions

➤ **Evaluate each expression. Show your work.**

1 $8x + 4$ when $x = 5$

2 $9(r + 2s)$ when $r = 3$ and $s = 2$

3 $m - \frac{7}{n}$ when $m = 9$ and $n = 3$

4 $9a - 10b$ when $a = \frac{3}{4}$ and $b = \frac{2}{3}$

5 $2x + 6(y + z)$ when $x = 4$, $y = 1$, and $z + 5$

6 $(p - q) \div 4$ when $p = 15$ and $q = 3$

Name:

Set 1 Ratio Language

➤ **Fill in the blanks to describe each ratio relationship.**

1 A recipe calls for 3 cups of oats and 2 cups of flour.

There are _____ cups of oats for every 2 cups of flour. The ratio of cups of

oats to cups of flour is _____ . The ratio of cups of flour to cups of oats is

_____ .

2 There are 8 cupcakes for every 4 guests.

There are _____ guests for every 8 cupcakes. The ratio of cupcakes to

guests is _____ . The ratio of guests to cupcakes is _____ .

3 A runner travels 1 mile for every 9 minutes he runs.

The ratio of miles run to minutes run is _____ . The ratio of minutes run to

miles run is _____ .

Set 2 Equivalent Ratios in Tables and Graphs

➤ **Complete the table, then plot points on the graph to represent the ratios for problems 1 and 2.**

1 A school cafeteria has 1 table for every 12 students.

Students	24			96
Tables	2	4	6	

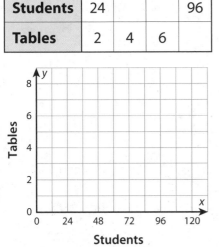

2 An applesauce recipe calls for 2 teaspoons of cinnamon for every 8 apples.

Apples	8	16	24	32
Cinnamon (teaspoons)				

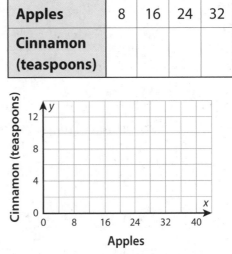

Set 3 Equivalent Ratios

➤ **Solve the problems. Show your work.**

1 Maria walks 16 meters every 10 seconds. How far does she walk in 45 seconds?

2 Brad swims 4 laps every 6 minutes. How long does it take him to swim 14 laps?

Set 4 Part-to-Part and Part-to-Whole Ratios

➤ **Solve the problems. Show your work.**

1 Kiana's soccer team's ratio of wins to losses is 5 : 3. Her team has played 24 games. How many games have they won?

2 A bracelet has two colors of beads. The ratio of green beads to blue beads is 2 : 7. There are 18 green beads. How many beads are there in total?

Set 5 Comparing Ratios

➤ **Solve the problem. Show your work.**

1 Anna and Jack make lemonade. Anna uses 2 cups of lemon juice with 9 cups of water. Jack uses 3 cups of lemon juice with 15 cups of water. Whose lemonade has a stronger lemon taste?

Set 6 Divide Fractions

➤ **Divide. Show your work for problems 1–6.**

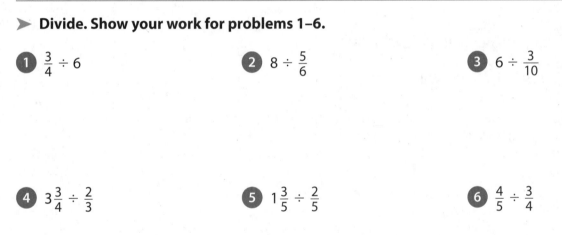

1 $\frac{3}{4} \div 6$

2 $8 \div \frac{5}{6}$

3 $6 \div \frac{3}{10}$

4 $3\frac{3}{4} \div \frac{2}{3}$

5 $1\frac{3}{5} \div \frac{2}{5}$

6 $\frac{4}{5} \div \frac{3}{4}$

7 Tyreek and his 4 friends equally split $3\frac{1}{3}$ cups of juice. How much juice does each person get?

Set 7 Numerical Expressions with Exponents

➤ **Write each multiplication expression as a power of the factor given for problems 1–3.**

1 $9 \cdot 9 \cdot 9 \cdot 9 =$ _____

2 $4 \cdot 4 =$ _____

3 $\frac{2}{3} \cdot \frac{2}{3} \cdot \frac{2}{3} =$ _____

➤ **Evaluate the expressions for problems 4–9. Show your work.**

4 6^3

5 2^6

6 $3 + 3^4$

7 $2^2 + 2^3$

8 $9^1 \cdot 4$

9 $\left(\frac{1}{3}\right)^4$

Set 8 Algebraic Expressions with Exponents

➤ **Evaluate each expression. Show your work.**

1 $2x^3$ when $x = 3$

2 $4 + n^2$ when $n = 6$

3 $8(1 + m^3)$ when $m = 10$

4 $(y - 5)^4$ when $y = 7$

5 $a^2 \div b^2$ when $a = 9$ and $b = 3$

6 $\left(\frac{x}{2}\right)^2 - 6$ when $x = 5$

Interactive Glossary/Glosario interactivo

English/Español	Example/Ejemplo	Notes/Notas

Aa

absolute value a number's distance from 0 on the number line. Absolute value is never negative.

valor absoluto distancia de un número desde 0 en la recta numérica. El valor absoluto nunca es negativo.

$|-3| = 3$
$|3| = 3$

---

acute angle an angle that measures more than 0° but less than 90°.

ángulo agudo ángulo que mide más de 0° pero menos de 90°.

---

acute triangle a triangle that has three acute angles.

triángulo acutángulo triángulo que tiene tres ángulos agudos.

---

additive inverses two numbers whose sum is zero. The additive inverse of a number is the opposite of that number, i.e., the additive inverse of a is $-a$.

inverso aditivo dos números cuya suma es cero. El inverso aditivo de un número es el opuesto de ese número; por ejemplo, el inverso aditivo de a es $-a$.

-2 and 2
$\frac{1}{2}$ and $-\frac{1}{2}$

---

algorithm a set of routine steps used to solve problems.

algoritmo conjunto de pasos rutinarios que se siguen para resolver problemas.

$$
\begin{array}{r}
17\ R\ 19 \\
31\overline{)546} \\
-\ 31\downarrow \\
\hline
236 \\
-\ 217 \\
\hline
19
\end{array}
$$

---

angle a geometric shape formed by two rays, lines, or line segments that meet at a common point.

ángulo figura geométrica formada por dos semirrectas, rectas o segmentos de recta que se encuentran en un punto común.

English/Español	Example/Ejemplo	Notes/Notas
area the amount of space inside a closed two-dimensional figure. Area is measured in square units such as square centimeters. **área** cantidad de espacio dentro de una figura bidimensional cerrada. El área se mide en unidades cuadradas, como los centímetros cuadrados.	6 units Area = 30 units² 5 units	
associative property of addition regrouping the terms does not change the value of the expression. **propiedad asociativa de la suma** reagrupar los términos no cambia el valor de la expresión.	$(a + b) + c = a + (b + c)$ $(2 + 3) + 4 = 2 + (3 + 4)$	
associative property of multiplication regrouping the terms does not change the value of the expression. **propiedad asociativa de la multiplicación** reagrupar los términos no cambia el valor de la expresión.	$(a \cdot b) \cdot c = a \cdot (b \cdot c)$ $(2 \cdot 3) \cdot 4 = 2 \cdot (3 \cdot 4)$	
axis a horizontal or vertical number line that determines a coordinate plane. The plural form is *axes*. **eje** recta numérica horizontal o vertical que determina un plano de coordenadas.	y y-axis 2 x-axis x −2 O 2 −2	

Bb

balance point the point that represents the center of a data set. In a two-variable data set, the coordinates of the balance point are the mean of each variable.

punto de equilibrio punto que representa el centro de un conjunto de datos. En un conjunto de datos de dos variables, las coordenadas del punto de equilibrio son la media de cada variable.

Data set: (1, 1), (3, 4), (5, 6), (7, 8)

$$\frac{1 + 3 + 5 + 7}{4} = 4$$

$$\frac{1 + 4 + 6 + 8}{4} = 4.75$$

Balance point: (4, 4.75)

---

base (of a parallelogram) a side of a parallelogram from which the height is measured.

base (de un paralelogramo) lado de un paralelogramo desde el que se mide la altura.

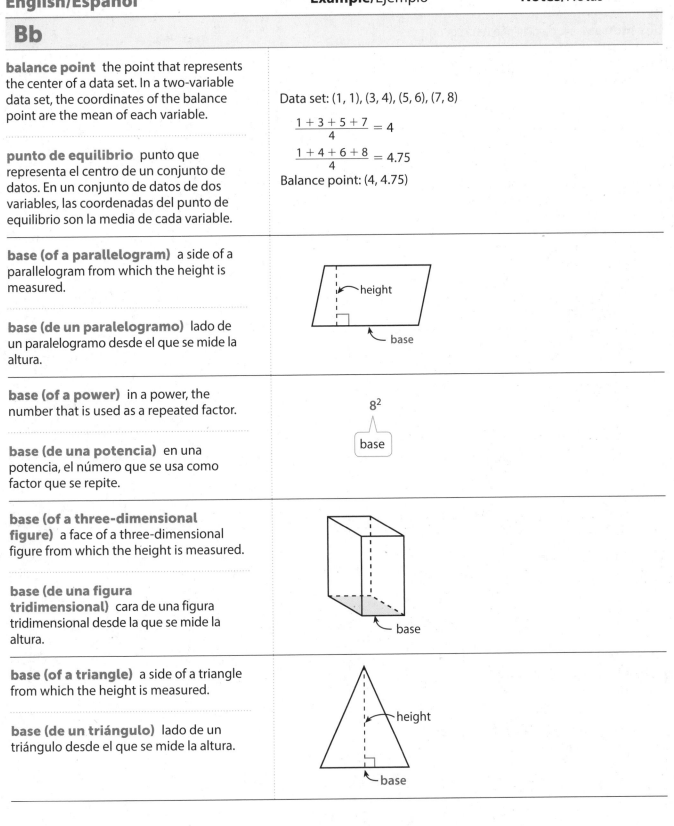

---

base (of a power) in a power, the number that is used as a repeated factor.

base (de una potencia) en una potencia, el número que se usa como factor que se repite.

8^2

base

---

base (of a three-dimensional figure) a face of a three-dimensional figure from which the height is measured.

base (de una figura tridimensional) cara de una figura tridimensional desde la que se mide la altura.

base

---

base (of a triangle) a side of a triangle from which the height is measured.

base (de un triángulo) lado de un triángulo desde el que se mide la altura.

height

base

English/Español	Example/Ejemplo	Notes/Notas

box plot a visual display of a data set on a number line that shows the minimum, the lower quartile, the median, the upper quartile, and the maximum. The sides of the box show the lower and upper quartiles and the line inside the box shows the median. Lines connect the box to the minimum and maximum values.

diagrama de caja representación visual de un conjunto de datos en una recta numérica que muestra el mínimo, el cuartil inferior, la mediana, el cuartil superior y el máximo. Los lados de la caja muestran los cuartiles inferior y superior y la recta del centro muestra la mediana. Las rectas conectan la caja con los valores mínimo y máximo.

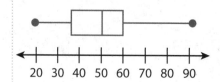

20 30 40 50 60 70 80 90

Cc

closed figure a two-dimensional figure that begins and ends at the same point.

figura cerrada figura bidimensional que comienza y termina en el mismo punto.

Closed figure   Open figure

cluster a group of data points that are close to each other.

agrupación conjunto de datos que están cerca unos de otros.

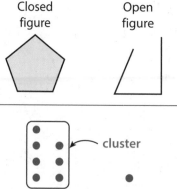

cluster

0 1 2 3 4

English/Español	Example/Ejemplo	Notes/Notas
coefficient a number that is multiplied by a variable.	$5x + 3$ coefficient	
coeficiente número que se multiplica por una variable.		
common denominator a number that is a common multiple of the denominators of two or more fractions.	A common denominator for $\frac{1}{2}$ and $\frac{3}{5}$ is 10 because $2 \cdot 5 = 10$.	
denominador común número que es múltiplo común de los denominadores de dos o más fracciones.		
commutative property of addition changing the order of the addends does not change the sum.	$a + b = b + a$ $4.1 + 7.5 = 7.5 + 4.1$	
propiedad conmutativa de la suma cambiar el orden de los sumandos no cambia el total.		
commutative property of multiplication changing the order of the factors does not change the product.	$ab = ba$ $4(7.5) = 7.5(4)$	
propiedad conmutativa de la multiplicación cambiar el orden de los factores no cambia el producto.		
compare to describe the relationship between the value or size of two numbers or quantities.	$-4 < 8.5$	
comparar describir la relación que hay entre el valor o el tamaño de dos números o cantidades.		
compose to make by combining parts. You can put together numbers to make a greater number or put together shapes to make a new shape.		
componer formar al combinar partes. Se pueden unir números para hacer un número mayor o unir figuras para formar una figura nueva.		

English/Español	Example/Ejemplo	Notes/Notas

composite number a number that has more than one pair of whole number factors.

número compuesto número que tiene más de un par de números enteros como factores.

16 is a composite number because 1 • 16, 2 • 8, and 4 • 4 all equal 16.

---

convert to write an equivalent measurement using a different unit.

convertir escribir una medida equivalente usando una unidad diferente.

60 in. is the same as 5 ft.

---

coordinate plane a two-dimensional space formed by two perpendicular number lines called *axes*.

plano de coordenadas espacio bidimensional formado por dos rectas numéricas perpendiculares llamadas ejes.

---

corresponding terms terms that have the same position in two related patterns. For example, the second term in one pattern and the second term in a related pattern are corresponding terms.

términos correspondientes términos que tienen la misma posición en dos patrones relacionados. Por ejemplo, el segundo término en un patrón y el segundo término en un patrón relacionado son términos correspondientes.

Pattern A: 12, 18, 24, 30

Pattern B: 6, 9, 12, 15

---

cube a rectangular prism in which each face of the prism is a square.

cubo prisma rectangular en el que cada cara del prisma es un cuadrado.

1 unit
1 unit
1 unit

Dd

data a set of collected information. Often numerical information such as a list of measurements.

datos conjunto de información reunida. Con frecuencia, información numérica como una lista de medidas.

Commute length (mi):

15, 22, 10.5, 21, 9.5

---

decimal a number containing a decimal point that separates a whole from fractional place values (tenths, hundredths, thousandths, and so on).

decimal número que tiene un punto decimal que separa un entero de los valores posicionales fraccionarios (décimas, centésimas, milésimas, etc.).

1.293

---

decompose to break into parts. You can break apart numbers and shapes.

descomponer separar en partes. Se puede separar en partes números y figuras.

---

degree (°) a unit used to measure angles.

grado (°) unidad que se usa para medir ángulos.

There are 360° in a circle.

---

denominator the number below the line in a fraction that tells the number of equal parts in the whole.

denominador número debajo de la línea en una fracción que indica el número de partes iguales que hay en el entero.

$\frac{3}{4}$

---

dependent variable a variable whose value depends on the value of a related independent variable.

variable dependiente variable cuyo valor depende del valor de una variable independiente relacionada.

$y = 5x$

The value of y depends on the value of x.

---

difference the result of subtraction.

diferencia resultado de la resta.

$$\begin{array}{r} 16.75 \\ -\ 15.70 \\ \hline 1.05 \end{array}$$

English/Español	Example/Ejemplo	Notes/Notas
digit a symbol used to write numbers. **dígito** símbolo que se usa para escribir números.	The digits are 0, 1, 2, 3, 4, 5, 6, 7, 8, and 9.	
dimension length in one direction. A figure may have one, two, or three dimensions. **dimensión** longitud en una dirección. Una figura puede tener una, dos o tres dimensiones.	5 in. 2 in. 3 in.	
distribution a representation that shows how often values in a data set occur. **distribución** representación que muestra la frecuencia con la que ocurren los valores en un conjunto de datos.		

Pet	Frequency
Bird	7
Cat	12
Dog	8
Snake	3

English/Español	Example/Ejemplo	Notes/Notas
distributive property multiplying each term in a sum or difference by a common factor does not change the value of the expression. **propiedad distributiva** multiplicar cada término de una suma o diferencia por un factor común no cambia el valor de la expresión.	$a(b + c) = ab + ac$ $5(4 + 2) = 5(4) + 5(2)$	
dividend the number that is divided by another number. **dividendo** número que se divide por otro número.	$22.5 \div 3 = 7.5$	
divisor the number by which another number is divided. **divisor** número por el que se divide otro número.	$22.5 \div 3 = 7.5$	

dot plot a data display that shows data as dots above a number line. A dot plot may also be called a *line plot*.

diagrama de puntos representación de datos que muestra datos como puntos sobre una *recta numérica*.

Ee

edge a line segment where two faces meet in a three-dimensional shape.

arista segmento de recta en el que dos caras se unen en una figura tridimensional.

edge

equal having the same value, same size, or same amount.

igual que tiene el mismo valor, el mismo tamaño o la misma cantidad.

$50 - 20 = 30$

$50 - 20$ is equal to 30.

equation a mathematical statement that uses an equal sign (=) to show that two expressions have the same value.

ecuación enunciado matemático que tiene un signo de igual (=) para mostrar que dos expresiones tienen el mismo valor.

$x + 4 = 15$

equilateral triangle a triangle that has all three sides the same length.

triángulo equilátero triángulo que tiene los tres lados de la misma longitud.

English/Español	Example/Ejemplo	Notes/Notas
equivalent having the same value. **equivalente** que tiene el mismo valor.	4 is equivalent to $\frac{8}{2}$.	
equivalent expressions two or more expressions in different forms that always name the same value. **expresiones equivalentes** dos o más expresiones en diferentes formas que siempre nombran el mismo valor.	$2(x + 4)$ is equivalent to $2x + 2(4)$ and $2x + 8$.	
equivalent fractions two or more different fractions that name the same part of a whole or the same point on the number line. **fracciones equivalentes** dos o más fracciones diferentes que nombran la misma parte de un entero o el mismo punto en la recta numérica.	$-\frac{5}{10}$ $\frac{4}{8}$ $-\frac{1}{2}$ $\frac{1}{2}$ -1 0 1	
equivalent ratios two ratios that express the same comparison. Multiplying both numbers in the ratio $a : b$ by a nonzero number n results in the equivalent ratio $na : nb$. **razones equivalentes** dos razones que expresan la misma comparación. Multiplicar ambos números en la razón $a : b$ por un número distinto de cero n da como resultado la razón equivalente $na : nb$.	$6 : 8$ is equivalent to $3 : 4$	
estimate (noun) a close guess made using mathematical thinking. **estimación** suposición aproximada que se hace por medio del razonamiento matemático.	$28 + 21 = ?$ $30 + 20 = 50$ 50 is an estimate of $28 + 21$.	
estimate (verb) to give an approximate number or answer based on mathematical thinking. **estimar** dar un número o respuesta aproximada basados en el razonamiento matemático.	$28 + 21$ is about 50.	

English/Español	Example/Ejemplo	Notes/Notas
evaluate to find the value of an expression. **evaluar** hallar el valor de una expresión.	The expression $4.5 \div (1 + 8)$ has a value of 0.5.	
exponent in a power, the number that shows how many times the base is used as a factor. **exponente** en una potencia, el número que muestra cuántas veces se usa la base como factor.	8^2 exponent	
exponential expression an expression that includes an exponent. **expresión exponencial** expresión que tiene un exponente.	$3x^3$	
expression a group of numbers, variables, and/or operation symbols that represents a mathematical relationship. An expression without variables, such as $3 + 4$, is called a *numerical expression*. An expression with variables, such as $5b^2$, is called an *algebraic expression*. **expresión** grupo de números, variables y/o símbolos de operaciones que representa una relación matemática. Una expresión sin variables, como $3 + 4$, se llama *expresión numérica*. Una expresión con variables, como $5b^2$, se llama *expresión algebraica*.	$\dfrac{32 - 4}{7}$ $3x + y - 9$	

Ff

face a flat surface of a solid shape.

cara superficie plana de una figura sólida.

face

factor a number, or expression with parentheses, that is multiplied.

factor número, o expresión entre paréntesis, que se multiplica.

$4 \times 5 = 20$
factors

factor pair two numbers that are multiplied together to give a product.

par de factores dos números que se multiplican para dar un producto.

$4 \times 5 = 20$
factor pair

factors of a number whole numbers that multiply together to get the given number.

factores de un número números enteros que se multiplican para obtener el número dado.

$4 \times 5 = 20$

4 and 5 are factors of 20.

formula a mathematical relationship that is expressed in the form of an equation.

fórmula relación matemática que se expresa en forma de ecuación.

$A = \ell w$

fraction a number that names equal parts of a whole. A fraction names a point on the number line and can also represent the division of two numbers.

fracción número que nombra partes iguales de un entero. Una fracción nombra un punto en la recta numérica y también puede representar la división de dos números.

$-\frac{1}{2}$ $\frac{4}{8}$

-1 0 1

English/Español	Example/Ejemplo	Notes/Notas
frequency a numerical count of how many times a data value occurs in a data set.	Data set: 12, 13, 12, 15, 12, 13, 15, 14, 12, 12	

Data Value	Frequency
12	5
13	2
14	1
15	2

frecuencia conteo numérico de cuántas veces ocurre un valor en un conjunto de datos.

Gg

gap an interval of the number line for which a distribution has no data values.

espacio intervalo de la recta numérica para el que una distribución no tiene valores.

greatest common factor (GCF) the greatest factor two or more numbers have in common.

GCF of 20 and 30: $2 \cdot 5$, or 10

$20 = 2 \cdot 2 \cdot 5$

$30 = 2 \cdot 3 \cdot 5$

máximo común divisor (M.C.D.) el mayor factor que dos o más números tienen en común.

English/Español	Example/Ejemplo	Notes/Notas
grouping symbol a symbol, such as braces {}, brackets [], or parentheses (), used to group parts of an expression that should be evaluated before others.	$3 \div (7 - 2) = 3 \div 5$ $$\frac{3}{7 - 2} = \frac{3}{5}$$	
símbolo de agrupación símbolo, como las llaves {}, los corchetes [] o los paréntesis (), que se usa para agrupar partes de una expresión que deben evaluarse antes que otras.		

Hh

height (of a parallelogram) the perpendicular distance from a base to the opposite side.	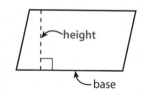	
altura (de un paralelogramo) distancia perpendicular desde una base hasta el lado opuesto.		
height (of a prism) the perpendicular distance from a base to the opposite base.	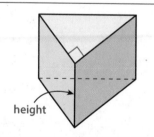	
altura (de un prisma) distancia perpendicular desde una base hasta la base opuesta.		

English/Español	Example/Ejemplo	Notes/Notas
height (of a triangle) the perpendicular distance from a base to the opposite vertex.		
altura (de un triángulo) distancia perpendicular desde una base hasta el vértice opuesto.	height base	
hexagon a polygon with exactly 6 sides and 6 angles.		
hexágono polígono que tiene exactamente 6 lados y 6 ángulos.		
histogram a data display similar to a bar graph. A histogram groups the data into equal-size intervals. The height of each bar represents the number of data points in that group.		
histograma presentación de datos parecida a una gráfica de barras. Un histograma agrupa los datos en intervalos de igual tamaño. La altura de cada barra representa el número de datos que hay en ese grupo.		

Ii

identity property of multiplication any number multiplied by 1 is itself.

propiedad de identidad de la multiplicación cualquier número multiplicado por 1 es el mismo número.

$3 \cdot 1 = 3$

---

independent variable a variable whose value is used to find the value of another variable. An independent variable determines the value of a dependent variable.

variable independiente variable cuyo valor se usa para hallar el valor de otra variable. Una variable independiente determina el valor de una variable dependiente.

$y = 5x$

The value of x is used to find the value of y.

---

inequality a mathematical statement that uses an inequality symbol ($<, >, \leq, \geq$) to show the relationship between values of expressions.

desigualdad enunciado matemático que muestra con un símbolo de desigualdad ($<, >, \leq, \geq$) la relación que existe entre los valores de las expresiones.

$4{,}384 > 3{,}448$

$x \geq -2$

---

integers the set of whole numbers and their opposites.

enteros (positivos y negativos) conjunto de números enteros y sus opuestos.

$-3, -1, 0, 2, 3$

---

interquartile range (IQR) the difference between the upper quartile and lower quartile.

rango entre cuartiles (REC) diferencia entre el cuartil superior y el cuartil inferior.

interquartile range

20 30 40 50 60 70 80 90

IQR: $60 - 35 = 25$

English/Español	Example/Ejemplo	Notes/Notas
inverse operations operations that undo each other. For example, addition and subtraction are inverse operations, and multiplication and division are inverse operations.	$300 \div 10 = 30$ $30 \times 10 = 300$	
operaciones inversas operaciones que se cancelan entre sí. Por ejemplo, la suma y la resta son operaciones inversas, y la multiplicación y la división son operaciones inversas.		
isosceles triangle a triangle that has at least two sides the same length.		
triángulo isósceles triángulo que tiene al menos dos lados de la misma longitud.	8 in. 8 in. 6 in.	

Ll

English/Español	Example/Ejemplo	Notes/Notas
least common multiple (LCM) the least multiple shared by two or more numbers.	LCM of 20 and 30: $2 \cdot 2 \cdot 3 \cdot 5$, or 60 $20 = 2 \cdot 2 \cdot 5$ $30 = 2 \cdot 3 \cdot 5$	
mínimo común múltiplo (m.c.m.) el menor múltiplo que comparten dos o más números.		
like terms two or more terms that have the same variable factors.	$2x^2$ and $4x^2$ 1.2 and 5.1 $6xy$ and xy	
términos semejantes dos o más términos que tienen los mismos factores variables.		

line a straight row of points that goes on forever in both directions.

recta línea recta de puntos que continúa infinitamente en ambas direcciones.

line of symmetry a line that divides a shape into two mirror images.

eje de simetría línea que divide a una figura en dos imágenes reflejadas.

line segment a straight row of points between two endpoints.

A ———————— B

segmento de recta fila recta de puntos entre dos extremos.

lower quartile the middle number between the minimum and the median in an ordered set of numbers. The lower quartile is also called the 1st quartile or Q1.

lower quartile

20 30 40 50 60 70 80 90

cuartil inferior el número del medio entre el mínimo y la mediana en un conjunto ordenado de números. El cuartil inferior también se llama primer cuartil, o Q1.

English/Español	Example/Ejemplo	Notes/Notas

Mm

maximum (of a data set) the greatest value in a data set.

máximo (de un conjunto de datos) mayor valor en un conjunto de datos.

Data set: 9, 10, 8, 9, 7

---

mean the sum of a set of values divided by the number of values. This is often called the *average*.

media suma de un conjunto de valores dividida por el número de valores. Suele llamarse *promedio*.

Data set: 9, 10, 8, 9, 7

Mean: $\dfrac{9 + 10 + 8 + 9 + 7}{5} = 8.6$

---

mean absolute deviation (MAD) the sum of the distances of each data point from the mean of the data set divided by the number of data points. It is always positive.

desviación media absoluta (DMA) suma de las distancias de cada dato desde la media del conjunto de datos dividido por el número de datos. Siempre es positiva.

Data set: 9, 10, 8, 9, 7

Mean: 8.6

MAD:

$\dfrac{0.4 + 1.4 + 0.6 + 0.4 + 1.7}{5} = 0.9$

---

measure of center a single number that summarizes what is typical for all the values in a data set. Mean and median are measures of center.

medida de tendencia central único número que resume qué es típico para todos los valores en un conjunto de datos. La media y la mediana son medidas de tendecia central.

Data set: 9, 10, 8, 9, 7

Mean: 8.6

Median: 9

---

measure of variability a single number that summarizes how much the values in a data set vary. Mean absolute deviation and interquartile range are measures of variability.

medida de variabilidad único número que resume cuánto varían los valores en un conjunto de datos. La desviación media absoluta y el rango entre cuartiles son medidas de variabilidad.

Data set: 9, 10, 8, 9, 7

MAD: 0.9

IQR: 1

English/Español	Example/Ejemplo	Notes/Notas
median the middle number, or the halfway point between the two middle numbers, in an ordered set of values.	Data set: 9, 10, 8, 9, 7 7, 8, **9**, 9, 10	
mediana el número del medio, o punto intermedio entre los dos números del medio, de un conjunto ordenado de valores.		
minimum (of a data set) the least value in a data set.	Data set: 9, 10, 8, 9, 7	
mínimo (de un conjunto de datos) valor mínimo en un conjunto de datos.		
multiple the product of a given number and any other whole number.	4, 8, 12, 16 are multiples of 4.	
múltiplo producto de un número dado y cualquier otro número entero.		
multiplicative comparison a comparison that tells how many times as many.	$\frac{1}{2} \times 6 = 3$ tells that 3 is $\frac{1}{2}$ times as many as 6 and that 3 is 6 times as many as $\frac{1}{2}$.	
comparación multiplicativa comparación que indica cuántas veces más.		
multiplicative inverse a number is the multiplicative inverse of another number if the product of the two numbers is 1.	3 and $\frac{1}{3}$	
inverso multiplicativo un número es el inverso multiplicativo de otro número si el producto de los dos números es 1.		

Nn

negative numbers numbers that are less than 0. They are located to the left of 0 on a horizontal number line and below 0 on a vertical number line.

números negativos números que son menores que 0. Se ubican a la izquierda del 0 en una recta numérica horizontal y debajo del 0 en una recta numérica vertical.

---

net a flat, "unfolded" representation of a three-dimensional shape.

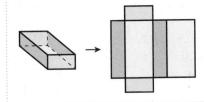

modelo plano representación plana "desplegada" de una figura tridimensional.

---

numerator the number above the line in a fraction that tells the number of equal parts that are being described.

$$\frac{3}{4}$$

numerador número que está sobre la línea en una fracción y que indica el número de partes iguales que se describen.

Oo

obtuse angle an angle that measures more than 90° but less than 180°.

ángulo obtuso ángulo que mide más de 90° pero menos de 180°.

obtuse triangle a triangle that has one obtuse angle.

triángulo obtusángulo triángulo que tiene un ángulo obtuso.

opposite numbers numbers that are the same distance from 0 on the number line but in opposite directions. Opposite numbers have the same numeral, but opposite signs.

números opuestos números que están a la misma distancia del 0 en la recta numérica pero en direcciones opuestas. Los números opuestos son el mismo número, pero con el signo opuesto.

−3 and 3

$-\frac{8}{15}$ and $\frac{8}{15}$

Order of Operations a set of rules that state the order in which operations should be performed to evaluate an expression.

orden de las operaciones conjunto de reglas que establecen el orden en el que deben hacerse las operaciones para evaluar una expresión.

Working from left to right:
1. Grouping symbols
2. Exponents
3. Multiplication/Division
4. Addition/Subtraction

ordered pair a pair of numbers, (x, y), that describes the location of a point in the coordinate plane. The x-coordinate gives the point's horizontal distance from the y-axis, and the y-coordinate gives the point's vertical distance from the x-axis.

par ordenado par de números, (x, y), que describen la ubicación de un punto en el plano de coordenadas. La coordenada x da la distancia horizontal del punto desde el eje y, y la coordenada y da la distancia vertical del punto desde el eje x.

(x, y)

x-coordinate y-coordinate

English/Español	Example/Ejemplo	Notes/Notas

origin the point (0, 0) in the coordinate plane where the *x*-axis and *y*-axis intersect.

origen el punto (0, 0) en el plano de coordenadas donde el eje *x* y el eje *y* se intersecan.

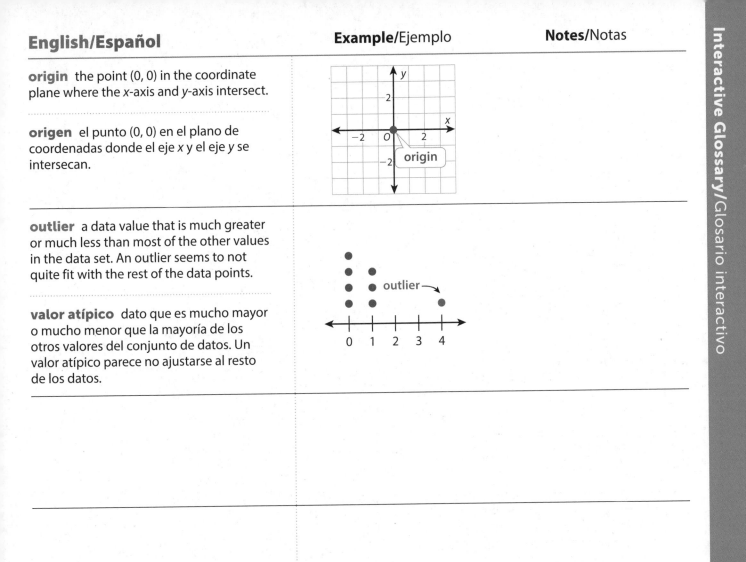

outlier a data value that is much greater or much less than most of the other values in the data set. An outlier seems to not quite fit with the rest of the data points.

valor atípico dato que es mucho mayor o mucho menor que la mayoría de los otros valores del conjunto de datos. Un valor atípico parece no ajustarse al resto de los datos.

Pp

parallel (∥) always the same distance apart and never meeting.

paralelos (∥) que están siempre a la misma distancia y nunca se encuentran.

$\overline{AB} \parallel \overline{CD}$ and $\overline{AD} \parallel \overline{BC}$

---

parallel lines lines that are always the same distance apart and never intersect.

rectas paralelas rectas que siempre están a la misma distancia y nunca se intersecan.

---

parallelogram a quadrilateral with opposite sides parallel and equal in length.

paralelogramo cuadrilátero que tiene lados opuestos paralelos y de la misma longitud.

---

partial products the products you get in each step of the partial-products strategy. You use place value to find partial products.

productos parciales productos que se obtienen en cada paso de la estrategia de productos parciales. Se usa el valor posicional para hallar productos parciales.

218×6
Partial products:
6×200, or 1,200,
6×10, or 60, and
6×8, or 48

---

partial quotients the quotients you get in each step of the partial-quotient strategy. You use place value to find partial quotients.

cocientes parciales cocientes que se obtienen en cada paso de la estrategia de cocientes parciales. Se usa el valor posicional para hallar cocientes parciales.

$2{,}124 \div 4$
Partial quotients:
$2{,}000 \div 4$, or 500,
$100 \div 4$, or 25, and
$24 \div 4$, or 6

---

partial sums the sums you get in each step of the partial-sums strategy. You use place value to find partial sums.

sumas parciales totales que se obtienen en cada paso de la estrategia de sumas parciales. Se usa el valor posicional para hallar sumas parciales.

$124 + 234$
Partial sums:
$100 + 200$, or 300,
$20 + 30$, or 50, and
$4 + 4$, or 8

English/Español	Example/Ejemplo	Notes/Notas
partial-products strategy a strategy used to multiply multi-digit numbers. **estrategia de productos parciales** estrategia que se usa para multiplicar números de varios dígitos.	$\begin{array}{r} 218 \\ \times \quad 6 \\ \hline 48 \\ 60 \\ + 1{,}200 \\ \hline 1{,}308 \end{array}$ (6 × 8 ones) (6 × 1 ten) (6 × 2 hundreds)	
partial-quotients strategy a strategy used to divide multi-digit numbers. **estrategia de cocientes parciales** estrategia que se usa para dividir números de varios dígitos.	$\begin{array}{r} 6 \\ 25 \\ 500 \\ 4)\overline{2{,}125} \\ -2{,}000 \\ \hline 125 \\ -100 \\ \hline 25 \\ -24 \\ \hline 1 \end{array}$ The quotient 531 is the sum of partial quotients (6, 25, and 500) and the remainder (1).	
partial-sums strategy a strategy used to add multi-digit numbers. **estrategia de sumas parciales** estrategia que se usa para sumar números de varios dígitos.	$\begin{array}{r} 312 \\ + 235 \\ \hline \end{array}$ Add the hundreds. 500 Add the tens. 40 Add the ones. $\underline{+\quad 7}$ 547	
peak in a distribution, the shape formed when many data points are at one value or group of values. **pico** en una distribución, la figura que se forma cuando los puntos de muchos datos están en un valor o grupo de valores.		
pentagon a polygon with exactly 5 sides and 5 angles. **pentágono** polígono que tiene exactamente 5 lados y 5 ángulos.		
per *for each* or *for every*. The word *per* can be used to express a rate, such as $2 per pound. **por** *por cada*. La palabra *por* se puede usar para expresar una tasa, como $2 por libra.	A price of $2 per pound means for every pound, you pay $2.	

English/Español	Example/Ejemplo	Notes/Notas
percent per 100. A percent is a rate per 100. A percent can be written using the percent symbol (%) and represented as a fraction or decimal.		
porcentaje por cada 100. Un porcentaje es una tasa por cada 100. Un porcentaje se puede escribir usando el símbolo de porcentaje (%) y se representa como fracción o decimal.	15% can be represented as $\frac{15}{100}$ or 0.15.	
perimeter the distance around a two-dimensional shape. The perimeter is equal to the sum of the lengths of the sides.	60 yd 40 yd 40 yd 60 yd Perimeter: 200 yd (60 yd + 40 yd + 60 yd + 40 yd)	
perímetro distancia alrededor de una figura bidimensional. El perímetro es igual a la suma de las longitudes de los lados.		
perpendicular (⊥) meeting to form right angles.	A B D C $\overline{AD} \perp \overline{CD}$	
perpendicular (⊥) unión donde se forman ángulos rectos.		
perpendicular lines two lines that meet to form a right angle, or a 90° angle.		
rectas perpendiculares dos rectas que se encuentran y forman un ángulo recto, o ángulo de 90°.		
place value the value of a digit based on its position in a number.		
valor posicional valor de un dígito que se basa en su posición en un número. Por ejemplo, el 2 en 3.52 está en la posición de las centésimas y tiene un valor de 2 centésimas, o 0.02.	The 2 in 3.52 is in the hundredths place and has a value of 2 hundredths or 0.02.	

English/Español	Example/Ejemplo	Notes/Notas
plane figure a two-dimensional figure, such as a circle, triangle, or rectangle. **figura plana** figura bidimensional, como un círculo, un triángulo o un rectángulo.		
point a single location in space. **punto** ubicación única en el espacio.	*A* ●	
polygon a two-dimensional closed figure made with three or more straight line segments that meet only at their endpoints. **polígono** figura bidimensional cerrada formada por tres o más segmentos de recta que se encuentran solo en sus extremos.		
positive numbers numbers that are greater than 0. They are located to the right of 0 on a horizontal number line and above 0 on a vertical number line. **números positivos** números que son mayores que 0. Se ubican a la derecha del 0 en una recta numérica horizontal y sobre el 0 en una recta numérica vertical.	−3 −2 −1 0 1 2 3	
power an expression with a base and an exponent. **potencia** expresión que tiene una base y un exponente.	8^2	
power of 10 a number that can be written as a product of 10s. **potencia de 10** número que se puede escribir como el producto de 10.	100 and 1,000 are powers of 10 because $100 = 10 \times 10$ and $1,000 = 10 \times 10 \times 10$.	

English/Español	Example/Ejemplo	Notes/Notas
prime number a whole number greater than 1 whose only factors are 1 and itself.	2, 3, 5, 7, 11, 13	
número primo número entero mayor que 1 cuyos únicos factores son 1 y sí mismo.		
prism a three-dimensional figure with two parallel bases that are the same size and shape. The other faces are parallelograms. A prism is named by the shape of the base.		
prisma figura tridimensional que tiene dos bases paralelas que tienen el mismo tamaño y la misma forma. Las otras caras son paralelogramos. La base determina el nombre del prisma.		
product the result of multiplication.	$3 \cdot 5 = 15$	
producto resultado de la multiplicación.		

Qq

quadrants the four regions of the coordinate plane that are formed when the x-axis and y-axis intersect at the origin.		
cuadrantes las cuatro regiones del plano de coordenadas que se forman cuando los ejes x y y se intersecan en el origen.		

English/Español	Example/Ejemplo	Notes/Notas

quadrilateral a polygon with exactly 4 sides and 4 angles.

cuadrilátero polígono que tiene exactamente 4 lados y 4 ángulos.

quotient the result of division.

$22.5 \div 3 = 7.5$

cociente resultado de la división.

Rr

range the difference between the greatest value (maximum) and the least value (minimum) in a data set.

Data set: 9, 10, 8, 9, 7

Range: $10 - 7 = 3$

rango diferencia entre el mayor valor (máximo) y el menor valor (mínimo) en un conjunto de datos.

rate a ratio tells the number of units of one quantity for 1 unit of another quantity. Rates are often expressed using the word *per*.

5 miles per hour

2 cups for every 1 serving

tasa razón que indica el número de unidades de una cantidad para 1 unidad de otra cantidad. Las razones suelen expresarse usando la palabra *por*.

ratio a way to compare two quantities when there are *a* units of one quantity for every *b* units of the other quantity. You can write the ratio in symbols as *a* : *b* and in words as *a to b*.

4 circles : 2 triangles

razón manera de comparar dos cantidades cuando hay *a* unidades de una cantidad por cada *b* unidades de la otra cantidad. Se puede escribir la razón en símbolos como *a* : *b* y en palabras como *a a b*.

rational number a number that can be expressed as the fraction $\frac{a}{b}$ or the opposite of $\frac{a}{b}$ where a and b are whole numbers and $b \neq 0$. Rational numbers can also be expressed as a decimal.

$\frac{3}{4}, -\frac{1}{8}, -3, 0, 1.2$

número racional número que se puede expresar como la fracción $\frac{a}{b}$ o la opuesta a $\frac{a}{b}$ en la que a y b son números enteros y $b \neq 0$. Los números racionales también se pueden expresar

ray a part of a line that has one endpoint and goes on forever in one direction.

semirrecta parte de una recta que tiene un extremo y continúa infinitamente en una dirección.

reciprocal for any nonzero number a, the reciprocal is $\frac{1}{a}$. The reciprocal of any fraction $\frac{a}{b}$ is $\frac{b}{a}$. Zero does not have a reciprocal. The reciprocal of a number is also called the *multiplicative inverse* of that number.

The reciprocal of $\frac{4}{5}$ is $\frac{5}{4}$.

The reciprocal of $\frac{1}{6}$ is 6.

The reciprocal of -8 is $-\frac{1}{8}$.

recíproco para cualquier número a distinto de cero, el recíproco es $\frac{1}{a}$. El recíproco de cualquier fracción $\frac{a}{b}$ es $\frac{b}{a}$. El cero no tiene recíproco. El recíproco de un número también se llama *inverso multiplicativo* de ese número.

rectangle a quadrilateral with 4 right angles. Opposite sides of a rectangle are the same length.

rectángulo cuadrilátero que tiene 4 ángulos rectos. Los lados opuestos de un rectángulo tienen la misma longitud.

English/Español	Example/Ejemplo	Notes/Notas
rectangular prism a prism where the bases are rectangles. **prisma rectangular** prisma en el que las bases son rectángulos.		
reflection a transformation that flips (reflects) a figure across a line to form a mirror image. **reflexión** transformación que gira (refleja) una figura del otro lado de una línea para formar una imagen reflejada.	A B	
remainder the amount left over when one number does not divide another number a whole number of times. **residuo** cantidad que queda cuando un número no divide a otro un número entero de veces.	$7 \div 2 = 3\,R\,1$ remainder	
rhombus a quadrilateral with all sides the same length. **rombo** cuadrilátero que tiene todos los lados de la misma longitud.		
right angle an angle that measures 90°. **ángulo recto** ángulo que mide 90°.		
right prism a prism where each base is perpendicular to the other faces. In a right prism, the faces that are not bases are rectangles. **prisma recto** prisma en el que cada base es perpendicular a las otras caras. En un prisma recto, las caras que no son bases son rectángulos.		

right rectangular prism a right prism where the bases and other faces are all rectangles.

prisma rectangular recto prisma recto en el que las bases y las otras caras son rectángulos.

right triangle a triangle with one right angle.

triángulo rectángulo triángulo que tiene un ángulo recto.

right triangular prism a right prism where the bases are triangles and the other faces are rectangles.

prisma triangular recto prisma recto en el que las bases son triángulos y las otras caras son rectángulos.

round to approximate the value of a number by finding the nearest ten, hundred, or other place value.

48 rounded to the nearest ten is 50.

redondear aproximar el valor de un número hallando la decena, la centena u otro valor posicional más cercano.

Ss

scale (on a graph) the value represented by the distance between one tick mark and the next on a number line.

escala (en una gráfica) valor representado por la distancia que hay entre una marca y la siguiente en una recta numérica.

scale = 5

scalene triangle a triangle that has no sides the same length.

triángulo escaleno triángulo que no tiene lados de la misma longitud.

side a line segment that forms part of a two-dimensional shape.

lado segmento de recta que forma parte de una figura bidimensional

side

skewed left when most of the data points of a distribution are clustered near the greater values.

asimétrica a la izquierda cuando la mayoría de los datos de una distribución se agrupan cerca de los valores más altos.

Skewed Left

skewed right when most of the data points of a distribution are clustered near the lesser values.

asimétrica a la derecha cuando la mayoría de los datos de una distribución se agrupan cerca de los valores más bajos.

Skewed Right

English/Español	Example/Ejemplo	Notes/Notas
solution of an equation a value that can be substituted for a variable to make an equation true. **solución de una ecuación** valor que puede sustituir a una variable para hacer que una ecuación sea verdadera.	The value 5 is the solution of the equation $19 = 4x - 1$ because $19 = 4(5) - 1$.	
solution of an inequality a value that can be substituted for a variable to make an inequality true. **solución de una desigualdad** valor que puede sustituir a una variable para hacer que una desigualdad sea verdadera.	All values of x less than 5 ($x < 5$) are solutions of the inequality $5x < 25$.	
square a quadrilateral with 4 right angles and 4 sides of equal length. **cuadrado** cuadrilátero que tiene 4 ángulos rectos y 4 lados de la misma longitud.		
statistical question a question that can be answered by collecting data that are expected to vary. **pregunta estadística** pregunta que se puede responder reuniendo datos que se espera que varíen.	What is the typical amount of rain in April?	
sum the result of addition. **total** resultado de la suma.	$24 + 35 = 59$	
surface area the sum of the areas of all the faces of a three-dimensional figure. **área total** suma de las áreas de todas las caras de una figura tridimensional.	5 units 4 units 5 units Surface Area: $2(4)(5) + 2(4)(5) + 2(5)(5) = 130$ units^2	

English/Español	Example/Ejemplo	Notes/Notas
symmetric when a distribution has the same shape on both sides of a middle point. **simétrico** cuando una distribución tiene la misma forma en ambos lados de un punto que está en el medio.	**Symmetric** 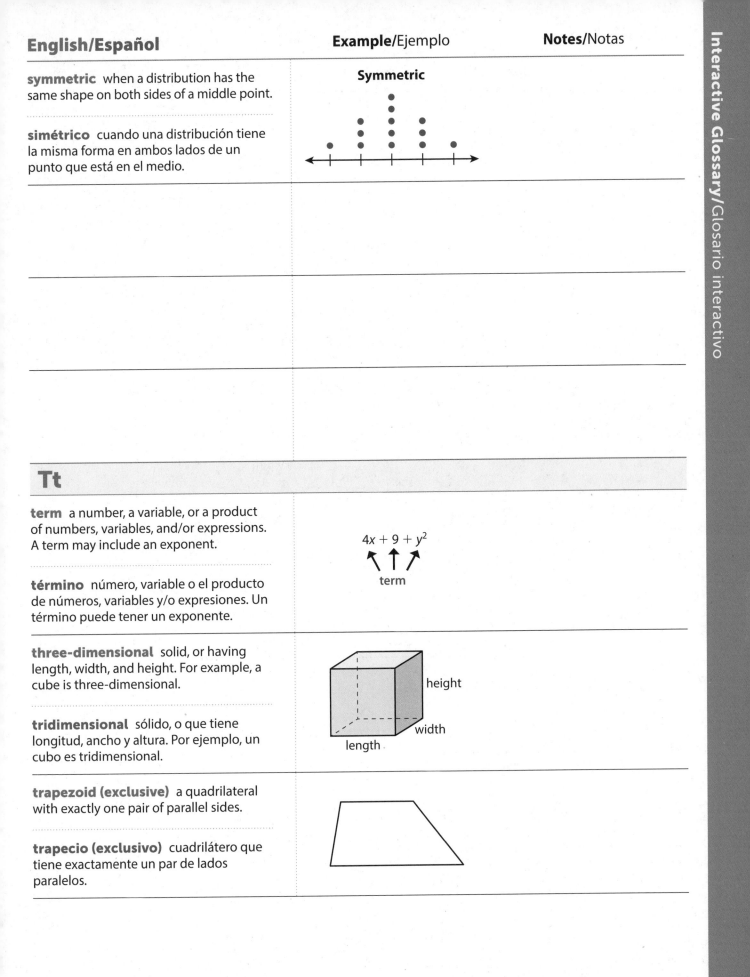	

Tt

English/Español	Example/Ejemplo	Notes/Notas
term a number, a variable, or a product of numbers, variables, and/or expressions. A term may include an exponent. **término** número, variable o el producto de números, variables y/o expresiones. Un término puede tener un exponente.	$4x + 9 + y^2$ ↖ ↑ ↗ term	
three-dimensional solid, or having length, width, and height. For example, a cube is three-dimensional. **tridimensional** sólido, o que tiene longitud, ancho y altura. Por ejemplo, un cubo es tridimensional.	height width length	
trapezoid (exclusive) a quadrilateral with exactly one pair of parallel sides. **trapecio (exclusivo)** cuadrilátero que tiene exactamente un par de lados paralelos.		

trapezoid (inclusive) a quadrilateral with at least one pair of parallel sides.

trapecio (inclusivo) cuadrilátero que tiene al menos un par de lados paralelos.

triangle a polygon with exactly 3 sides and 3 angles.

triángulo polígono que tiene exactamente 3 lados y 3 ángulos.

triangular prism a prism where the bases are triangles.

prisma triangular prisma en el que las bases son triángulos.

two-dimensional flat, or having measurement in two directions, like length and width. For example, a rectangle is two-dimensional.

bidimensional plano, o que tiene medidas en dos direcciones, como longitud y ancho. Por ejemplo, un rectángulo es bidimensional.

width

length

Uu

unit fraction a fraction with a numerator of 1. Other fractions are built from unit fractions.

$$\frac{1}{5}$$

fracción unitaria fracción que tiene un numerador de 1. Otras fracciones se construyen a partir de fracciones unitarias.

unit rate the numerical part of a rate. For the ratio $a : b$, the unit rate is the quotient $\frac{a}{b}$.

Rate: 3 miles per hour

Unit rate: 3

tasa por unidad parte numérica de una tasa. Para la razón $a : b$, la tasa por unidad es el cociente $\frac{a}{b}$.

unknown the value you need to find to solve a problem.

$$20.5 + x = 30$$

incógnita valor que hay que hallar para resolver un problema.

upper quartile the middle number between the median and the maximum in an ordered set of numbers. The upper quartile is also called the 3rd quartile or Q3.

upper quartile

20 30 40 50 60 70 80 90

cuartil superior número del medio entre la mediana y el máximo en un conjunto ordenado de números. El cuartil superior también se llama tercer cuartil, o Q3.

Vv

variability how spread out or close together values in a data set are.

variabilidad la dispersión o cercanía de los valores en un conjunto de datos.

Gavin's Handstand Times

There is high variability in Gavin's handstand times.

variable a letter that represents an unknown number. In some cases, a variable may represent more than one number.

variable letra que representa un número desconocido. En algunos casos, una variable puede representar más de un número.

$$3x + 9 = 90$$

vertex the point where two rays, lines, or line segments meet to form an angle.

vértice punto en el que dos semirrectas, rectas o segmentos de recta se encuentran y forman un ángulo.

vertex

volume the amount of space inside a solid figure. Volume is measured in cubic units such as cubic inches.

volumen cantidad de espacio dentro de una figura sólida. El volumen se mide en unidades cúbicas como las pulgadas cúbicas.

volume: 24 units³

Ww

whole numbers the numbers 0, 1, 2, 3, 4, . . . Whole numbers are nonnegative and have no fractional part.

0, 8, 187

números enteros los números 0, 1, 2, 3, 4, . . . Los números enteros no son negativos y no tienen partes fraccionarias.

Xx

x-axis the horizontal number line in the coordinate plane.

eje x recta numérica horizontal en el plano de coordenadas.

x-coordinate the first number in an ordered pair. It tells the point's horizontal distance from the *y*-axis.

(x, y)

x-coordinate

coordenada x primer número en un par ordenado. Indica la distancia horizontal del punto al eje *y*.

Yy

y-axis the vertical number line in the coordinate plane.

eje y recta numérica vertical en el plano de coordenadas.

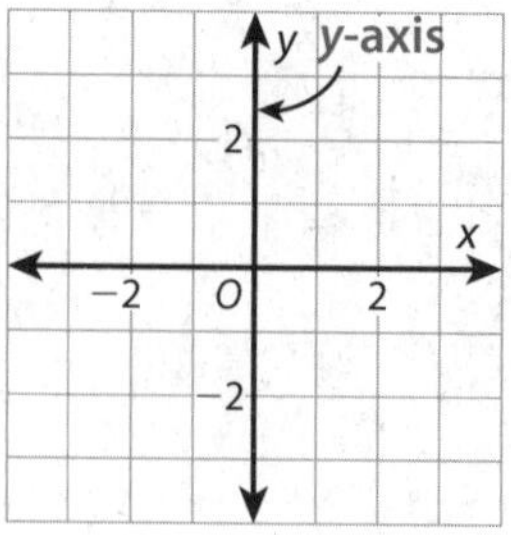

---

y-coordinate the second number in an ordered pair. It tells the point's vertical distance from the x-axis.

coordenada y el segundo número en un par ordenado. Indica la distancia vertical del punto al eje x.

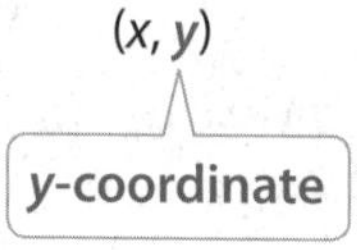

(x, y)

y-coordinate

Credits

Acknowledgment

Common Core State Standards © 2010. National Governors Association Center for Best Practices and Council of Chief State School Officers. All rights reserved.

Photography Credits

Cover: Song Heming/stock.adobe.com
Back Cover: 54 yanik88/Shutterstock, 3DMAVR/Shutterstock; 324 Glass and Nature/Shutterstock, Sari ONeal/Shutterstock
Text: ii, 96 Lukiyanova Natalia frenta/Shutterstock; ii, 120 redtbird02/Shutterstock, Kriengsuk Prasroetsung/Shutterstock; iii, 161 Olga Danylenko/Shutterstock; iii, 180 Rainbow4527/Shutterstock; iii, 194 Feaspb/Shutterstock, Roman Borodaev/Shutterstock; iv, 272 Matthias G. Ziegler/Shutterstock; v, 364 Maridav/Shutterstock, Production Perig/Shutterstock; v, 410 Vaclav Volrab/Shutterstock; vi, 494 Gino Santa Maria/Shutterstock; vi, 496 Jiri Hera/Shutterstock.com; vi, 509 Mrinal Pal. Shutterstock, Robert Biedermann/Shutterstock; vii, 560 Palmer Kane LLC/Shutterstock, Dmitry Naumov/Shutterstock; vii, 582 Jojoo64/Shutterstock; vii, 590 ToffeePhoto/Shutterstock, Iryna Dobrovynska/Shutterstock; viii, 664 vnlit/Shutterstock, Scisetti Alfio/Shutterstock; viii, 689 Gerald A. DeBoer/Shutterstock; viii, 735 YP_Studio/Shutterstock; 1, 41 Comaniciu Dan/Shutterstock; 3 marekuliasz/Shutterstock; 4 Bankrx/Shutterstock; 5 Japan Stock Photography/Alamy Stock Photo; 8 adike/Shutterstock; 9 sripfoto/Shutterstock, NASA/JPL-Caltech/Space Science Institute; 12 saaton/Shutterstock, little birdie/Shutterstock; 13 foto-select/Shutterstock.com; 19 IROOM STOCK/Shutterstock; 20, 229 chinasong/Shutterstock; 21 Krasovski Dmitri/Shutterstock; 24 7Crafts/Shutterstock; 25 I.B.Me/Shutterstock; 31 CD Lenzen/Shutterstock; 32 Jozef Sowa/Shutterstock; 42 Chonlawut/Shutterstock; 43 GoWithLight/Shutterstock; 47 Andrey Starostin/Shutterstock; 52 alleski/Shutterstock; 61 Lorena Huerta/Shutterstock; 63 Artbox/Shutterstock; 64 goir/Shutterstock; 65 Arthur Salimullin/Shutterstock; 69 Brent Hofacker/Shutterstock; 70 AGCuesta/Shutterstock; 72 AS Food Studio/Shutterstock; 74, 201 lzf/Shutterstock; 75 Den Rozhnovsky/Shutterstock; 76 Vladyslav Danlin/Shutterstock; 80 Tony Savino/Shutterstock; 83 chuckchee/Shutterstock; 85 Mikadun/Shutterstock; 87 Kathrin Richter/FOAP/Getty Images; 90 PolyPloiid/Shutterstock; 97 Eleni Mavrandoni/Shutterstock; 98 Sirin_bird/Shutterstock; 108 An Nguyen/Shutterstock; 109 FabrikaSimf/Shutterstock, stefanphotozemun/Shutterstock; 112 trabantos/Shutterstock.com; 113 David Fine/FEMA; 114 Jason Yoder/Shutterstock; 116 Nadezhda Nesterova/Shutterstock; 119, 129, 362, 366 Eric Isselee/Shutterstock, 119 MuratGungut/Shutterstock; 124 OSTILL is Franck Camhi/Shutterstock; 127 Nantawat Chotsuwan/Shutterstock; 129, 132 Diane Garcia/Shutterstock; 129, 132 pfuegler-photo/Shutterstock; 129 Ljupco Smokovski/Shutterstock, LittlePerfectStock/Shutterstock, Tsekhmister/Shutterstock; 135 RiumaLab/Shutterstock; 136 Rustic/Shutterstock, Inegvin/Shutterstock, Kovtun Dmitriy/Shutterstock, photomaster/Shutterstock; 137 PhotoSongserm/Shutterstock, Andrey Esin/Shutterstock, Alexander Baumann/Shutterstock, Anya Hess/Shutterstock; 143, 195 Ocskay Bence/Shutterstock; 145 Edy Wibowo/Shutterstock; 147 Normana Karia/Shutterstock; 150 Vaclav Hroch/Shutterstock; 151 Spiroview Inc/Shutterstock, Somchai Som/Shutterstock, Andrei Kuzmik/Shutterstock, jackhollingsworth.com/Shutterstock, Alexander Mak/Shutterstock; 154 M. Rohana/Shutterstock; 156 Suzanne Tucker/Shutterstock; 157 Rachel Moon/Shutterstock; 158 Benhamin Simeneta/Shutterstock; 160 Alexandru Chiriac/Shutterstock; 166 Oleksandr Osipov/Shutterstock; 167 Pavel1964/Shutterstock; 168 Rob Hainer/Shutterstock; 169 pelfophoto/Shutterstock; 172 Mike Flippo/Shutterstock; 173 ArliftAtoz2205/Shutterstock.com; 174 donatas1205/Shutterstock; 176 stockphoto-graf/Shutterstock; 178 welcomia/Shutterstock; 179 Roberto Galan/Shutterstock.com; 185 evrymmnt/Shutterstock; 186, 672 sirtravelalot/Shutterstock, 186 theerapol sri-in/Shutterstock; 188, 476, 737 Brocreative/Shutterstock; 190 MiVa/Shutterstock; 197 RG-vc/Shutterstock; 198 Adcharin Chitthammachuk/Shutterstock; 200 Graeme Dawes/Shutterstock, ZaZa Studio/Shutterstock; 203 Rachel Juliet Lerch/Shutterstock; 204 Slavica Stajic/Shutterstock; 206 kosam/Shutterstock, Tiger Images/Shutterstock; 207 A_stockphoto/Shutterstock; 208 MaxyM/Shutterstock; 209 KREUS/Shutterstock, Evgeny Prokofyev/Shutterstock; 212 akiyoko/Shutterstock, Andrzej Rostek/Shutterstock; 213 Tippman98x/Shutterstock.com, Diana Johanna Velasquez/Alamy Stock Photo; 214 iStock.com/Bastiaan Slabbers; 216 Arina P Habich/Shutterstock; 218 irin-k/Shutterstock, Erkki Makkonen/Shutterstock; 219 Moonborne/Shutterstock; 220 Tsekhmister/Shutterstock; 223 DONOT6_STUDIO/Shutterstock, Daniel Prudek/Shutterstock; 224 Cultura Creative (RF)/Alamy Stock Photo; 230 cybrain/Shutterstock; 231 lucadp/Shutterstock; 234 luskiv/Shutterstock; 235, 236 Cathy Keifer/Shutterstock; 235 Leonardo Garofalo/Shutterstock; 239 iStock.com/EdwardMosser, Rashevskyi Viacheslav/Shutterstock; 241 Viktor1/Shutterstock; 242 iStock.com/evemilla; 250 Microgen/Shutterstock;

251 ILYA AKINSHIN/Shutterstock, Kuttelvaserova Stuchelova/Shutterstock; 253 Eric Broder Van Dyke/Shutterstock; 256 CkyBe/Shutterstock, Tony Stock/Shutterstock; 257 Napat/Shutterstock, SOMMAI/Shutterstock; 259 Megapixel/Shutterstock, MilkBottle/Shutterstock, Slava_Kovtun/Shutterstock; 265, 308 Enshpil/Shutterstock; 267 Joshua Resnick/Shutterstock; 268 AlenKadr/Shutterstock, Vitalina Rybakova/Shutterstock; 269 AN Images/Shutterstock; 270 LanaSweet/Shutterstock; 273 Irina Burakova/Shutterstock; 274 Thorsten Spoerlein/Shutterstock; 278 Don Mammoser/Shutterstock; 279, 406, 761 New Africa/Shutterstock; 280 gmstockstudio/Shutterstock, Oleg Voronische/Shutterstock; 281 Indian Food Images/Shutterstock; 284 Katherine Austin/Shutterstock; 285 William Silver/Shutterstock; 286 FooTToo/Shutterstock; 288 Alexey Boldin/Shutterstock; 290 kungverylucky/Shutterstock, SeeCee/Shutterstock; 291 Hollygraphic/Shutterstock; 292 Andril A/Shutterstock; 298 kai celvin/Shutterstock; 309 Tanupong Wittayanukullak/Shutterstock, NewFabrika/Shutterstock; 312 fotoknips/Shutterstock; 313, 314 Baloncici/Shutterstock, Yurkina Alexandar/Shutterstock; 314 iStock.com/EHStock; 318 Christopher Boswell/Shutterstock; 319 Anansing/Shutterstock, Becky Starsmore/Shutterstock; 320 domnitsky/Shutterstock; 322 hardqor4ik/Shutterstock; 327 Mikbiz/Shutterstock; 329, 332 karelnoppe/Shutterstock, Tashal/Shutterstock; 334 Rozhnovskaya Tanya/Shutterstock, Tarzhanova/Shutterstock; 335 Dan Kosmayer/Shutterstock, Matt Benoit/Shutterstock; 336, 465 Africa Studio/Shutterstock; 336 Guiyuan Chen/Shutterstock, Dan Kosmayer/Shutterstock, andersphoto/Shutterstock, Nataly Studio/Shutterstock, bigacis/Shutterstock, Danny Smythe/Shutterstock, baibaz/Shutterstock; 337 NYS/Shutterstock, gkrphoto/Shutterstock; 343, 385 KRIACHKO OLEKSII/Shutterstock; 345 Elena Rostunova/Shutterstock; 347, 348 AlesiaKan/Shutterstock; 347 Bas Nastassia/Shutterstock, Tatyaby/Shutterstock; 352 Ivan Calamonte/Shutterstock; 354 Nadia Young/Shutterstock; 356 Sensvector/Shutterstock, Johann Helgason/Shutterstock; 357 GreenArt/Shutterstock; 358 Collins93/Shutterstock; 362 Anna Kraynova/Shutterstock; 363 frantic00/Shutterstock; 368 ACHPF/Shutterstock.com; 369, 370 studiovin/Shutterstock; 369 Bomshtein/Shutterstock, stuar/Shutterstock; 372 24Novembers/Shutterstock; 374 Markus Mainka/Shutterstock; 375 Byelikova Oksana/Shutterstock.com; 376 a katz/Shutterstock.com; 378 Heliopixel/Shutterstock; 380 bluedog studio/Shutterstock, PetlinDmitry/Shutterstock; 384 photosnyc/Shutterstock; 386 Dimj/Shutterstock; 387 mariait/Shutterstock; 388 hans.slegers/Shutterstock, Zoom Team/Shutterstock; 390 Rimma Bondarenko/Shutterstock, Dewin Indew/Shutterstock; 392 f11photo/Shutterstock, MarkVanDykePhotography/Shutterstock, Tshooter/Shutterstock; 394 PaweenaS/Shutterstock; 396 on_france/Shutterstock; 397 V_E/Shutterstock; 398 zsolt_uveges/Shutterstock; 399 FarisHDZQ/Shutterstock; 403, 525 Fotografiecor.nl/Shutterstock; 404 furtseff/Shutterstock; 406 Lec Neo/Shutterstock; 408 sl_photo/Shutterstock; 409 maxpro/Shutterstock; 412 Lipskiy/Shutterstock; 413 muratart/Shutterstock; 417 Vasyl Shulga/Shutterstock; 418 Tim_Walters2017/Shutterstock; 419, 422 PremiumArt/Shutterstock, Victoria Tsukanova/Shutterstock, lgrapop/Shutterstock; 419 Sergey Nivens/Shutterstock; 423, 426, 427 NASA; 425 Juergen Faelchle/Shutterstock; 426 HiSunnySky/Shutterstock, AVS-Images/Shutterstock, photomak/Shutterstock, NASA/Reid Wiseman; 427 3Dsculptor/Shutterstock; 433, 503 Denis Belitsky/Shutterstock; 440 arsa35/Shutterstock, Art 27/Shutterstock; 441 Gorondenkoff/Shutterstock; 442 Proxima Studio/Shutterstock; 446 Tienuskin/Shutterstock; 447, 448 RedKoala/Shutterstock, Rueankam Jompijit/Shutterstock; 450 jocic/Shutterstock, Susse_n/Shutterstock, Nancy Hixson/Shutterstock; 452 Salenta/Shutterstock, Oliver Denker/Shutterstock; 456 iStock.com/Todor Tsvetkov, Normana Karia/Shutterstock; 458 Russ Heinl/Shutterstock; 463 Peter Milto/Shutterstock; 468 Morinka/Shutterstock; 475 solarseven/Shutterstock; 476 Razym/Shutterstock, Gocili/Shutterstock, mapichai/Shutterstock, kajiwori/Shutterstock; 481 LifetimeStock/Shutterstock; 482 Martin Hejzlar/Shutterstock; 484 Kalos2/Shutterstock, arka38/Shutterstock; 486 Hortimages/Shutterstock; 487 Kit Leong/Shutterstock; 490 shutter_o/Shutterstock; 492 nevodka/Shutterstock; 493 chaoss/Shutterstock; 498 Shpadaruk Aleksei/Shutterstock, Bokyo.Pictures/Shutterstock; 502 FXQuadro/Shutterstock; 504 Brian A. Jackson/Shutterstock; 505 Sinem Babacan/Shutterstock; 508 Igor Kyrlytsya/Shutterstock; 510 2630ben/Shutterstock; 512 Kisialiou Yury/Shutterstock; 514 Kerry Hargrove/Shutterstock; 515, 516 dand_art99/Shutterstock, Piyawat Nandeenopparit/Shutterstock; 515 Joe Gough/Shutterstock; 519 beboy/Shutterstock; 522 Nomad_Soul/Shutterstock; 524 Chase Dekker/Shutterstock; 530, 532 MightyRabittCrew/Shutterstock; 530 K Woodgyer/Shutterstock, WoodysPhotos/Shutterstock, Mile Atanasov/Shutterstock; 531 iStock.com/Frelia; 532 Skellen/Shutterstock, ARTBALANCE/Shutterstock, nexusby/Shutterstock; 533 Master1305/Shutterstock, Watchduck/Wikimedia Commons/CC BY 4.0; 539, 621 roger ashford/Shutterstock; 541 Damsea/Shutterstock; 542 Daniel Prudek/Shutterstock, 542 RnDmS/Shutterstock; 552 NeonLight/Shutterstock;

Data Sets

336 https://nutritiondata.self.com; 336 FoodData Central (2019). U.S. Department of Agriculture, Agricultural Research Service. Retrieved from fdc.nal.usda.gov.; 336 https://www.nutritionix.com